SAINTS ON THE SEAS

VOLUME SEVENTEEN

UNIVERSITY OF UTAH PUBLICATIONS IN THE AMERICAN WEST

Emigrant Ship Leaving Liverpool.
Frederick Piercy. *Courtesy Church Archives, Church of Jesus Christ of Latter-day Saints.*

SAINTS ON THE SEAS

A Maritime History of Mormon Migration

1830–1890

By Conway B. Sonne

UNIVERSITY OF UTAH PRESS / SALT LAKE CITY / 1983

Volume Seventeen of the University of Utah
Publications in the American West, under the editorial direction
of the American West Center—S. Lyman Tyler, Director
Brigham D. Madsen, General Editor

© 1983 by Conway B. Sonne
Published by the University of Utah Press
Salt Lake City, Utah 84112
Printed in the United States of America

Library of Congress Cataloguing-in-Publication Data

Sonne, Conway B. (Conway Ballantyne), 1917–
    Saints on the seas.

    (University of Utah publications in the American
West; v. 17)
    Bibliography: p.
    Includes index.
    1. Mormon Church—History—19th century. 2. United
States—Emigration and immigration—History—19th
century. 3. Mormon Church—Missions—History—19th
century. 4. Converts, Mormon—History—19th century.
5. Navigation—History—19th century. I. Title.
II. Series.
BX8611.S75   1983   289.3'09   83-3604

ISBN 0-87480-684-4

Paperback reprint edition
2005 2004 2003 2002 2001
3 2 1

To my sons—Scott, Alan, Marc, and Carl—
who shared my enthusiasm

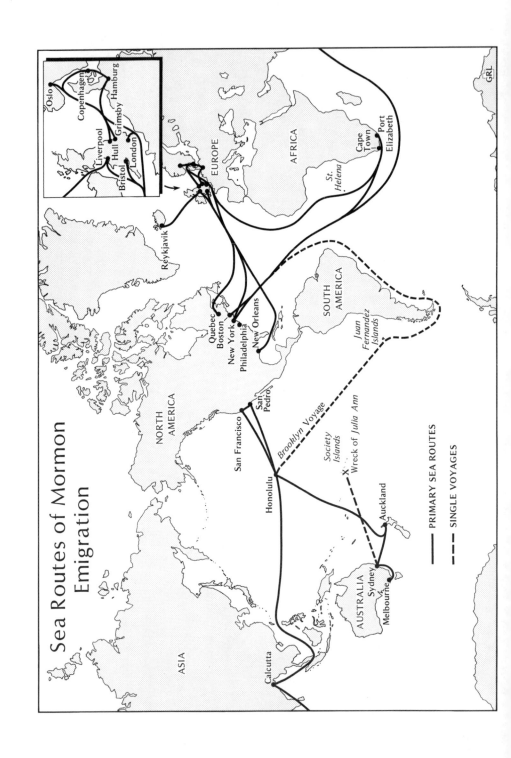

Sea Routes of Mormon Emigration

PRIMARY SEA ROUTES

SINGLE VOYAGES

Oslo
Copenhagen
Hamburg
Grimsby
Liverpool
Hull
Bristol
London

Reykjavik

EUROPE

AFRICA

St. Helena

Cape Town
Port Elizabeth

SOUTH AMERICA

Juan Fernandez Islands

Quebec
Boston
New York
Philadelphia
New Orleans

NORTH AMERICA

San Pedro

San Francisco

Brooklyn Voyage

Society Islands

Wreck of Julia Ann

Honolulu

Auckland

ASIA

AUSTRALIA
Sydney
Melbourne

Calcutta

GRL

Contents

Maps

Preface

To a considerable extent sailing and steam vessels shaped the course of American civilization. Water transportation opened the New World, planted a diverse and adventurous population on its shores, and nourished towns and cities with trade and communication. Ships and steamboats not only moved large numbers of people but also sustained them in remote places. Likewise, the Church of Jesus Christ of Latter-day Saints (Mormon) and the cultural development of its adherents owe an incalculable debt to the water craft that brought an infusion of converts from widely varied backgrounds to the American West.

Yet little has been written about the rich maritime tradition in the Mormon Church. The purpose of this volume is to describe the migration of Latter-day Saints over water during the period from 1830 through 1890. This migration can be divided into two broad movements. The first was the outflow of Mormon missionaries to foreign lands. These were not professional preachers, but lay members of the church who had been ordained to the priesthood and called from all walks of life to proselyte abroad. They either supported themselves, depended on aid from friends and family, or traveled "without purse or scrip" like the early Christian saints. The second movement was the resulting inflow of converts to Mormonism—the harvest of missionary enterprise, the thousands who eagerly responded to the beckoning of Zion.

Since these two movements were intertwined in complex reality but flowed in opposite directions, the study treats them separately. A topical format is used, with each section developed chronologically. The opening chapter, for example, covers the significant voyages of the missionaries in three types of vessels—windships, riverboats, and steamships—together with the conditions they encountered. In contrast to their converts, who emigrated in organized companies, the missionaries were largely on their own and crossed the water individually or in small groups.

The remaining chapters focus on the emigration of converts to America. In sequence these chapters discuss the "gathering" and its first stages, with European Saints traveling to Liverpool, the principal port of embarkation for the Atlantic crossing; the transocean passages under sail; river transportation aboard steamboats before expansion of the railroad westward; the later Atlantic and Pacific ocean passages aboard the faster steamships; and the half-century emigration in summary in the chapter "Ebb Tide."

For convenience the massive data developed in this study are summarized in the Appendixes. Appendix 1, for example, lists organized emigrant voyages by the vessel's name, rig, registry, tonnage, master, number of Latter-day Saint passengers, ports and dates of departure and arrival, number of days in passage, and emigrant company leader. The appendixes also include detailed statistics concerning the passages, the vessels themselves, shipbuilding locations, steamship lines, passengers transported, and certain shipmasters.

This work is a marriage of two loves—maritime lore and Mormon history. It began many years ago and evolved into a long search among Mormon Church archives, federal and foreign government archives, special library collections, contemporary newspapers, journals, personal letters and records, and other primary sources.

About 325 ocean and river craft yielded to research, all of which played a vital part in the global movement of missionaries and converts. Inevitably a few vessels eluded me, but the great majority and the most important were identified with certainty. Yet, as one would expect in a study of this scope, frustrating difficulties were encountered. Records, for example, were often incomplete, inaccurate, and illegible. In such cases information had to be developed from other sources. Since ships sailed under many flags— American, British, German, Dutch, Danish, Norwegian, and French—and were usually registered only in their home ports, it was sometimes necessary to search in different countries. Furthermore, ship data were not always consistent. Tonnages could be reported on several bases, such as gross, net, old, new, and deadweight. Over the years the registered tonnage, rig, and dimensions of a vessel could change. Handwriting in old records created problems, particularly when accompanied by misspellings. Even the names of vessels were spelled differently in various sources; for instance, the name of the brig *Tarquinia* appears four ways, and the ships *Tyrian*, *Athena*, and *Alesto* are reported incorrectly in some records.

Occasionally the popularity of some names for ships complicated identification. *Lloyd's Register* listed more than thirty-five vessels under *Hope*, for example, the name of one Mormon emigrant ship. Such common names required the piecing together of scattered facts to ensure proper identification.

Ship departure and arrival dates were not always readily available. There are gaps in the National Archives' passenger lists, especially for the earlier years. These dates and related facts had to be developed largely from newspaper files, such as the *New York Commercial Advertiser, Daily Alta California,* and *Daily Picayne* in New Orleans.

It was also impossible to determine the precise number of emigrants, since Mormon emigrant companies usually included a few returning missionaries and occasionally non-Mormon relatives or friends. In addition, some converts are known to have emigrated independently, although details are lacking in most instances. All in all, total passengers involved in the Mormon emigration are estimated at 91,600. If adjustment is made for returning elders and non-Mormons in the companies, it can be assumed that more than 85,000 Mormon converts emigrated to America from 1840 through 1890.

This book owes much to many institutions and individuals who are listed in the acknowledgments. Special credit, however, should be given to the midwifery of Dr. Leonard J. Arrington and Dr. Davis Bitton, who followed the progress of the research, offered excellent suggestions, and graciously lent their encouragement and support. It is also appropriate to recognize the fine editorial touch of Trudy McMurrin. Let me also add a particular word of thanks to one who helped in so many ways, my wife, Elaine W. Sonne.

CONWAY B. SONNE

Introduction

To understand fully the Mormon migration over water, one must know something of the turbulent history of the Church of Jesus Christ of Latter-day Saints. This church was born during the religious ferment of the early 1800s. It was a time of hell-fire and damnation preaching, frenzied exhortation, and flights of religious fancy. Sects of all kinds sprouted like poppies on the Yankee landscape. As waves of revivalism swept over the eastern United States, zealous clerics vied with one another in proclaiming their particular creed and exclusive formula for salvation.

During the heat of this evangelism and contention a teenage youth in western New York made a startling announcement. Joseph Smith said that he had received a series of visions and angelic visitations and that he was called to establish the Gospel in its fullness. Sometime later he claimed, through divine guidance, to have unearthed a collection of gold plates which had been buried in a nearby hill. By miraculous means he translated the hieroglyphics found on the plates, with Oliver Cowdery acting as scribe. The translation was published as the Book of Mormon, purportedly a religious chronicle of pre-Columbian inhabitants in the Western Hemisphere. This volume of more than five hundred pages tells of the migrations of three peoples—the Jaredites, Nephites, and Mulekites—from the Old to the New World. It describes their religious practices, apostasies, recurring wars, and eventual destruction of their civilizations. Survivors presumably mixed with other immigrants and became ancestors of the Indians in the Americas.

Yet it was not just the Book of Mormon that led to the founding of the Mormon Church. There were other revelations as well, and by supernatural means the Aaronic and Melchizedek priesthoods were conferred upon Joseph Smith and Oliver Cowdery. These lay priesthoods established the ecclesiastical authority and administrative machinery of the new religion.

On April 6, 1830, a group of six men met in Fayette, New York, and formally organized the church. Joseph Smith was named its president and Prophet, Seer, and Revelator. It was not long before a hierarchy was created consisting of the First Presidency, a Quorum of Twelve Apostles, a First Council of Seventy, a Presiding Bishopric, and a Patriarch to the Church. Geographically, an organization of stakes, wards, branches, and missions soon evolved.

In the dynamics of Mormonism migration became a key element. It was a church on the move, reminiscent of the migratory patterns recorded in the Book of Mormon. The new faith produced migrations in two directions: a proselyting enterprise to recruit converts at home and abroad and a "gathering" of Saints in Zion. This Zion was the American frontier, particularly Missouri, Illinois, and later Utah.

To win converts, missionaries were sent into the world, and as a result, the church grew with surprising rapidity. Among the first missionaries were the Prophet himself, his brother Samuel H. Smith, and Oliver Cowdery. Yet the greatest proselyting responsibility was given to the Twelve Apostles, also referred to as a "traveling high council" or "traveling elders." Some apostles were notably successful in their efforts: Brigham Young, Heber C. Kimball, Wilford Woodruff, Orson Pratt, Parley P. Pratt, John Taylor, Orson Hyde, Lorenzo Snow, and Erastus Snow. Many other missionaries who were not apostles were likewise successful, including such colorful personalities as Dan Jones, Ola N. Liljenquist, and Orson Spencer.

During the early years their number was small, but by the end of the first decade about six hundred missionaries had been called. Each served from a few months to as long as six years, and many completed more than one mission. From 1830 through 1890—the first sixty years of the church— about 7,500 men were called into the mission field. In this same period church membership increased to more than 200,000, including some 85,000 overseas converts who emigrated to America. Since only a fraction of the total missionaries crossed the oceans, their harvest was remarkable.

It was an untrained ministry, except for a few former Protestant ministers who had been converted. Men of the lay priesthood were called, often without warning, to proselyte in the far corners of the world. Some were husbands and fathers, who in answering the call left their families in the "care of the Lord." As in the early Christian church, missionaries usually traveled in pairs, which provided a measure of security, companionship, and the availability of a witness. Missionaries customarily traveled "without purse or scrip" and thus relied on their faith that sustenance would be forthcoming. It was a humbling and trying experience, yet through this system many thousands were converted and inspired to gather in Zion.

Of all the Mormon doctrines perhaps none had a more profound influence than the gathering—a concept rooted in the Old Testament, in the dreams of the ancient Hebrews and in their yearnings for a golden age. Over the centuries, during the glory years and long periods of bondage and dispersion, the prophets of Israel and Judah kept alive the hopes and aspirations of their people. From Moses to Malachi the theme was unchanged. The Lord would redeem and gather his people, and they would live in peace and freedom.

Echoes of the gathering are also found in the New Testament, in the promises of Jesus. Matthew wrote, "And he shall send his angels with a great sound of a trumpet, and they shall gather together his elect from the four winds." John recorded that "there shall be one fold, and one shepherd." Inherent in the gathering was the belief that Christ would return and reign on the earth. To gather in Zion, therefore, was a mystical call. It captured the hearts and minds of those who believed and brought them together as nothing else.

To the Mormons the gathering was both spiritual and temporal. It was spiritual in that converts felt they were no longer lost sheep but had in truth been restored to the fold, that at last they had found the true Gospel and were accepted in the Lord's house. This spirit of the gathering permeated the literature, discourses, and music of the church. As taught in the Book of Mormon and by Joseph Smith, a gathering was necessary to build the Kingdom of God. Furthermore, the "keys" for that purpose had been committed to the church. Without the gathering, without its congenial environment for carrying out the Divine Plan, the Saints could not receive all of the saving ordinances and blessings.

After their baptism many converts said they experienced a compelling desire to leave family and friends and travel to Zion. They attributed this nostalgic longing to the influence of the Spirit, beckoning them to abandon the past and start afresh in a promised land. To the devout, Zion was not only an inheritance but a sanctuary for the "pure in heart" as well.

On the other hand the gathering was temporal. It was a place, America, where the Saints could build the Kingdom of God and work out their own salvation without distractions. They could escape from the Gentile, that is, non-Mormon, world with its temptations and evils. They could erect temples and perform sacred ordinances. In reality, the gathering channeled religious zeal into action. It was a disciplined movement of people. Such people were not just spiritually transformed; they were physically transported to their Zion in a land "choice above all the lands of the earth."

During these years of energetic missionary activity and increasing Mormon immigration, the church became the target of much opposition. Perhaps it was inevitable that a religion spawned in controversy would in itself become the center of controversy. From the outset Mormon doctrines had collided with many orthodox beliefs. Yet it was one thing to challenge other Christian churches on theological grounds, but quite something else to present a perceived economic and political threat. As a result of the gathering, the Saints through their cohesiveness and unity were a growing temporal power. In large measure it was the success of the Mormon Church in winning converts—sometimes whole congregations converted together—that alarmed its rivals. If Mormon ranks had not swelled so quickly, there would probably have been much less hostility.

In any case, the early history of the Mormons was one of relentless persecution, and the Latter-day Saints themselves were not always blameless. During these years episodes of violence and tragedy were almost commonplace—whippings, kidnappings, burnings, the Haun's Mill Massacre, the murders of Joseph and Hyrum Smith, expulsion of the Saints from Missouri and Illinois, the sufferings at Winter Quarters, Nebraska, the Utah invasion of Johnston's Army, and the subsequent Mountain Meadows Massacre. It is not necessary to catalogue the attacks upon missionaries and converts, for it is clear that the gathering was set against a backdrop of persecution.

After the Saints were permanently settled in the Great Basin, opposition grew less violent but more effective. The leading adversary was now Washington. To increase its control over the territory of Utah, the federal government began a campaign to stamp out polygamy—the doctrine that, more than any other, had outraged non-Mormons. Sensing that this issue was the Achilles' heel of the church, between 1862 and 1887 politicians armed themselves with a series of anti-polygamy laws, and each succeeding law contained increasingly severe penalties. Finally the Edmunds-Tucker Act of 1887—the harshest of all—dissolved the church as a legal entity, escheated its assets, and abolished certain civil rights.

No longer could the Mormons withstand the full weight of the federal government, which was legislating the church out of existence and hindering immigration. Then on October 6, 1890, the church issued the famed Manifesto banning plural marriages. It was a landmark in Mormon history and the dawn of a new era. The Manifesto inaugurated a real change of direction. Controversy over polygamy abated. Mormons regained their civil rights and the church was preserved. In 1896 Utah was admitted as the forty-fifth state of the Union.

As the Mormon Church adjusted to the world around it, some changes were inevitable. These changes were more in method than in substance, however. Its proselyting became even more energetic, and young men—and eventually women—fulfilled missions in growing numbers.

Yet even more significant was the changing concept of the gathering. After 1890 the church placed less emphasis on immigration to America. In 1911 the First Presidency sent a message forcefully urging overseas Mormons not to emigrate but to build the Kingdom on their native soil. Rather than bringing converts to Zion, the church began bringing Zion to the converts. To facilitate the new policy, recognizing that the Temple with its sacred ordinances was a magnet for gathering, the church commenced building temples in foreign lands where there were sizable memberships, including Canada, England, Switzerland, New Zealand, Brazil, Mexico, and Japan.

Although a few Saints would continue to emigrate, after more than half a century of intense activity, organized emigration was virtually dead before 1900. Those who chose to leave their homelands traveled individually or in small groups, sometimes with returning missionaries. The winds had shifted. While converts were still being gleaned in Europe, missions were reaping more bounteous harvests in Asia, Latin America, and the Pacific areas. The time of gathering had now passed, but it had served its purpose. The idea of the gathering had laid the groundwork for a world religion.

Under the command of Captain Nathaniel Brown Palmer of Stonington, Connecticut (insert), the 895-ton packet ship *Garrick* sailed from New York on July 1, 1837, carrying the first Mormon missionaries overseas to Liverpool. *Courtesy The Peabody Museum of Salem.*

One

A Call Across the Deep

Big and bearded, Captain Nathaniel B. Palmer, America's foremost shipmaster and an early explorer of Antarctica, appeared on the quarter-deck of the packet ship *Garrick*, pride of the Dramatic Line. He raised the speaking-trumpet in his hand and in a clear, firm voice shouted his orders. The wind was right and the square-rigger strained at the lines holding her to the South Street pier. As the great topsails filled, the lines were cast off. The halyards flattened to the breeze. The crew hoisted the jibs and loosened the spanker. The vessel eased backward into the East River, her stern swinging to the north and clearing the docks. The maneuver brought admiring nods and cheers from the spectators, who recognized the master mariner's skill. With her bow pointing toward the Atlantic Ocean, the *Garrick* anchored in the river until late morning. Then—at ten o'clock—the steam tug slowly towed her out of the New York harbor as far as Sandy Hook. There her sails and courses were swiftly spread, and the white-winged craft bound for England gathered speed in the wind.

It was July 1, 1837. Aboard this packet were the first Mormon missionaries called to Europe. Their efforts and those of the hundreds who followed were to create a rising tide of religious migration. "Captain Nat" had heard of the strange faith and was naturally curious about these seven passengers. On the historic voyage to Liverpool he became friendly with the witty, powerfully built Heber C. Kimball, the soft-spoken Orson Hyde, and the rotund Dr. Willard Richards. Kimball and Hyde were members of the Quorum of Twelve Apostles of the new church. These Yankees were accompanied by an Englishman, Joseph Fielding, and three Canadians—John Goodson, Isaac Russell, and John Snyder. During the nineteen-day crossing the genial and burly skipper won the missonaries' affection and respect. Nine months later Kimball, Hyde, and Russell returned to New

[1]

York on the same ship. Captain Palmer, a sincere Christian, encouraged the elders to preach on shipboard and treated them with consideration and kindness.[1]

In 1839 apostles Wilford Woodruff and John Taylor with Theodore Turley and several other elders sailed from New York as steerage passengers on the packet ship *Oxford*, commanded by another famous mariner, Captain John Rathbone.[2] In early 1840 Heber C. Kimball again sailed for England with fellow apostles Brigham Young, Orson Pratt, Parley P. Pratt, and the youthful George A. Smith. Reuben Hedlock traveled with them aboard the popular packet ship *Patrick Henry*, her master the colorful Captain Joseph C. Delano of the Black Ball Line. In his journal Brigham Young said that the elders "paid $18 each for a steerage passage, furnished our own provisions and bedding and paid the cook $1 each for cooking. . . . I was sick nearly all the way and confined to my berth."[3] After a 28-day voyage the ship arrived at Liverpool.

The opening of the British Mission was just a beginning. Soon other missionaries were sailing the seas to more distant lands. Some of these journeys were veritable odysseys, and none was more remarkable than Orson Hyde's ambitious mission to Palestine. He and John E. Page accepted a call from Joseph Smith, the Mormon prophet, to travel to Jerusalem and dedicate the Holy Land for the prophesied return of the Jews. Although they were called in April of 1840, their progress was slow and Page eventually lost the spirit of his mission. Finally in January 1841—eight months later—Hyde acquired another companion, George J. Adams, and the two sailed for Liverpool, crossing the Atlantic aboard the square-rigged *United States*. Adams remained in the British Isles to preach in Manchester, Birmingham, and other English cities.

On June 20 Hyde left London, traveling alone. He crossed the English Channel to Holland aboard the "fine steamer" *Batavier*. The trip was stormy and he wrote that never had he suffered more from seasickness.[4] At Rotterdam Hyde met a Jewish rabbi, but neither could speak the other's language. Despite this obstacle, the undaunted elder preached to him as best he could. He also published in Dutch five hundred copies of a tract he had written, *An Address to the Hebrews*. He presented a copy to the rabbi and distributed others in The Hague and Amsterdam. There is little doubt that Orson Hyde was the first Mormon missionary to preach on the European continent.

Leaving the picturesque Netherlands, he traveled by coach to Arnhem and then by steamboat up the Rhine. He sojourned in Bavaria to study the German language, which he apparently mastered in eight days. From there he seems to have sailed down the Danube to Constantinople, that sprawling metropolis of ancient mosques and towering minarets. He then traveled to

Smyrna, Beirut, and finally Jerusalem. In a letter to Parley P. Pratt he described some of his hardships:

> When we left Smyrna for Beyrout, we only took in stores for one week, thinking that would surely be sufficient, as the voyage is usually made in four days; but we were nineteen days on the passage. A number of days I ate snails gathered from the rocks, while our vessel was becalmed in the midst of several small and uninhabited islands, but the greatest difficulty was, I could not get enough of them. I was so weak and exhausted that I could not go on shore after the slight exertion of drawing on my boots.[5]

On October 24, 1841, after many trials and privations on land and sea, Hyde stood on the slope of the Mount of Olives, gave a prayer dedicating the land of Palestine as the home of the Jews, and erected a mound of stones where the Temple had been. He then made his solitary way to Egypt, to Cairo and Alexandria, cities of stifling heat, swarming flies, and teeming populations. At Alexandria he boarded a vessel and sailed for Trieste, where the ship was quarantined. Of this period he wrote,

> I feel . . . as though I wished to write a few lines more on this the last day of my confinement on ship board; where I have spent the last fifty-six days: six days in the harbor of Alexandria—twenty-two days on our passage—and twenty-eight here in quarantine. . . . Let me now tell you something about a thunderstorm at sea. I have crossed the Atlantic three times—once the German and Black seas, and all about the Levante, besides sailing much on American waters; but never, no, never before did I witness nature in such a rage on the deep, as once on this last voyage off the Island of Candia [Crete], about the 7th of December. The sun sat behind the rising bulwarks of a dark and gloomy cloud as though he would not look upon the scene that awaited us . . . the breath of the monster reached us; all hands aloft furling sails . . . the sea began to roll in upon our weatherbeam and lash the hull of our ship, tossing her from surge to surge with as much ease as a giant would sport with an infant.[6]

This adventurous apostle, an eloquent orator who had memorized the Bible in three languages, survived border wars, seasickness, hunger, and perils from pirates and nature. After his return to Liverpool, Hyde was appointed president of an emigrant company that sailed to New Orleans aboard the square-rigger *Medford*. He reached his Nauvoo home in December 1842—after traveling some 20,000 miles and an absence of nearly three years.[7]

Another epic journey began in October 1843, when Addison Pratt, Noah Rogers, Benjamin F. Grouard, and Knowlton F. Hanks sailed from

New Bedford, Massachusetts, aboard the 346-ton whaleship *Timoleon*, bound for the Society Islands. The ship, which had made about a dozen whaling expeditions, was under the command of hard-drinking Captain William Plaskett. Misfortune struck early in the voyage. Elder Hanks, who suffered from consumption, became seriously ill and died. He was the first missionary to be buried at sea. But during the passage the missionaries converted two of the passengers, a Methodist minister and his wife. The whaler took a course to the Cape Verde Islands, there acquiring fresh fruit, and then beat her way through the stormy waters off the Cape of Good Hope. Into the Indian Ocean she moved at a whale-hunting pace past Cape Van Diemen off Australia and skirted Tasmania before bringing the three missionaries to Tubuai after 203 days at sea. Addison Pratt received some useful gifts from his fellow passengers and remained at Tubuai while his companions continued with the *Timoleon* to Tahiti—a passage of four more days, making their voyage the longest yet for any Mormon missionaries.[8]

To these Mormons from New England this cluster of mountainous islands in the Pacific with their ancient volcanoes and lofty peaks carpeted in lush greenery opened a strange new world. At this time the Society Islands were torn by skirmishes between the natives and French soldiers who were busy subduing a resisting population. Catholic and Protestant missionaries were also busy enthusiastically working to save the souls of less than enthusiastic Polynesians, and the established clergy regarded the Mormons as interlopers. Nevertheless, Noah Rogers found lodging in a native home for two dollars a week and began the task of learning the language. In their preaching the Mormons followed an island-hopping program, traveling from one island to another in small sailing craft such as the 40-ton schooner *Artarevedre*.[9] After a year of moderately successful proselyting the missionaries read in a newspaper of the murders of Joseph and Hyrum Smith and the mobs threatening the Saints in Illinois. Alarmed for the safety of their families, the elders decided that Rogers would return to Nauvoo.

Rogers arranged passage on the American whaleship *Three Brothers*, skippered by Captain Mitchell, and boarded the vessel on July 1, 1845. Two days later the Nantucket whaler sailed from Papeete, Tahiti, on her way home from a four-year whaling voyage. She stopped briefly at Tubuai, but Rogers missed seeing Addison Pratt, who was visiting another island and returned just after the ship sailed, a bitter disappointment. During the homeward passage Captain Mitchell permitted Rogers to preach on shipboard, and seven or eight believed. Even the master professed belief; but "finding that he must obey also, he became bitter, which rendered part of the voyage disagreeable."[10] With the wind blowing hard at Cape Horn, the sturdy whaler rounded the treacherous area through snow squalls and biting cold. After doubling the Cape the ship passed the Falkland Islands and some days later sighted a loaded slaver from Africa sailing off the coast of Brazil. On November 6, after a 126-day passage, Rogers landed at Nantucket, giving him the distinction of completing the first Mormon missionary journey around the world. A few months later he joined the Saints in the exodus from Nauvoo, but he died from exposure at Mount Pisgah, Iowa.[11]

As for Addison Pratt, he remained in Tahiti until 1847, when he made a remarkable voyage to San Francisco aboard the 56-ton schooner *Providence* commanded by a personal friend, Captain Lewis T. Sajat. The Tahitian vessel made the passage, after a brief stop in Honolulu, in about 75 days. (It is interesting that more than a century later a group of Mormon missionaries sailed a 50-ton schooner-rigged diesel yacht from Wilmington, California, to Tahiti, almost duplicating Pratt's voyage in reverse. The yacht was given Addison Pratt's Polynesian name, Paraita.)[12] In Pratt's absence, Benjamin Grouard was in charge of the mission. Grouard, who, like Pratt, was an experienced sailor before his baptism, had married a Tahitian woman.

In 1850 Pratt was called on another mission to the Society Islands. Arranging passage on the brig *Frederick*, possibly of Tahitian registry, he sailed from San Francisco and landed at Tahiti in May. Six months later he was joined by his wife and four daughters as well as another group of new missionaries. Shortly after his return, with the help of the natives Pratt built an 80-ton schooner, the *Ravaai* ("fisher"), a suitable vessel for carrying the missionaries between islands.

The Mormons were now making headway among both the native and European populations. Hundreds of islanders had been baptized, a situation which created much anxiety in official circles. Then came a change in the government, and French administrators denied the elders permission to remain in the Islands. Pratt and Grouard sold the *Ravaai* and with the proceeds purchased passage on the American bark *Callao*. The 168-ton vessel sailed from Papeete on May 16, 1852. After a 43-day voyage the *Callao* arrived at San Francisco, her manifest listing a cargo of 165,000 oranges and passengers "Pratt, lady and 4 daughters" and "Greward, lady and 4 children."[13]

During the 1840s a growing number of missionaries landed in the British Isles. On December 6, 1844, Apostle Wilford Woodruff, Dan Jones, Hiram Clark, Milton Holmes, Leonard Wilford Hardy, and several of their wives sailed from New York on the packet ship *John R. Skiddy*, skippered by the highly respected Captain William Skiddy of the Swallowtail Line. After a rough, month-long passage the contingent landed at Liverpool. The following year Dan Jones organized the Welsh Mission and proved to be one of the most prolific missionaries in Mormon history. After a highly successful year as head of the British Mission, Apostle Woodruff returned to New York in March 1846, crossing the Atlantic in the slow square-rigger *Ashburton*. He wrote of that "terrible time at sea" but stated that he was "perfectly satisfied with our voyage" under the able Captain William Howland.[14]

In March 1850 Apostle Lorenzo Snow, a small man with a gentle spirit and indomitable will, made a pleasant passage from New York aboard the ship *Shannon*. He traveled on to Italy and sent missionaries to India and Malta. In May of that year Apostle John Taylor, John Pack, and Curtis E. Bolton sailed from New York to Liverpool in 23 days on the new packet ship *Jacob A. Westervelt* commanded by Captain William R. Hoodless.[15]

The Pacific Ocean drew more missionaries as well. On November 15, 1850, ten Mormon elders set out for the Sandwich Islands aboard the British bark *Imaum of Muscat*. In Sacramento Apostle Charles C. Rich had met with them and appointed Hiram Clark president of the Sandwich Islands, or Hawaiian Mission. It was Clark's third mission call. Because of headwinds the vessel did not get under way until the twenty-second—a delay that did not please Captain James Isaac Riches because it meant feeding his passengers while in port. The elders paid $40 each for passage, less a 5 percent discount, for accommodations between decks. They furnished their own bedding. The food was "uninviting," and it was so dark between decks that it took several minutes for their eyes to adjust to the faint light. As the *Imaum* beat her way out of the harbor through long, rolling waves, the master found himself with seasick passengers, facing angry black clouds. Fearing the coming storm, the pilot turned back and left the British master in strange waters off a dangerous coast.

George Q. Cannon found humor in the precarious situation, however, writing that "we were all suffering severely from the effects of sea-sickness, and notwithstanding the dangers . . . the sense of the ridiculous, in my case —only one bucket among us for every purpose—overcame fear, and I could not help laughing. . . . Right in the midst of our sickness we heard the startling cry from the mate of 'Breakers ahead,' and that we were close upon them. At any other time this would have excited us; but we were so sick we did not mind it." In any event, the ship escaped crashing on the rocks, and Captain Riches with his Malay crew brought the *Imaum of Muscat* into Honolulu harbor on December 12.[16]

Another dynamic leader—Apostle Parley P. Pratt—was called to open a new mission in South America. With his wife Phebe and Rufus C. Allen he sailed from San Francisco on September 5, 1851, aboard the American bark *Henry Kelsey*, a 197-ton three-master. Pratt described the voyage as "tedious and disagreeable." He recorded that the skipper, apparently

Captain C. E. Sampson, was a miser who fed the passengers moldy bread full of worms and bugs and rotten beef and pork. At one time the small vessel almost met disaster when she ran too close to shore. After 64 days at sea the missionaries landed at Valparaiso, Chile, where they faced insurmountable obstacles. A raging civil war, religious hostility, language difficulties, and a lack of funds compelled them finally to leave the country.

On March 5, 1852, the missionaries boarded the 213-ton brig *Dracut*. The return voyage was also unpleasant. Poor and scanty food as well as bad sailing weather prompted Pratt to write these despairing words: "We are hungry, and weary, and lonesome, and disconsolate. . . . The most horrid blasphemies resound in our ears every day in the cabin and on deck, from captain and mate together, with gambling and blackguardism."[17] After 75 days at sea—a journey of more than 5,000 miles—the Mormon party eagerly disembarked at San Francisco.

The most ambitious missionary enterprise, however, originated on August 28, 1852, at a special conference of the church held in Salt Lake City. From the pulpit 106 men were called on missions to almost all parts of the globe. Six were assigned to the United States, four to Nova Scotia and other Canadian provinces, two to South America, four to the West Indies, thirty-nine to Great Britain, one to France, four to Germany, three to Prussia, two to Gibraltar, one to Denmark, two to Norway, nine to India, four to China, three to Siam, three to South Africa, ten to Australia, and nine to the Sandwich Islands.[18]

No really complete records of the early missionary journeys exist, but the dedication and courage of these elders, and their families, opened an important door on the world. Some missions, particularly those in the Far East, were unsuccessful; but in Europe, South Africa, Hawaii, Australia, and New Zealand seeds were planted for a plentiful future harvest of converts. Yet the adventures—and sometimes misadventures—of these stalwarts are sagas in themselves.

Richard Ballantyne, a tall, austere Scotsman, was such a missionary. At a time when his fortunes were at their worst, he was one of the 106 called without warning. He left his family almost destitute and traveled westward truly without purse or scrip. Twelve others were to accompany him to India. Crossing the desert to California, he arrived at San Pedro and sailed to San Francisco on the small brig *Col. Fremont*. At this tumultuous seaport, buzzing with goldseekers and adventurers, the elders, financed by local church members, engaged passage to India on the Yankee clipper ship *Monsoon*. Commanded by Captain Zenas Winsor of Duxbury, Massachusetts, who took a liking to the stout-hearted missionaries, this trim craft carried the thirteen Mormons for about 85 days and almost 11,000 miles to Calcutta. The *Monsoon*'s log is very sketchy, but Richard Ballantyne's journal is descriptive.[19] His pen gives such vignettes as the following:

> Jany. 29, 1853 Saturday. After Breakfast we attended to singing and prayer. . . . Today in the afternoon put out to sea and took the last view of San Francisco and the American Continent for a few years. This land on which the Zion of God is to be built up in this generation and where at the present time the Saints are located in the Great Basin of North America. Their we left our friends, our families, our wives, children, Mothers, Sisters and brothers. . . .
>
> This evening was taken with sea sickness which continued untill Monday the 31st when it appeared that I was affected with the Small Pox. I have probably taken the Contagion in the house of Bro Hazen Kimball, whose wife was just recovering from a severe attack of the disease at the time I arrived in San Francisco.

Elder Ballantyne was violently ill for several weeks. He suffered severe pains in his head, chest, and back and weakness, sleeplessness, and loss of appetite. In about five days pustules erupted over his body, and in his feverish condition he felt that he was being seized upon "as if by some power . . . [that] could destroy me." During his sickness his missionary companions patiently cared for him, especially Robert Skelton, who nursed him with "unwearied care and kindness . . . exposing himself to the contagion." Elder Levi Savage was similarly afflicted, and the two missionaries were isolated in their cabin. The disease apparently spread no further.

Ballantyne described their treatment at the hands of Captain Zenas Winsor and his men:

> A good cheerful spirit also seems to prevail on the vessel from Captain to crew, and scarce a profane word has been heard since we came on board. The Captain allows us every priviledge that we can desire, is sociable, and furnishes excellent, healthy diet three times aday. We have fresh bread morning and evening with potatoes, meat, butter, cheese, etc. And at noon have soup, plumb or Rice pudding, potatoes, meat, etc. with tea and coffee morning and evening to those who drink it. Many of the brethren don't use it, preferring to observe the Word of Wisdom.

The *Monsoon* had favorable winds, much to the surprise of the captain. She sailed past the Sandwich Islands, several other small islands, crossed the International Date Line, and was approaching the Philippines. Then one day Captain Winsor offered an interesting proposition, which Ballantyne noted in his journal: "The Captain of the vessel proposed that if all the brethren would throw their tobacco over board he would set the example. It was agreed to by all, and the tobacco being carefully collected and put in a package together, was deposited in the mighty deep to the no small joy of those who have not been using the article. . . . In the evening the Captain treated the Company with wine, Brandy and whisky to make merry over the Tobacco scrape. Very temperately used."

As the ship passed by the Philippines, the missionaries observed some flying fish, a cow fish weighing about 150 pounds, and a strange fowl. The bird was large, between the size of duck and goose, with a very "dark brow, a little white about the tail, long wings. . . . We generally see this sea Fowl a great distance from land and in all probability its home is on the waters."

On March 10, with the vessel now about three thousand miles from Calcutta, Ballantyne reported the only unpleasantness with the crew:

> Today the sailors refused painting the outside of the vessel. One of them stated that they were afraid to do it, lest they might fall into the sea. Another Complained of being misused. The Captain informed them that up to this time he had been fully satisfied with them, but if they now refused to obey orders they should have no more pay. The sailors retired and did not Comply with the order. . . . All parties seem to have got along in a quiet and peaceable manner thus far. A better behaved set of seamen I never before saw . . . .
> Friday, 11th . . . . Today the Sailors have agreed to paint the outside of the Ship as required by the Captain.

Several days later the *Monsoon* sailed within about thirty miles of the coast of Cochin China, but from that distance all that could be seen were low, irregular mountains. The weather was hot, squally with rainstorms. During the night the weather grew worse, with an almost continuous torrent of rain. Then a "singular luminous flame was seen, during the night, on the top of the masts. It was supposed to be an accumulation of electric fluids, which in Equatorial regions frequently collect and present the appearance of a luminous body. Mariners call it the 'Tacky Lantern'."

As the vessel entered the South China Sea, she encountered a yellow scum on the water resembling sawdust. "Today the Captain drew up some of it in a pail and pronounced it an animal substance. . . . As we had no Microscope we could not determine the existence of life. A number of Small water snakes were seen yesterday. Day before the Captain Harpooned a large Cowfish. Probably 250 lbs. It had a young fish fully formed inside. In length about two feet. . . . The meat resembled beef . . . quite palatable, and wholesome."

The scenery was changing. Passing through the Straits of Singapore, the missionaries could see heavy foliage, green mountains. Then there came in sight a lighthouse shaped like a pillar, encircled with a cornice and topped with a beautiful dome. Singapore provided further excitement as it was a "delightful and imposing aspect." There were many vessels of all nations anchored in the harbor, the large white Government House, and the British army barracks with a tall pole from which the Union Jack fluttered.

Then began the 500-mile passage through the Straits of Malacca, sailing past Chinese and Malay junks. It was a hazardous voyage, but in a few weeks the ship ascended the Hooghly River to Calcutta. The Scotsman was appalled at this Indian city. Never had he seen such poverty, filth, disease, and death. It was a huge, teeming city of palaces and penury, reeking with foul odors and swarming with beggars.

Nathaniel V. Jones, who had been elected mission president, assigned Richard Ballantyne and Robert Skelton to serve in Madras, but obtaining passage was a different matter. Only one vessel was scheduled to make the voyage before the monsoon season began, the 404-ton square-rigged *John Brightman*, skippered by Captain Thomas D. Scott. However, Captain Scott wanted nothing to do with the Mormons. After repeated pleas Richard Ballantyne promised the mariner a safe passage in the name of the Lord if he would accept the two missionaries as passengers, and upon that unusual promise Captain Scott agreed. Following the Hooghly out of Calcutta, the ship moved carefully. At the narrowest and most dangerous part of the river, there suddenly appeared another vessel headed directly for the *John Brightman*. A collision seemed unavoidable. Beside himself with anger and fear, Captain Scott reminded the elder of his promise. Ballantyne reassured him that the ships would pass safely. Then the two vessels, miraculously it seemed, separated and passed without colliding. From that time the elders enjoyed the complete confidence and friendship of the master.

Yet the voyage was far from over. After the ship had reached the open sea, the heavens grew black and then exploded in the fury of a hurricane. The sea heaved insanely. Two sailors were washed overboard but rescued. Passengers were seasick and terrified. The captain's log contained such entries as, "Ship pitching very heavy and taking in much water. Surging waves over the vessel. Head Knees and rails all washed away . . . . Lightning. Tremendous squall from the N.W. Split the fore-top-sail and fore topmast stay-sail tore to pieces. Carried away the forsheet. 6 A.M. Blowing a hurricane from the N.W. with a tremendous sea from the South. . . . Much water lashing over all . . . tearing the Copper off her bottom."[20] The storms subsided, and the crippled ship dropped anchor in the Madras Roads on July 24, 1853. At Madras a thankful Captain Scott gave Richard Ballantyne a pair of shoes, some money, paid for his passengers' board and room at the Madras House, and financed the publication of 2,000 missionary tracts.

After a year in Madras—a year of hardship, dysentery, fevers, and persecution—Richard Ballantyne boarded the snow-rigged *Royal Thistle*, which flew the British flag. His illness and weakness moved Captain Robert Wright to provide him with free cabin passage to London. It was a 134-day voyage around the Cape of Good Hope. At times the vessel was bedeviled by raging storms and frustrating calms. Then the white cliffs of Dover came into view, and the small two-master made her way up the River Thames to anchor at London on December 6, 1854. The following month Ballantyne was appointed president of an emigrant company that sailed from Liverpool aboard the American ship *Charles Buck*. After a 56-day passage the square-rigger reached New Orleans on March 14, 1855. Two days later the Mormon emigrants were traveling up the Mississippi River aboard the side-wheeler *Michigan*, docking at St. Louis after 11 days. There the missionary formed a wagon train and brought his company safely across the plains to Utah. Richard Ballantyne was reunited with his family after an absence of almost three years. His odyssey was historic. He was the first Mormon missionary to travel westward around the world without purse or scrip, a feat only Noah Rogers had achieved, a decade earlier from the other direction. Ballantyne was on shipboard approximately 320 days plus 11 days on the Mississippi. Rogers had spent approximately 333 days on the water, excluding inter-island travel, during his mission.[21]

For the other members of the East Indian Mission, history reveals only occasional glimpses of their sea journeys. In June 1853 Elam Ludington (sometimes spelled Luddington) and Levi Savage sailed from Calcutta for Rangoon aboard the *Fire Queen*, but the vessel sprang a leak and had to return to port. Robert Owens, who had been assigned to Madras, was a troublesome missionary who undermined Richard Ballantyne's work. Serious moral charges were brought against him, but apparently he repented and was reinstated. In July of 1854 he was back in Calcutta. There he boarded the British ship *Hyderabad* and worked his passage to Australia, arriving two months later. He then embarked on the small British steamer *Hellespont* for Tasmania, the first Mormon elder in that land. What took him there, however, is a mystery. In April of 1855 this enigmatic wanderer was on his way from Melbourne on the ill-starred American brig *Tarquinia*, a 210-ton craft that was to be condemned as unseaworthy at Honolulu, leaving her passengers—including 72 Mormons—to their own resources.[22]

Other missionaries were homeward bound, among them William Willes, sent to India and Burma almost four years earlier by Lorenzo Snow. He sailed from Singapore aboard the small British bark *Gazelle*. Four and a half months later, on March 1, 1855, this three-master with its gazelle figurehead docked at Liverpool. Elder Willes praised Captain George

Leslie, who had "behaved with much kindness, and permitted me to testify, and distribute the Word, among the crew."[23]

There was also Samuel A. Woolley. On November 1, 1854, he sailed out of Calcutta down the unpredictable Hooghly River into the Bay of Bengal for a pleasant and uneventful voyage of 100 days to Boston aboard the American clipper ship *John Gilpin*. In contrast, the return trip of Chauncey W. West and Benjamin F. Dewey was filled with peril and adventure. West had been president of the Siam Mission, but had found his destination blocked by political strife in Burma. He and Dewey sailed to Ceylon, but after finding few listeners they took a ship to Bombay. Leaving Bombay early in 1854 on the British bark *Cressy*, the two elders apparently worked for their passage as deck hands. During the voyage the vessel was becalmed, struck a reef, was exposed to hostile natives, had one of her small boats attacked by a shark, weathered severe heat, survived a frightening typhoon, and arrived in Macao in leaky condition with her master dying. The missionaries then engaged passage to California on the *Hiageer*, but after boarding this bark West declared that he had dreamed the vessel was wrecked. Twice more he had the same dream. Whatever doubts he may have had were removed when Elder Dewey said that he had dreamed the same dream "thrice." They canceled their passage and made another booking on the British ship *John Gray*. A few days after boarding the second vessel for a 53-day voyage to San Francisco, they were informed that the *Hiageer* was lost.[24]

There was also a rare coincidence. An old friend of the missionaries, Captain Zenas Winsor, had skippered the clipper ship *Monsoon* which three years earlier had carried Amos Milton Musser and twelve other elders from San Francisco to Calcutta. This missionary, while trying to engage passage for a "Brother Adams" who was hospitalized and later died, chanced to meet the Yankee mariner again in Calcutta. After learning of Adams's death, Captain Winsor offered Musser first-class cabin passage to London aboard his new clipper ship *Viking*. She sailed from Calcutta March 3, 1856, and arrived at London 138 days later. Musser wrote of his friendship and admiration for Captain Winsor and added that "notwithstanding the great length of the voyage from Calcutta, I must acknowledge, I have never before spent a more pleasant and agreeable time at sea."[25]

Soon to join the exclusive fraternity of those who had encircled the globe—Rogers, Ballantyne, Woolley, and Musser—was the stout-hearted Truman Leonard. After his arrival at Calcutta on the *Monsoon*, this elder spent about seven months near and around Calcutta, that grimy, tumultuous, squalid pesthole. It was a city he was glad to leave, and with Musser he made the sea journey around the subcontinent's cape to Bombay. For the

Captain Zenas Winsor of Duxbury, Massachusetts, skippered two American clipper ships that carried missionaries of the East Indian Mission—the 774-ton *Monsoon* in 1853 and the 1,349-ton *Viking*, shown above. *Courtesy New Bedford Whaling Museum.*

next year and a half he preached his way as far up the coast as Karachi, carrying his message to anyone who would listen—elite Brahmans, turbaned Sikhs, zealous Muslims, and devout Buddhists. He passed among untouchables, merchants, farmers, soldiers, and priests; through villages with mud and straw huts, trade centers with noisy bazaars, and wealthy estates. Yet few listened. Discouraged, he finally arranged to work for his passage to Liverpool, where he boarded the ship *Enoch Train* with a large company of Mormon emigrants, arriving in Boston May 1, 1856, after 39 days at sea.[26]

The last missionary to leave India was the dauntless Robert Skelton, who had nursed and cared for Richard Ballantyne through his frequent illnesses. Their mission had resulted in a dozen baptisms, one convert being ordained an elder, preaching "in almost every nook and corner of that large city" Madras, and the publishing of a monthly paper and a number of tracts and news articles.[27] Skelton sailed from Calcutta in May 1856 on the British ship *Earl of Eglinton*, bound for China.[28]

Among the 106 missionaries called in August 1852 were Hosea Stout, James Lewis, and Chapman Duncan, who were assigned to proselyte in China. After traveling overland to California the elders took the coastal steamer *Sea Bird* from San Pedro to San Francisco. There they had difficulty obtaining passage to China. Finally, Captain Jacob Bouten of the

Dutch bark *Jan van Hoorn* agreed to take them on his vessel for $80 each, which was donated by local Mormons. The bark sailed through the Golden Gate March 9, 1853, for an uneventful voyage which Stout faithfully recorded in his diary. There was only one other cabin passenger, but sixty Chinese were cramped in the lower deck "like so many sick pigs." After 48 days at sea, the *Jan van Hoorn* dropped anchor at Hong Kong on April 27.[29]

Their efforts in China were unproductive. After less than two months the missionaries packed their bags and sailed on June 22 from Hong Kong aboard the British square-rigger *Rose of Sharon*. Their passage cost $55 each, but the elders supplied their own provisions. Among the passengers were thirty-seven Chinese men, two cooks, two doctors, and forty-nine Chinese women recruited for prostitution. During the voyage Stout described in his diary an albatross dinner provided by the master, a battle between a whale and a thresher shark, and a religious ceremony of the Chinese courtesans invoking the aid of their gods to improve the sailing weather. After 62 days the 788-ton ship anchored off San Francisco on August 22, the three elders going ashore the next day.[30]

In addition to the missionaries called in 1852 to labor in India and China, two other groups were assigned to Hawaii and Australia. These elders were among the thirty who had come from San Pedro to San Francisco in January 1853 aboard the brig *Col. Fremont*. While those departing for other destinations were arranging their passage across the Pacific, the Hawaii-bound missionaries made their booking on the 677-ton Yankee square-rigger *Huntress*, skippered by her builder, Captain James L. Lambert. This vessel had just made the sea journey from Boston around Cape Horn in 146 days. On January 29 the *Huntress* cleared the port of San Francisco with her nine Mormon passengers: Benjamin F. Johnson, Nathan Tanner, Thomas Karren, William McBride, Ephraim Green, James Lawson, Reddin A. Allred, Reddick N. Allred, and Egerton Snyder. After 19 uneventful days on the water the group landed at Honolulu, where they were welcomed by President Philip B. Lewis and other elders already in the mission.[31]

There were other voyages to and from Hawaii. In September 1854, for example, sixteen-year-old Joseph F. Smith made a "somewhat disagreeable" voyage to Honolulu with a group of missionaries aboard the 370-ton clipper schooner *Vaquero*, a vessel noted for her fast runs in the Pacific. Smith, who quickly mastered the Hawaiian language and demonstrated a gift for healing, later became the sixth president of the Mormon Church.[32] Three years later the *Vaquero* reappeared in Mormon chronicles as the vessel that transported from Australia to California seven discouraged elders who were returning home without being properly released.[33]

In October 1854 the 415-ton American ship *Ianthe*, built in 1840 and skippered by Captain Grant Dubs, sailed from San Francisco to Hawaii on her way to Hong Kong. Her passengers included a new contingent of missionaries to the Islands, Henry P. Richards, Washington B. Rogers, Orson K. Whitney, John A. West, Joseph A. Peck, Smith B. Thurston, and William King. It was a pleasant voyage of 20 days. Two months later John T. Caine and Edward Partridge made the same passage in 22 days on the brig *Susan Abigail*. This two-master of only 159 tons was commanded by Captain Todd. The *Susan Abigail* became a curious footnote in Civil War history when, as part of a whaling fleet in the Bering Strait, she was captured and sunk on June 23, 1865, by the ship-rigged and steam-driven Confederate raider *Shenandoah*, whose officers were unaware that the war had ended at Appomattox two months earlier.[34]

Several other sailing vessels were utilized by missionaries in Hawaii, among them the noted clipper ship *Francis A. Palmer*. In January 1855 James Lawson, who had traveled to Hawaii two years earlier, became ill and returned to San Francisco on this American ship. After a 13-day voyage Lawson's appearance was so shabby that the California Saints donated clothing and money to make him "appear respectable on the streets." In April 1856 James Graham and John S. Eldredge, returning from Australia, engaged passage at Honolulu on the "Francis Palmer"— apparently the same vessel, although the *Daily Alta California* reported her as a bark when she arrived on April 23. (It was not uncommon for sailing ships to change rig.) Later that year John T. Caine made a 23-day return voyage to San Francisco on this ship, and in 1862 her name is mentioned again as the ship that carried Elder George Sims to Liverpool.[35]

Three years after his arrival in Honolulu, Joseph F. Smith left Hawaii with a group of elders in October 1857 aboard the bark *Yankee*, commanded by Captain James Smith. The *Daily Alta California* noted her reaching San Francisco on October 23—a 16-day passage. Among the last of the sailing craft mentioned in Hawaiian Mission records was the bark *Onward*, a 303-ton trader. The *Daily Alta California* reported her arrival in San Francisco on May 16, 1864, under Captain Hemstead, "22 days from Honolulu." Among her passengers on this voyage were apostles Ezra Taft Benson and Lorenzo Snow, returning from a brief visit to the Islands.[36]

When the 195-ton Tasmanian bark *Petrel* anchored in the beautiful Sydney harbor on October 30, 1851, two resolute Mormon elders—John Murdock and Charles W. Wandell—brought ashore the Book of Mormon and their hope of a spiritual conquest of the land "down under." They had traveled 8,000 miles from San Francisco across the tossing Pacific for almost eight weeks. It was a reasonably good voyage for these pioneer missionaries to Australia, and they considered shipmaster John Blackburn "a gentle-man." On June 2, 1852, leaving Wandell to preside over the mission, Murdock sailed for home aboard the British square-rigged *Harmony*, commanded by Captain George Banks. She was a remarkable ship of 525 tons, built in 1809, and she plied the seas for more than half a century. The *Daily Alta California* reported her arrival in San Francisco on October 9, "120 days from Sydney, via Monterey 7 days." She had encountered strong and continued head gales after leaving Sydney and more heavy weather off Monterey.[37]

On February 2, 1853, ten more missionaries left San Francisco aboard the British bark *Pacific*. Little is known of this vessel except that she was listed at 355 tons and skippered by a Captain Matthews. The missionary party consisted of Augustus Farnham, William Hyde, Josiah W. Fleming, Burr Frost, Absalom P. Dowdle, James Graham, John S. Eldredge, J. Norton, John Hyde, and Paul Smith. The elders apparently had cabin accommodations. Shortly after sailing Absalom Dowdle came down with smallpox. Although the doctor tried to keep the illness secret and isolated other cases developed. Fortunately all of the afflicted recovered. On February 20 the *Pacific* narrowly escaped shipwreck at Christmas Island. The whaleship *Robert Pulsipher* of New Bedford was not so successful, however. She was wrecked with 650 barrels of oil and 32 persons on board. Elder Fleming wrote, "We took one whaling boat, the second mate, the doctor and eight hands on our vessel."[38] The remaining survivors decided to make for shore in a small boat. The next day the *Pacific* crossed the equator, and then on March 1 anchored at Samoa for several days. After the voyage resumed, a passenger caught an eight-foot shark, and Paul Smith became ill with canker. On March 31 the *Pacific* entered the mouth of Sydney harbor, but was quarantined for seven days because of the smallpox aboard.

In late 1856 ten more elders sailed from San Francisco aboard the 164-ton British bark *General Wool*, under the command of Captain Fuller, and after "a very tedious passage" of 94 days arrived at Melbourne, Australia. About the same time George S. Clark and Andrew J. Stewart made a 65-day passage from San Francisco to Melbourne on the French clipper bark *Foederis Arca*. The Melbourne newspaper *Argus* of December 13, 1856, reported: "Dec. 12. 'Foderis Area,' French barque, 390 tons, C. Hauvean, from San Francisco, 8th October." No other details of the voyage are known. These journeys were among the last made under canvas by the missionaries to Australia.[39]

On the other side of the world missionaries were expanding their activities in the British Isles and Europe, reaping thousands of converts. Crossing the Atlantic under sail was growing less attractive, however, as the faster steamships increased in popularity. Yet passenger fares for the windships were so much lower than those of the steamers that many missionaries of the fifties and sixties endured the longer and less pleasant voyages of sailing craft.

At the 1852 special conference two missionaries had been called to Gibraltar. Crossing the plains from Utah and selling their animals in Missouri to finance their journey, Edward Stevenson and Nathan T. Porter, with some other elders, sailed from New York on November 17, 1852, aboard the 1,146-ton Yankee packet ship *American Union*. They landed at Liverpool 49 days later—unusually slow time for an eastward passage. From there Stevenson and Porter continued to Southampton, where they took the British paddle-wheel steamer *Iberia* of the P.&O. Line along the coast of Portugal and Spain to their Gibraltar destination.

It is unfortunate that so little is known of one missionary sea adventure. Sometime in 1864 Bendt Jensen Eriksen, an emigrant elder from Denmark, had completed his mission call and was bound for America on the ship *Louis Napoleon*, possibly of British registry. In midocean the vessel caught fire and was lost. Eriksen and other passengers found themselves adrift in a small boat and faced with the perils of a cold and surging Atlantic, its gusty winds and unpredictable weather. For three days they floated in a lifeboat before being rescued by a passing ship. Eriksen lost all of his belongings and arrived at New York penniless.[40]

In 1852 three missionaries were called to South Africa—Jesse Haven, Leonard I. Smith, and William H. Walker. These elders put their affairs in order, left their wives and families, crossed the plains eastward from Utah, sailed to Liverpool, and then at London booked passage on the 358-ton British bark *Domitia*. The vessel had been built a year earlier in Scotland with one deck and a female figurehead and was skippered by Captain J. R. McDowell. The Mormons, who were the only passengers, shared two cabins. On February 11, 1853, the bark was towed down the Thames into the open sea.

The first evening the missionaries retired to a stateroom and prayed and exchanged blessings. Although the voyage of more than nine weeks was uneventful, Haven recorded several incidents:

> We frequently saw flying fish. One day we saw a whale. If the swallow of a whale is no bigger than 3 inches in diameter, the size that whalers say it is, Jonah must have been a very small man. . . . At other times, porpoises or sea-hogs were very plentiful about the ship. One day the first mate harpooned one. . . . It weighed about 300 lbs. At another time we saw a shark following the vessel. The mates and sailors succeeded in capturing him. He weighed something like 150 lbs. . . . The sailors cut off the tail. They say the strength is in the tail.

He also described the initiatory rites of those crossing the equator for the first time. The indignities consisted of "Neptune" shaving the neophyte with an iron hoop and throwing water on him. Afterwards the captain gave the sailors a bottle of brandy which was quickly consumed. Otherwise, there were few breaks in the shipboard tedium. It was April 18 when the *Domitia* dropped anchor off Cape Town and the South African Mission was born.[41]

On December 15, 1855, after more than two and a half years in South Africa, President Haven boarded the 96-ton schooner *Cleopatra* at Cape Town and began his homeward journey. This small two-masted craft, which was owned by South Africans and commanded by Captain Thomas Ford, made her way to London by late February or early March.

William Walker and Leonard I. Smith had left a short time earlier. Several Mormon converts—John Stock, Thomas Parker, and Charles Roper—had decided to purchase rather than charter the 169-ton brig *Unity* for £2,500. The brig had been built in 1848 at Whitehaven, England, and the master might have been a Captain Way. The purchase was necessitated by the difficulty in booking passage on other ships. Persecution of the Mormons—attributable in part to their success—had become so intense that no master was willing to accept them as passengers except in the lowliest steerage berths at exorbitant fares. The purchase, according to Walker, caused "a great stir among the people. They began to boast and say . . . 'Mormons' could not get from this land of Africa. Editors were amazed; hireling priests disfigured their faces with a sly grin." On November 28, 1855, the "Mormon ship" sailed from Algoa Bay. Walker and Smith were accompanied by fifteen emigrating Saints, evidence of their success. The *Unity* stopped at St. Helena, where the two elders preached the Gospel and distributed Mormon literature, and arrived at London two months after leaving Port Elizabeth.[42]

The South African Mission grew slowly but steadily. Other missionaries came and went. They were pelted with abuse and occasionally with stones, but their baptisms translated into at least seven emigrant companies that sailed for Zion. Then the mission became inactive and was not reopened until about forty years later.

No maritime chronicle would be complete without recognition of the role of steamboats in missionary journeys. From the beginning the young elders traveled extensively over America's inland waterways. In fact, much of the nation's economy was built around its river system, and it was not until the railroads locked their steel bands over western commerce that reliance on the country's rivers and canals declined. Of the various watercourses, traffic was heaviest on the Mississippi, Missouri, Ohio, and Hudson rivers. Yet the St. Lawrence, Allegheny, Monongahela, Delaware, Sacramento, and Illinois were also important connecting links; and the Erie Canal was a lifeline between the Atlantic Ocean and the Great Lakes. In the years when river travel was both convenient and economical, missionaries depended greatly on these ribbons of water.

Steamboat trips were often risky, however, particularly in the winter and spring. Accidents took their toll in both human life and river craft. There were many hazards—snags, floating debris, shifting sandbars, changing currents, floods, ice, fires, collisions, and boiler explosions. River pilots were vital, men who knew every twist and turn and had a developed instinct for danger. But even under the guidance of these professionals, steamboat longevity—especially on the Mississippi and the Missouri—was an insurance nightmare.

As the body of the Mormon Church moved westward, missionaries were generally moving eastward. Prominent among these early elders was Heber C. Kimball, who was ordained an apostle in February 1835. In September of that year, returning from one of his journeys, he arrived by stage at Buffalo, New York. There he met several other apostles. They boarded the 367-ton steamer *United States*, but had traveled only as far as Dunkirk when the side-wheeler struck a rock, springing a leak. The vessel continued with difficulty to Erie, Pennsylvania, but soon was forced to run on to a sandbar to avoid sinking. The passengers were transferred to another steamboat which took them to Fairport. The following year Kimball traveled the St. Lawrence River from Sackets Harbor to Ogdensburg, New York, on another steamboat of the same name.[43]

In 1837 Kimball's fellow apostle Brigham Young, returning from a mission to the eastern states, came from Buffalo to Fairport, Ohio, over Lake Erie on the famous 358-ton side-wheeler *Daniel Webster*. Two years later Kimball and Young and several companions set out on their mission to England by taking the 391-ton side-wheeler *Columbus* from Fairport to Buffalo. Brigham Young wrote that the "boat stopped at Erie . . . and coming out of the harbor she ran against the pier, which was covered with an immense body of ice. She struck it with such force that she ran right up on the ice . . . and remained a short time, and then slid backwards into the water without much damage."[44]

Returning from England in 1841, Brigham Young, Heber C. Kimball, and John Taylor met with an accident aboard the 107-ton *Cicero* while steaming from Pittsburgh down the Ohio River. The little side-wheeler ran aground on a sandbar, where she remained a day and a night, the passengers being able to go ashore. This mishap was followed by the accidental scalding of a woman and two children when condensed steam was released from the boiler. The unlucky craft ran aground on yet another

Above and facing page, top: Rare 1850s photographs of Mormon missionaries arriving at foreign ports aboard sailing vessels. In the early years the elders usually traveled "without purse or scrip" and occasionally worked on shipboard for their passage.

Bottom: In the late nineteenth century the steamship *Australia* carried Mormon missionaries to Pacific ports and brought their converts from Australia and New Zealand to California. *All, courtesy Church Archives, Church of Jesus Christ of Latter-day Saints.*

sandbar. During the trip Captain Thomas O'Connor was "very kind" to the three apostles. At Cincinnati they transferred to the 157-ton *Mermaid*, also a side-wheeler. The river trip took three weeks, and on July 1 their families, their prophet, and the Saints warmly welcomed the missionaries at Nauvoo.[45]

In July of 1843, after having been sustained as president of the Quorum of Twelve Apostles, Brigham Young, accompanied by Wilford Woodruff, George A. Smith, and E. P. Maginn, left Nauvoo on another mission. They traveled on the steamer *Rapids* to St. Louis and at Cincinnati took the steamboat *Adelaide* for Pittsburgh, but had to leave that vessel when she ran aground on a sandbar. During this mission the elders traveled on steamers, canal boats, and even skiffs. On their homeward journey, after extensive preaching in the East, Brigham Young, Heber C. Kimball, George A. Smith, and some other missionaries took a canal boat from Philadelphia on October 4, 1843. Four days later they boarded the small side-wheeler *Raritan* for St. Louis. Because the river was low, the steamboat was grounded on sandbars for a time. "Sister Cobb, who accompanied us from Boston, had a child very sick, who died in Cincinnati," wrote Brigham Young. The grieving mother had the child put "in a tin coffin and took it with her." The missionaries transferred to the 189-ton side-wheeler *Nautilus* and "reached St. Louis on the 19th, where we reshipped for Nauvoo, and arrived on the 22nd."[46]

On May 21, 1844, approximately a hundred elders, including apostles Brigham Young and Heber C. Kimball, embarked on a unique mission to promote the candidacy of Joseph Smith for president of the United States. As these missionaries left Nauvoo aboard the 128-ton side-wheeler *Osprey*, spectators on the wharf cheered and shouted, "Joseph Smith, the next President of the United States!"[47] The small riverboat under the command of Captain G. C. Anderson arrived at St. Louis the next day. On the twenty-third the Mormon party left St. Louis aboard the 295-ton side-wheeler *Louis Philippe*, docking at Cincinnati the twenty-sixth. On June 4 Brigham Young, Franklin D. Richards, and L. Brooks traveled down the Pennsylvania and Ohio Canal to Warren aboard the packet *Erie*. They continued to Kirtland, Ohio, the scene of their former persecution, and then on by steamer to Buffalo, by rail to Albany, by steamer again to New York, and then to Boston. It was on July 16 at Salem, Massachusetts, that Brigham Young learned of the murders of Joseph and Hyrum Smith.[48]

During this period Heber C. Kimball and Lyman Wight left St. Louis for Washington. They went on to Philadelphia and from there took the steamboat *Balloon* back to Wilmington, Delaware, for a conference. Kimball described this as "one of the most pleasant trips in our life." The missionaries returned by rail and then went on to Boston to join Brigham

Young at Salem, where they were told that the Smith brothers had been martyred June 27.[49]

The Prophet was dead, but the church and its missionary system was very much alive. Mormonism had never lacked leaders, and those leaders—headed by Brigham Young—were determined to execute the plans of their fallen architect. Not the least of those plans was to preach the Word to all nations and peoples. Soon missionaries were again on the move, many of them being transported by steamboat to American seaports. On August 28, 1844, for example, Apostle Wilford Woodruff, Hiram Clark, Dan Jones, and their families left for Chicago, where they boarded the propeller-driven steam schooner *Oswego* and sailed across Lake Erie, through the Williams Canal, and over Lake Ontario. They made their way to New York, where they took passage to England aboard the ship *John R. Skiddy*.[50]

There were occasional missionary deaths on the rivers. In the spring of 1848, after proselyting through the eastern states, Mephibosheth Sirrine became ill with consumption. He started home aboard the side-wheeler *Niagara*, but on the way his condition worsened until he died at the mouth of the Ohio River. Another fatality was Moroni Bigelow, one of the few who traveled on steamboats after the railroads had displaced much of the river traffic. He too had been preaching in the East. In 1870 he was traveling on the steamer *Mary McDonald* on the Missouri River between Camden and Wellington, Missouri, when he fell overboard and was drowned.[51]

Steamboats played a minor role on the West Coast. The most popular craft were the *Senator* and the *West Point*. George Q. Cannon and six other elders traveled aboard these side-wheelers down the Sacramento River from the gold fields to San Francisco in 1850. Other missionaries undoubtedly made similar trips for years.[52]

During the last half of the nineteenth century a transportation revolution was well under way. The steamboat was giving way to the railroad and fewer missionaries would know the labored chugging of the side-wheeler belching billows of smoke from twin stacks as her paddles thrashed against uncertain river currents. Likewise, the age of sail was passing in the wake of the steamship, and fewer missionaries would know the excitement and adventure of windships. The flapping of canvas, the humming shrouds, the wind howling through the rigging, and the creaking of wooden masts and hulls would soon live only in memory. Less easily forgotten would be the monotonous weeks and months at sea, stale food and water, damp quarters, and decks awash and slippery. Times were indeed changing.

Among the first elders to cross the Atlantic under steam was John T. McAllister. He and some other missionaries sailed from Philadelphia for Liverpool on the Inman Line SS *Glasgow*, arriving October 25, 1851. He would be away from home three and a half years.[53] On May 8, 1852, Apostle Erastus Snow, who had opened the Scandinavian Mission, and Apostle Franklin D. Richards, who had presided over the British Mission, departed from Liverpool on the side-wheel paddle steamer *Africa*, the last wooden ship built for the Cunard Line, making a 12-day passage to New York. Apostle Lorenzo Snow left Liverpool on May 12, 1852, on the wooden paddle steamer *Niagara* in an 11-day passage to New York. The *Niagara* had carried a small emigrant company across the Atlantic to America two months earlier, the first company to travel in a steamship. This steamer made approximately a hundred crossings for Cunard under the British flag. Another steamer was noted for a historic death. On August 21, 1853, Willard Snow, who had succeeded his brother Erastus as president of the Scandinavian Mission, died aboard the British paddle-wheel steamer *Transit* in the North Sea traveling between Copenhagen and England.[54]

Occasional missionary voyages on steamships continued in the 1850s. For example, in July 1856 William Miller and possibly other elders sailed from New York to Liverpool in eleven days on the American paddle-wheeler *Atlantic* of the Collins Line. When United States troops invaded Utah in 1857, most missionaries were called home. Traveling incognito, apostles Orson Pratt and Ezra T. Benson, accompanied by Alexander McRae, William Miller, and some other missionaries, arranged passage on another Collins liner, the *Baltic*. She left Liverpool on October 14 of that year and made an 11-day passage to New York. In February 1858 Joseph W. Young, Lorenzo Hatch, and Seymour B. Young also sailed from Liverpool to New York in a 15-day passage aboard the Inman Line steamer *City of Washington*.[55]

Over the next decade missionaries increasingly relied on steamships. In 1860 Francis M. Lyman sailed from New York to Liverpool on the *Edinburgh* of the Inman Line, and Jesse N. Smith with his companions sailed on the Inman *City of Baltimore* from New York to Liverpool in twelve stormy days at sea. In 1863 the Cunard ocean liner *Etna* provided return passage from Liverpool to New York for a party of missionaries that included Martin Wood, a 13-day voyage.[56] The American Civil War, in full flame at this time, did not seriously dampen the overseas mission program. It is significant that missionaries generally traveled in British vessels, however, for American ships were being attacked by the Confederate Navy in Atlantic waters.

During this period, on April 27, 1863, there was a tragedy far removed from the war scene. At San Pedro, California, two Mormon elders bound for Hawaii—Hiram S. Kimball and Thomas Atkinson—boarded the 83-ton steam tender *Ada Hancock*. This small craft was ferrying passengers from the wharf to the steamship *Senator*, which was anchored about five miles from shore. After steaming about a thousand yards the *Ada Hancock* exploded and was literally blown to pieces. About forty passengers were killed, including the two missionaries.[57]

Among the steamships that carried missionaries over the oceans were the *Kangaroo* out of Australia and England flying the British flag and the Cunard liner *Australasian*, which once transported Jesse N. Smith. Both vessels seem to have been used by missionaries between 1860 and 1870. Jesse Yelton Cherry, and probably some other elders, sailed from New York to Liverpool in the summer of 1864 aboard the British steamer *Virginia* of the National Line. In 1867 Apostle Brigham Young, Jr., was released as president of the European Mission, and he and his family crossed the Atlantic from Liverpool to New York in ten days aboard the *Scotia*, the last Cunard paddle-steamer. The following year George Teasdale, Albert Carrington, and Jesse N. Smith took the steamer *City of Antwerp* of the Inman Line from New York to Liverpool.[58]

In November of 1879 four Mormon missionaries experienced near disaster at sea. Crossing the Atlantic with the elders among her passengers, the steamer *Arizona* of the Guion Line crashed into a huge iceberg at high speed. She mounted a submerged ridge and rocked the berg, which enabled her to slide off, in the process telescoping twenty-five feet of the bow. Fortunately, the vessel was able to make her way to Saint John's, Newfoundland, where repairs were made. No lives were lost in the mishap.[59] Over a ten-year span the *Arizona* carried nine Mormon emigrant companies to America.

Two years later Feramorz Little Young became ill during his mission to Mexico, and his return passage was arranged on the American steamer *Knickerbocker*. The vessel sailed from Vera Cruz, and when she was about a hundred miles from Havana, Elder Young died and was buried at sea.[60]

Between the years 1870 and 1890 missionaries usually preferred traveling to Liverpool aboard the passenger liners that transported Mormon emigrant companies. Among the most popular steamships were the *Minnesota, Nevada, Wisconsin,* and *Wyoming*—all operated by the Guion Line. Steamships were used in other waters; in 1883, for example, Walter R. Barber, suffering from consumption, sailed from Auckland, New Zealand, to San Francisco aboard the American steamer *City of New York* in a three-week voyage. In 1885 John P. Ibsen, a missionary in Denmark, was deported under police escort at Copenhagen and crossed the North Sea to England on board the small but sturdy British steamer *Milo*.[61] The following year William T. Stewart, president of the New Zealand part of the Australasian Mission, returned to San Francisco from Auckland aboard the British steamship *Mararoa*. In 1887 the steamer *Zealandia* of the Oceanic Steamship Co. carried six missionaries from San Francisco to Auckland.

A few weeks later, on July 1, Joseph F. Smith, second counselor to President John Taylor, his wife, and William W. Cluff sailed from Honolulu for San Francisco as passengers on the American liner *Mariposa*—a trip of only eight days.[62] The steamer *Australia*, built in Scotland, transported missionaries to various Pacific ports for at least two decades.

For more than half a century hundreds of Mormon missionaries had crossed the oceans and seas under sail and later under steam. They entered foreign lands and preached. Organized missions sprang into being—the British, Society Islands, Welsh, Scandinavian, French, Italian, Swiss, Sandwich or Hawaiian Islands, Australasian, East Indian, Malta, Gibraltar, German, South African, Siam, Netherlands, Mexican, Turkish, and Samoan. The dedication and zeal of these elders brought them hardship, persecution, and often personal danger.

Such ordinary men—often with little formal schooling and with many human frailties—differed from other men in one element: they were kindled with an extraordinary purpose. They believed that they were God's messengers of a new revelation and that they were chosen instruments in fulfilling the prophesied gathering. Their efforts bore fruit, for they set in motion a religious migration of tens of thousands. Crossing the waters of the world, these thousands of believers—like the mariners of old—had found a star of promise and followed it to a haven in Zion.

Two

The Gathering

When the first missionaries were sent to the British Isles, the Mormon Prophet Joseph Smith instructed them to "remain silent concerning the gathering . . . until such time as the work was fully established, and it should be clearly made manifest by the Spirit to do otherwise."[1] By 1840 about 2,000 converts had been made in the British Mission. In April of that year the apostles met in Preston, England, with Brigham Young presiding and decided that the work was sufficiently established to announce the doctrine of the gathering.[2] From that time the missionaries preached and the Saints practiced the principle. This belief in the gathering to Zion of the seed of Israel—or all peoples who accept the Gospel as taught by the Mormon Church—was the impelling force that brought the migration of Saints across the Atlantic and Pacific oceans and the seas between to the New World. Joseph Smith formally stated in the Tenth Article of Faith: "We believe in the literal gathering of Israel and in the restoration of the Ten Tribes; that Zion will be built upon this [the American] continent."[3] That missionary message was to be carried to every "nation, kindred, tongue, and people."

From 1840 America was Zion to thousands of overseas converts. They left their homes, uprooted their lives, parted from families and friends, and began new lives under a religious discipline that committed them to a future of exacting obedience, dedication, and sacrifice. That discipline was centered around apostolic authority and a lay priesthood system. Yet there was more. Mormonism was a many-faceted religion, one that blended the spiritual and temporal with considerable success.

In the spiritual realm, the convert accepted not only traditional Christian values and the Bible as God's word but also the Book of Mormon and Joseph Smith's revelations as scripture. He embraced such concepts as the

[27]

pre-existence, man's eternal progression, a belief that man is a spiritual child of God inheriting his Parent's divine potential, that life should be joyful, that salvation comes through knowledge and personal development, that the heavens are open, and—most important—that God speaks today as in times past. There were also Mormon beliefs about the millennium, baptism and temple ordinances for both the living and the dead, and the Word of Wisdom. Whether one considers the Mormon faith as eclectic or as primitive Christianity restored, it did offer something for almost everyone.

While its theology often created controversy, the practices of the church were sometimes startling. For example, within a few years cooperative economics would find expression in the church's United Order experiments in communal living—experiments that were bold and idealistic, but short-lived. Then there was plural marriage. After its public announcement in 1852, this doctrine was vigorously attacked from almost all sides—often within the church itself. It created a storm that raged for decades. Yet despite controversy the Mormon organization was dynamic, and the church grew. Its doctrines were sufficiently compelling to motivate the gathering; and from the four winds inspired men, women, and children traveled to the Mormon Mecca. At first this Mecca was Nauvoo, Illinois, then after 1847, the Salt Lake Valley. Their determination is evident in the early Mormon hymn "Ye Elders of Israel":

> O Babylon, O Babylon, we bid thee farewell,
> We're going to the mountains of Ephraim to dwell.
>
> We'll go to the poor, like our Captain of old,
> And visit the weary, the hungry and cold;
> We'll heal up their wounds, and we'll dry up their tears,
> And lead them to Zion to dwell there for years.[4]

The emotions of these emigrants were expressed in this statement of one participant: "I believed in the principal of the gathering and felt it my duty to go although it was a severe trial to me, in my feelings to leave my native land and the pleasing associations that I had formed there; but my heart was fixed. I knew in whom I had trusted and with the fire of Israel's God burning in my bosom, I forsook my home."[5]

Although spiritually inspired, the gathering itself was stark reality. The movement of Mormons from the Old World to Zion was a formidable challenge. Complex planning was necessary, for a swelling number of diverse and inexperienced converts had to cross thousands of miles of water and land to settle in Illinois and eventually Utah. These emigrants were an amalgam of many differing cultures and languages. They migrated in groups from the British Isles, Scandinavia, Germany, Holland, Switzerland, Italy, France, South Africa, Gibraltar, Australia, and New Zealand.[6]

They also represented a wide range of skills. Between 1850 and 1854 James Linforth listed over 300 "professions and occupations" of the emigrants sailing from Liverpool. Although the rosters included 3 chemists, a dentist, a physician, and 5 schoolmasters, most emigrants were from the less skilled vocations. Among them were 457 laborers of all kinds, 226 miners, 120 farmers, 96 shoemakers, 74 tailors, 73 masons, 55 carpenters, 47 blacksmiths, 46 engineers, 43 gardeners, 41 mariners (including 5 master mariners and a naval officer), 38 joiners, 30 sawyers, 28 clerks, 23 bricklayers, and 21 butchers.[7]

As part of the great westward migration to America, the Mormons crossed more than sea and land. They literally crossed the boundaries of mind, blood, and class. Most had never traveled more than a few miles from their homes, but they were fired with a faith and a purpose. Their migration was unique. It formed a cycle of proselyting and pioneering, conversion and movement. No longer were the words "Kingdom of God" and "Promised Land" just scriptural phrases—they were part of the lexicon of the gathering.

With confidence in their authority, the priesthood system, and prophetic destiny, the apostles in England lost no time in planning the details of the migration; and the details were numerous. They had to solve the problems of routing, scheduling, timing arrivals and departures to minimize on-shore lodging expense, provisioning the emigrants for the voyages, chartering the most seaworthy vessels, providing experienced leadership during the journey, organizing the emigrants themselves, establishing acceptable rules of deportment, utilizing the talents and skills available, and financing a very costly undertaking.

Under the strong and practical leadership of Brigham Young and his fellow apostles an effective system evolved. A shipping agency was established at Liverpool and later at other ports. A communications network was created through the missionaries and various mission publications, including the *Millennial Star* in Liverpool, *Skandinaviens Stjerne* in Copenhagen, *L' Etoile du Deseret* in Paris, and others. Discipline was enforced in the emigrant companies. While backsliders and the disaffected apostatized or were excommunicated, those who endured and found their way to Zion demonstrated their mental and physical stamina, spiritual fervor, and loyalty. The gathering was for the tried and tested.

Contemporaries were often impressed by the logistical planning of the Mormon leaders, and the migration became so well organized that its success and safety record were unprecedented. These leaders not only anticipated problems but learned from their mistakes as well. Their instructions to emigrating Saints clearly revealed a desire to profit from experience. As a result, not one organized company of Mormon emigrants was lost crossing the Atlantic, and only one company was shipwrecked in the Pacific Ocean.

Church leaders chartered the emigrant ships, usually negotiating the most favorable rates; and the emigrants generally found their vessel awaiting their arrival. Many actually went on board the same day they arrived by train at Liverpool and were able to sleep in their berths or on deck. Others might lodge temporarily with local church members or in boarding houses if there were a delay in boarding. This careful planning spared the converts the risks and expense of waiting in a port city where they could fall prey to confidence men and swindlers.

Among the first decisions was the choice of routes to the New World. Until 1855 there was no rail network linking the Atlantic Ocean and the Mississippi River. Emigrants could sail up the St. Lawrence River to Quebec and then travel by steamboat on the lakes, rivers, and canals to the Midwest. Or they could arrive at an eastern United States port such as New York, Philadelphia, or Boston. From these cities they could make their way through the Erie Canal and Great Lakes or down the Ohio to the Mississippi River. By far the easiest route—though about two weeks longer by sea—was sailing from Liverpool to New Orleans and then transshipping by riverboat up the Mississippi and Missouri rivers. It is significant that from 1840 to early 1855 there were 81 passages of Mormon emigrant companies from Liverpool to New Orleans compared with five from Liverpool to New York, two from Bristol to Quebec, and one from Liverpool to Boston (see Appendix 1 for extensive data on the passages of emigrant companies). This southern route offered many natural advantages during those years. A lively trade had developed between Liverpool and New Orleans. The former shipped manufactured goods and emigrants to the South, and New Orleans provided return cargoes of cotton and sugar to industrialized England. For the Mormons the New Orleans route was ice-free in winter, cheaper, and for the time a convenient access up the Mississippi to Illinois and points west.

From the outset it was clear that the task of transporting thousands of Saints to America required financial resources beyond what many individual emigrants, the British Mission, and possibly even the church itself could provide. There were three classes of emigrants: those who could finance themselves, those who needed partial assistance, and those who had to depend entirely on outside financial support. For their emigration converts were expected to travel to Liverpool, to buy provisions for the long ocean voyage to America and the steamboat or rail trip to the Midwest, and to have some reserve cash on hand for stopovers at Liverpool or American cities. The fare to New Orleans, for example, might be as low as £4 and for the steamboat journey 15s, and many—if not most—Mormon emigrants financed their own way. Some accumulated savings from meager wages. Others sold their possessions, and still others made cash settlements on their inheritances.[8]

For the less fortunate many financing schemes were considered, and it was evident that a pooling of the resources of both the poor and the rich was needed. Before leaving Nauvoo the Saints recognized their responsibilities in the gathering and made a solemn covenant in the Temple that any individual without means, if he so desired, would be brought to Zion. In September 1849 Brigham Young proposed the creation of a Perpetual Emigrating Fund Company to administer a revolving cooperative fund to finance needy emigrants. This agency would collect donations of money, wagons, livestock, food, and clothing from the Saints wherever they might be located. At the October Conference in Salt Lake City, Heber C. Kimball presented the plan, which was unanimously accepted by the membership. A committee to raise the Perpetual Emigrating Fund, or P.E.F. as it was called, was formed, consisting of Willard Snow, John S. Fullmer, Lorenzo Snow, John D. Lee, and Franklin D. Richards. About $5,000 was soon raised, and Bishop Edward Hunter carried that sum to Iowa to outfit the poor Saints in the "Pottawattamie lands."[9] In 1850 the Perpetual Emigrating Fund Company was incorporated by the General Assembly of the State of Deseret, its administration under the direction of the First Presidency of the church. Before it was dissolved in 1887, the P.E.F. assisted about 50,000 persons, including as many as one half of the converts from foreign countries.[10]

Any assistance given through the Fund was considered a loan to be repaid as soon as possible after the convert's arrival in Utah. The plan enabled Mormons already living in Utah to send for their friends in the Old World by making deposits in Salt Lake Valley to cover the cost of transportation. Some Saints received only partial financing from the P.E.F. The church offered a Ten Pound Plan, under which the Fund paid all costs of passage but charged each adult £10 and each child less than a year old £5. Later this approach evolved into the Thirteen and Fifteen Pound Plans, reflecting higher transportation costs. Other Saints were financed entirely by the P.E.F. Many—but not all—repaid these loans in full.[11]

When the Perpetual Emigrating Fund was introduced overseas, the British converts promptly responded with donations. The individual contributions ranged from a few pence to £400. By July 1854 donations in Great Britain totaled more than £6,800. In addition, missions on the continent of Europe and even a few in Asia deposited £280 with the British agency, bringing the total to £7,113. On January 10, 1852, the first P.E.F. emigrants—sixty-nine of them—sailed from Liverpool bound for New Orleans aboard the American ship *Kennebec*.[12] By the end of 1855 the number of emigrants financed by the P.E.F. had grown to 2,885.[13]

From every maritime nation thousands of vessels of all kinds sailed in and out of Liverpool each year. During the nineteenth century this thriving English harbor in the Mersey estuary was unrivaled in world trade, and it was the principal port of embarkation for Mormon emigrants. This "View of Liverpool from the South West" (1847) pictures a sprawling city with acres of crowded docks, swing bridges, and fireproof warehouses. *Courtesy National Maritime Museum, Greenwich.*

Yet the financial aid provided through the P.E.F. was only part of the cooperative effort. Before the Fund was established, many individuals had contributed generously to finance the emigration of the poor. Thomas Jeremy, for example, paid the transportation of three persons besides his own family in 1849. It is said that Christopher Arthur's father, a baker, paid the way for forty converts. Christopher Layton, on his second voyage to America in 1850, used his profits from selling horses in California to pay passage for his bride, six relatives, and forty-six friends. An Elder Jennings donated £100 to assist forty-five Birmingham Saints in the 1860s. In Scandinavia Anders Eliason of Ennerkulen, Sweden, paid passage to Utah for one hundred converts. Ola N. Liljenquist, a master tailor from Copenhagen, Denmark, and the only burgher among the Mormons, was criticized by officials in 1852 because he stood passport security for so many emigrating Saints. He was reminded that he could be prosecuted and jailed for signing beyond his capacity, but he continued to provide guarantees for the next four years, until his own departure.[14] These incidents were multiplied many times, and the spirit of the gathering inspired an outpouring of private assistance to the "Lord's poor."

No seaport was more important in the Mormon migration than Liverpool. Since the great majority of emigrants came from the United Kingdom and the European continent, this vibrant city was the principal staging area for their Atlantic crossing. Of the 333 identified voyages of Mormon emigrant companies through 1890, Liverpool was the port of embarkation for 289. Other companies sailed from Bristol and London, England, Le Havre, Hamburg, Amsterdam, Calcutta, Melbourne and Sydney, Australia, Auckland, New Zealand, Port Elizabeth, South Africa; and—if the famous voyage of the ship *Brooklyn* to San Francisco is included—from New York.[15]

Liverpool had many natural advantages. It was centrally located between Great Britain and Ireland. It was quite accessible by rail from London and the eastern ports of England, such as Hull and Grimsby. The harbor had easily navigable channels, being situated just a few miles up the Mersey Estuary from the Irish Sea and Liverpool Bay. Liverpool was also a day's sail nearer in distance to America and, because of the delays in moving up and down the English Channel and River Thames, several days nearer in time than London.

Arriving at Liverpool, the Mormon convert found a crescent-shaped harbor thriving on marine traffic. Upwards of 20,000 vessels entered and left the River Mersey each year. Liverpool grew up on the east bank of the estuary opposite Birkenhead on the west bank. The traveler would see a forest of masts, for the harbor was filled with craft of every description. There were sleek clipper ships, square-rigged packets from America, schooners, barks, barkentines, brigs, snows, sloops, steamers, tugs, and fishing boats—all crowded in and around the docks anchored in the Mersey, or moving in or out of the estuary. Colorful pennants and flags of many nations flew in the breeze, and the docks were lined with ornamented bows and figureheads.

The nineteenth century was Liverpool's golden age. In the previous century the city had become the hub of the notorious Liverpool Triangle. This term was applied to a three-cornered trade. Ships sailing out of Liverpool carried trinkets and cheap cotton goods to West Africa in exchange for black slaves. These slaves were transported to the West Indies and sold for cargoes of sugar, cotton, and other raw materials. Early in the nineteenth century this triangular trade ceased, and Liverpool was revitalized by the flowering industrial revolution and the phenomenon of westward emigration.

Once again Liverpool became a port bursting with activity. By 1840 its population had grown to over 200,000. The focal point of commercial life was the Pier Head, which was adjacent to the floating landing stage used to disembark passengers from ships of all flags. Liverpool was well on the way toward constructing some of the finest dock facilities in the world. These docks formed a belt along the waterfront and were given such names as Prince's, Victoria, Waterloo, George's, Albert, and King's. There were basically three kinds of docks: wet docks which retained water through a system of gates, permitting large ships to float up to the pier, dry docks which became dry as the tide receded, and graving docks in which the water could be controlled to facilitate the repair of ships. Incoming vessels were not always able to find dock space or had to anchor offshore until the tide changed. Brigham Young recorded upon his arrival at Liverpool on April 6, 1840, "We landed in Liverpool; I got into a boat with Elders Kimball and P.P. Pratt, and when I landed on the shore I gave a loud shout of hosannah. We procured a room at No. 8, Union-street. The ship failing to get into the dock with the tide, I sent a boat for brothers O. Pratt, Geo. A. Smith and R. Hedlock."[16]

Liverpool was expanding its docks, warehouses, and sheds along the water's edge but the city itself was also being built up. Along the dock area were rows of artisans' houses, and over the years a Custom House, St. Georges' Hall, Victoria Tower, a Town Hall, Lyceum, and railroad station on Lime Street would be built. The city was a mixture of old and new. Its gray drabness belied the energy and verve of its people, increased considerably by an inflow of Irish workers. Its streets were alive with American, English, African, Asian, and other foreign seamen seeking their diversions from pubs, panderers, and prostitutes. One visitor said, "In Liverpool decent chaps owned ships, fairly decent chaps broked cotton, almost decent chaps broked corn—the rest just didn't exist."[17]

A rival of London, Liverpool was a city of almost everything—yet all things were not favorable. Tides in the harbor could range up to twenty-nine feet. Winters were often severe, although ice seldom caused navigational problems in the Mersey. Winds were frequently contrary. Since these winds during the winter months could reach gale force from the west and northwest, sailing packets sometimes delayed their scheduled departures for several days. Eventually tugs were used to tow the ships out of the estuary. Delays could also be caused by the frequent fogs that blanketed the harbor and city. Despite these drawbacks, mariners regarded Liverpool as one of the finest ports in the world.

The Mormon emigrant saw in Liverpool a city of contrasts. The rich and poor were worlds apart. It was a haven of churches but a home of brothels. It was overcrowded, rambunctious, and tough. For all of its virtues and vices, Liverpool had a cosmopolitan excitement; and the Mormon convert experienced mingled hope and anxiety in his strange surroundings. To him Liverpool was the place of the first gathering, the springboard to Zion. In keeping with the flight of the fabulous bird *Liver*, from which its name was supposedly derived, from 1840 on this great port winged its way solidly into Mormon history.

For more than a decade the Mormon emigration consisted entirely of British converts, and with the exception of two sailings from Bristol these Saints gathered at and later sailed from Liverpool. Emigrating Mormons from all parts of the British Isles traveled to this port by rail and coastal steamers. Among these coastal vessels was the 409-ton steamship *Troubador* of Liverpool. Early in 1849 Daniel Jones, a native Welshman and one of the most successful missionaries in Mormon history, gathered a group of Saints at Swansea, Wales. Under the direction of this remarkable elder—remarkable in that he was college educated, a master mariner, orator, and trusted friend of Joseph Smith—the Welsh Mormons boarded the *Troubador*. Hundreds of spectators crowded the wharf to see them off. As the steamer moved down the river into Swansea Bay, the emigrants sang lustily and responded to the cheers of the onlookers. The *Troubador* entered St. George's Channel and sailed through the Irish Sea to Liverpool. On February 25 these Saints embarked on the ship *Buena Vista* bound for America.[18]

The first Mormon emigrants from Scandinavia—nine persons—left Copenhagen, traveling by stage, steamboat, and ferry until they arrived at Rendsburg in Holstein on February 2, 1852. These Saints then took the train to Altona, Germany, where they were received by Elder George P. Dykes, a former officer of the Mormon Battalion and one of the earliest

The *John Bull*, a well-known British paddle steamer, carried the first Scandinavian Mormon emigrants across the North Sea to England in 1852. This steamship sailed the turbulent European waters for more than forty years. *Courtesy National Maritime Museum, Greenwich.*

missionaries in Scandinavia. After dinner he took the nine Danes aboard an old 398-ton British steamer, the *John Bull.* On February 4 this paddle-wheeler sailed for London, arriving the next morning. The emigrants journeyed by train to Liverpool, where they joined nineteen other Danish Saints, and on March 11 the twenty-eight Scandinavians sailed for New Orleans aboard the American square-rigger *Italy.*[19]

Later that year John E. Forsgren, temporarily in charge of the Scandinavian Mission, assembled 293 converts in Copenhagen for emigration to Utah. On December 20, 1852, these Scandinavian Saints boarded the 167-ton paddle-wheel steamer *Obotrit*—registered at Wismar, Germany— and a jeering rabble gathered at the wharf to see their departure. The spectators shouted obscenities and cursed the emigrants for following "that Swedish Mormon Priest" Forsgren to Utah. At four o'clock that afternoon the small steamer pulled away from the custom house headed for Kiel, Holstein. After a stormy passage the *Obotrit* and her cramped and miserable passengers arrived at Kiel the evening of the twenty-second.[20]

Two days later these Saints boarded the 460-ton British paddle-wheeler *Lion* and floated with the tide down the Elbe River to Cuxhaven, Germany. There the steamer dropped anchor because of the fog, and the emigrants celebrated Christmas Eve on shipboard. On Christmas Day the *Lion* steamed to the mouth of the river but found her progress slowed by head winds. It was midnight before the vessel reached the open sea. The next day the ship passed Helgoland and encountered a North Sea gale. The wind increased to hurricane force, ripping the bridge and gunwale to pieces and smashing and washing overboard the goods stored on deck. Sailors said they had never experienced such a storm in the North Sea. After the storm's fury was spent, the *Lion* steamed into the harbor at Hull, England. Her arrival was greeted with surprise, for it was reported that about 150 vessels had been lost in the storm and the *Lion* was believed to have been among them.[21]

About a year later three hundred Scandinavian Saints boarded the Danish steamship *Slesvig* in Copenhagen. As the Mormons departed on December 22, 1853, a large, hostile crowd once again collected on the wharf, shouting derisively. After the iron paddle-wheeler had left the harbor, Elder Peter O. Hansen was assaulted by the mob and slightly injured as he was walking back to the Mission Office. The steamer's course took her to Kiel, Glückstadt, and Hull. From there the Saints went by rail to Liverpool, where they boarded the ship *Jessie Munn* for America.[22] The 298-ton *Slesvig* transported another company of Mormons from Copenhagen to Hull in late November 1854, with stops at Kiel and Hamburg, Germany.[23]

On December 26, 1853, a company of 378 Scandinavian Mormons under the direction of Hans Peter Olsen, a missionary returning from the island of Bornholm, sailed from Copenhagen aboard the small iron-hulled steamer *Eideren*, owned by the Royal Danish Post Service. These emigrants traveled to Kiel, Glückstadt, and then to Hull. From Hull they took a train to Liverpool, where an unidentified fever caused the deaths of twenty-two children. The examining physician also refused to permit fifteen other emigrants to board the American ship *Benjamin Adams* with the rest of the company.[24]

There is no other body of water quite like the North Sea. It is often unpredictable, violent, and treacherous—and particularly so during the winter months. Of all the North Sea passages made by Mormon emigrants, probably none was as terrifying as that of the small Danish steamer *Cimbria*. It began November 24, 1854. Some 300 Scandinavian Saints were crowded on board when the 132-ton paddle-wheeler sailed out of the Copenhagen harbor. Although the sea was very rough, the *Cimbria* reached Fredrikshavn on the east coast of Jutland the following morning. There 149 additional emigrants from Aalborg and Vendsyssel joined the company, further crowding the 160-foot ship.

On November 26 the steamer resumed her voyage, and the weather was fair until the next afternoon. Then a strong wind came up, and its

CIMBRIA

EIDEREN

SLESVIG

Many Scandinavian and German emigrants described the North Sea passage to England as their most terrifying experience. These small Danish ships of under 500 tons encountered unpredictable and often violent storms in this crossing. The paddle-wheeler

AURORA

L. N. HVIDT

GEISIR

Cimbria made a particularly perilous voyage in 1854, being driven back to port several times before finally reaching Hull, England, a month later. *All, courtesy Danish Maritime Museum.*

rising fury forced the captain to seek haven in the nearest Norwegian port. He put into Mandal, an excellent harbor sheltered by high and steep granite cliffs. Here the Norwegians offered the Saints accommodations on shore for several days until the wind diminished. The elders preached to some of the villagers, and several were later converted.

On December 7 the *Cimbria* once again put to sea, but the improved weather soon changed for the worse. Before the end of the day a violent storm struck. The waves became mountainous, and the wind shrieked through the rigging. Tons of water crashed over the bow, shattering the bulwarks and some boxes on deck. The captain once more sought safety in Mandal's harbor, but the strong currents and winds made it too danger-ous to head toward Norway. The vessel returned to Fredrikshavn, where she anchored on the ninth. During this storm the emigrants huddled below decks, suffering from the cold, the pitching of the ship, and seasickness. Once on shore again, a few of the less hardy refused to travel farther, but most of the Saints recovered their courage and even held public meetings.

It was not until December 20 that the captain felt the weather would permit setting out again for England. For a day the sea was favorable, but the following night the storm returned with the appalling savagery of a mindless beast. Great masses of water threatened to capsize the little steamer, and the twisting troughs between waves seemed designed to break her back. For hours the *Cimbria* battled the ferocity of the winds and the high seas, while the miserable passengers were too cold and sick and too busy holding on to their bunks, tables, or anything secure to think of much else but prayer and survival. The vessel, shuddering and quivering with each wave, tried to turn back for a third time. Then, in the afternoon of the twenty-second, the wind veered to the north. The captain changed course and continued on to Hull. On December 24 the battered steamer with her exhausted crew and thankful passengers anchored in the River Humber. The following day—Christmas—the Scandinavian Saints traveled by rail from Hull to Liverpool, where they boarded the Yankee square-rigger *James Nesmith* bound for New Orleans.[25]

Within a few days of the departure of the *Slesvig* and *Cimbria* another Danish paddle steamer, the *Geisir*, sailed from Copenhagen with a smaller company of Saints. Apparently the storm did not seriously delay the pas-sage, since the vessel arrived at Hull, December 7, 1854.[26]

Canute Peterson, an elder returning from a four-year mission in his native Norway, sailed from Copenhagen on December 29, 1855, aboard the Danish paddle-wheeler *Løven* with 447 Scandinavian Saints in his charge. This steamer of only 94 registered tons must have been very crowded. In any case, the voyage was reported as pleasant, indicating that there was a window of good weather during the winter storm season. The vessel called at the ports of Kiel and Glückstadt on her way to Grimsby. From Grimsby the emigrants traveled to Liverpool, where they were joined by thirty Italian and forty-two British Mormons and embarked on the American ship *John J. Boyd* bound for New York.[27]

During the next several years other Mormon companies emigrated from Scandinavia. On April 11, 1857, for example, Saints from Christiania (Oslo), Norway sailed to Copenhagen aboard the Norwegian steamship *Viken*. In a calm sea the vessel arrived at the Danish port the following day. After a five-day delay this company—about 540 emigrants under the direction of Hector C. Haight, president of the Scandinavian Mission—boarded the Danish screw steamer *L. N. Hvidt* and traveled to Grimsby. From that English port they traveled by train to Liverpool, leaving a few days later aboard the American ship *Westmoreland* for Philadelphia. Two years later the *L. N. Hvidt* transported another Mormon company from Copenhagen to Grimsby. On April 1, 1859, this 328-ton steamer left Copenhagen, but encountered heavy seas and strong winds. It was not until April 6 that the 355 Scandinavian Saints arrived at Grimsby. This company, which was under the direction of elders Carl Widerborg and Niels Wilhelmsen, went by rail to Liverpool, where they joined an almost equal number of British and Swiss emigrants and boarded the square-rigged *William Tapscott* bound for New York.[28] About a year later the German screw steamer *Pauline* brought a group of Saints from Copenhagen to Grimsby, arriving in England on May 5, 1860, after a 3-day passage. These Saints also sailed from Liverpool on the *William Tapscott*, for the vessel's second voyage carrying a Mormon company.[29]

During April and May of 1863 at least four steamships carried Scandinavians to England. On April 13, a group of twenty-eight Norwegian Mormons sailed from Christiania aboard the Swedish screw steamer *Excellencen Toll* (also called *Excellencen*). It was a rough passage to Copenhagen, where the vessel docked on the fifteenth. On April 30 about 200 Saints gathered in Copenhagen and embarked on the Danish screw steamship *Aurora*, apparently bound for Kiel. From there these emigrants traveled by rail to Altona and then on foot to Hamburg, Germany. On May 1 some 600 Scandinavian Saints had assembled in Hamburg and sailed for England aboard the British screw steamer *Roland*. It was a crowded but smooth passage to Grimsby, where the emigrants arrived May 3 and took the train to Liverpool. There they boarded the American square-riggers *B. S. Kimball* and *Consignment* and crossed the Atlantic to New York. Another small party of seven adults and six children traveled directly from Stavenger, Norway, to Hull aboard the Danish screw steamer *Skandinavien*, arriving May 4, 1863. These emigrants joined the Mormon company that embarked on the *B. S. Kimball*.[30]

Many of the steamers carrying the Mormon emigrants to England in the years ahead are not identified by name or the names are confused. For example, a company of 630 Scandinavian Saints sailed from Copenhagen June 13, 1868, aboard a steamer named "Hansia" which arrived at Hull on June 16. It is likely that the name was a misspelling of *Hansa*, a German screw steamship of 2,992 tons that sailed out of Bremen for England.[31] Another German steamer used by the Mormons was the *Otto*, a vessel known to have transported 397 Saints from Copenhagen to Lubeck, Germany, early in 1872—a group reported to have been in good spirits and enthusiastic about their journey to Zion.[32]

Through the year 1890 nearly a quarter of the Mormon emigrants to America were Scandinavians. There were also smaller numbers of Germans, Swiss, Italians, and other Europeans, and except for eight companies that sailed from Hamburg directly to America, most of these emigrants crossed the North Sea in small steamers to England for transshipment to American ports. Liverpool became the first leg in their trek to Zion.

Three

Windships and *Mariners*

With an American flag flying from her spanker gaff, a two-decked packet ship of the Black Ball Line glided slowly out of the Liverpool harbor and down the River Mersey. She was the *Britannia*. Built in New York City fourteen years earlier, the 630-ton square-rigger was the first packet to exceed 600 tons. She would die in two more years, her epitaph "lost at sea." As the crew responded to the sharp commands of Captain Enoch Cook, a veteran master mariner, the black hulled *Britannia* pointed her weathered billethead toward the Irish Sea.

This Atlantic run was unusual, however. On this Saturday, June 6, 1840, a group of forty-one excited Mormons were among the passengers— excited about their future and, most of all, the journey to Zion. Their leader, Elder John Moon, was deep in thought as he watched the docks of Liverpool fade in the distance. On June 1 he had been called and set apart to preside over these converts by two Mormon apostles, Brigham Young and Heber C. Kimball, who also blessed the departing Saints and "commended them to the Lord."[1] It was the first organized Mormon company to emigrate to America. Forty-four days later, after three days in quarantine, these emigrants landed at New York "safe and in good spirits," thankful for having survived three storms and considerable seasickness.[2]

The Mormon migration was under way. Historic as it was, it was not the number of emigrants that was significant. In the next half century the Mormons accounted for fewer than one hundred thousand of some fourteen million overseas emigrants to the United States. The significance was rather in their religious purpose, their remarkable organization, and their lasting impact on the development of the American West. In their gathering, in answering the call to Zion, the foreign-born Saints played an important part in colonizing several hundred towns and cities in the United

[43]

The packet ship *Britannia* of the Black Ball Line, registered at 630 tons, sailed from Liverpool to New York on June 6, 1840, with the first company of Mormon emigrants. Two years later this square-rigger was lost at sea. *Courtesy The Mariners Museum, Newport News, Virginia.*

States. From their past, lived largely in green and watered lands, their future would be lived carving settlements from inhospitable country under the most adverse conditions, and their adversaries would be legion: desolate desert, harsh climate, frightening droughts, rapacious grasshoppers, restless Indians, and a hostile federal government. Yet they would survive, and the Mormon Church has flourished to this day and has derived much of its vitality from the legacy of these culturally diverse and dedicated converts.

While differing in some ways from other emigrants, the Mormons shared the hazards of crossing the oceans under both canvas and steam. These passages fall into two periods. During the first twenty-eight years, approximately 150 windships transported the emigrant companies. Over the next twenty-two years, 21 steamships provided their passage. Through the year 1890 there were 333 known voyages of Mormon companies— 176 in sailing craft and 157 in transoceanic steamers. (See Appendix 2 for data concerning number of passages and registered tonnages.)

Of the 176 voyages under sail, 154 were made in full-rigged ships. Eighteen crossings were made in barks, three in brigs, and one in a barkentine. These sailing vessels ranged from 183 to 1,979 tons, increasing gradually in size over the years. The windships carried Mormon companies numbering from five to 974 emigrants and averaging about 160 in the 1840s, 270 in the 1850s, and 430 in the 1860s. Four out of five of the passages were made under the American flag, for it was the golden age of the United States merchant marine. Vessels of all kinds with the American ensign snapping in the wind were winging their way across the seas all over the globe, threatening the supremacy of British shipping—particularly in the packet, or passenger, trade.[3]

A word of explanation concerning the different kinds of sailing craft used by the emigrants may be useful. The distinguishing feature of a vessel is the rig, or the way the masts and sails are fitted to the hull. The two basic rigs are fore-and-aft, or the sails running lengthwise of the hull, and square, or the sails hanging across the hull. The nine principal kinds of windships all represent variations in rig based on these two types.

Although the word "ship" is applied generally to any large vessel, a seaman applies the term specifically to a craft with three or more masts mounted with square sails. All ships also carried jibs and staysails, which are triangular sails between the masts and between the foremast and bowsprit that help in keeping a steady course. Most ships also carried a spanker, a fore-and-aft sail behind the mizzenmast. The bark has three or more masts, with the foremast and mainmast square-rigged and the mizzenmast fore-and-aft or schooner-rigged. The barkentine likewise usually has three masts with the foremast square-rigged and the others fore-and-aft rigged.

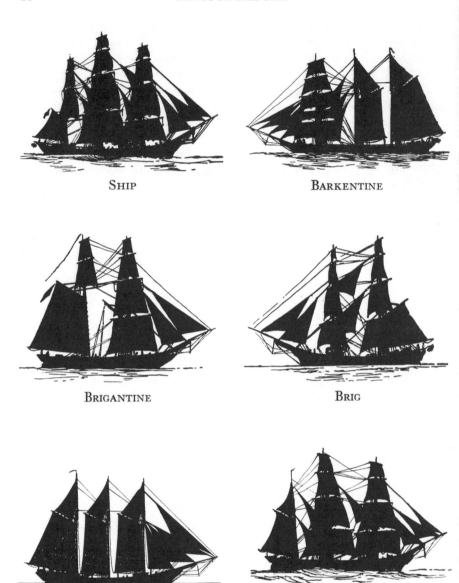

SHIP

BARKENTINE

BRIGANTINE

BRIG

SCHOONER

BARK

These drawings illustrate the principal types of sailing vessels that carried Mormons across the oceans. *Courtesy The Peabody Museum of Salem, Massachusetts.*

The brig has two square-rigged masts with a fore-and-aft sail on her mainmast, but despite this fore-and-aft sail, she is considered a square-rigger. A brigantine's foremast is square-rigged like a full-rigged brig, but the mainmast carries a fore-and-aft mainsail. A schooner is rigged with fore-and-aft sails on two or more masts.[4]

Full-rigged ships dominated the ocean trade. They carried the largest spread of canvas and were the work horses of the seas, combining strength and speed. For this reason these beautiful square-riggers were employed extensively in the packet service. The American clipper ship eventually evolved as the ultimate in both speed and beauty, becoming famous during the California Gold Rush and the colorful period of trade in the Orient.

North American forests ranging along the Atlantic seaboard were a natural source of timber for shipbuilding. With wood for ships so readily accessible, it was inevitable that the East Coast and the Maritime Provinces of Canada would turn to shipbuilding. The early settlers soon became handy with the shipwright's tools—axes, augers, adzes, saws, and mauls. Their master craftsmen learned the secrets of constructing a vessel that could survive the wild seas, extremes of temperature, and the ravages of weather and salt water, and soon the skills of the Yankee shipwrights were unsurpassed. It was under their expert hands that the sailing vessels used by the Mormon emigrants took shape.

One hundred forty-six of the sailing craft that carried Mormon emigrant companies have been identified, the majority built in the United States. New England had become the shipbuilding center of America, and Maine and the Kennebec River region boasted the finest shipyards in New England. Of the 121 sailing vessels built in the United States, Maine alone produced 62—more than half. Massachusetts built 25, New York 16, New Hampshire 9, Pennsylvania 5, Connecticut 3, and New Jersey 1. (See Appendix 3 for all locations, names of builders, and years ships were built.)

In Maine the town of Bath was famous for its skilled shipwrights. Bath's rich maritime history reaches into the earliest Colonial times, and perhaps no area in the New World contributed more to seafaring and shipbuilding. This reputation is confirmed in the ships used by Mormon emigrants as nearly a score of communities around the Kennebec River shared in the production of these emigrant vessels.[5]

Of particular importance were the shipbuilders and shipowners, for they were a breed apart. These individuals personified Yankee enterprise, ruggedly independent and shrewdly resourceful. Many combined the boldness and skills of merchant, mariner, and practical engineer. In earlier times some evolved from general store owners, to importers of overseas merchandise, to part owners of ships, and then to shipbuilders, to expand their trade. Others started their careers before the mast, rising to ship's officers, then to master mariners, and eventually to part owners or owners of their own ships. Very often a vessel was built on shares divided among various owners, including the master, into quarters, eighths, sixteenths, thirty-seconds, and so on. The hailing port was usually the residence of the managing owner. It is well to remember that these shipbuilders, ship-owners, and masters were first and foremost merchants who bought and sold cargoes and transported passengers throughout the world. Their fleets were appropriately the merchant marine. It was also not unusual for a builder to hold a master's license and command a vessel on her maiden voyage.[6]

Among these Yankee shipbuilders was Johnson Rideout of Bath, one of the few who constructed vessels in a large shiphouse. He began his career as a day laborer, became a shipwright's apprentice, and soon emerged as one of the most respected shipbuilders in Maine. He was a skilled craftsman and knew the science and art of building ships as well as any. Four Rideout-built ships were part of the Mormon migration: the 1,258-ton *Cynosure*, which carried two Mormon companies, the 926-ton *Kennebec*, the 623-ton *Liverpool*, and the smaller *Tremont*.[7]

Levi Houghton started as a merchant provisioning vessels preparing for sea. He engaged in the cotton trade out of New Orleans and imported manufactured goods and raw materials from Europe. As an importer, he took shares in vessels built at Bath, and soon he was building for himself. One of his square-riggers was the 577-ton *Hanover*, which carried about 200 Saints to New Orleans in 1842 and seven years later met her end at the mouth of the Kennebec River in a severe snowstorm. His contemporary Thomas Harward was also a prominent Bath shipbuilder and owner. Harward had been a major in the militia during the War of 1812 and would live to an age of 102. He built the 815-ton ship *Rockaway*, which brought Mormon companies to New Orleans in 1852 and 1855.

The Patten brothers, John and George F., built the 813-ton *Falcon* and the 590-ton *Sheffield*, each of which brought an emigrant company. John had an adventurous life at sea. While sailing before the mast during the War of 1812, he had the unusual distinction of being captured four times—by the French and the English—and recaptured by the Americans. He was also a privateer until the peace was concluded. George served as a captain in the militia in those years. These brothers were successful shipbuilders in Bath, turning out one or two vessels a year for their own operation. Their fleet was one of the largest of its day, and their house flag—a blue anchor on a white field—was known throughout the world.

Captain William Drummond, another master mariner and prominent Bath shipbuilder, produced, with his associates, such fine, large ships as the 1,170-ton *Benjamin Adams*, the 1,736-ton clipper *Emerald Isle*, which brought three Mormon companies to New York, and the 1,525-ton *William Tapscott,* which also transported three companies. These ships were among the most important in the Mormon emigration. Other Bath builders who turned out ships used by the Mormons were Willard Hall, who built the 1,363-ton *Caravan,* and John Larabee, who constructed the medium-sized *Italy* and *Marshfield.*

Kennebunk, Maine, was also an active shipbuilding village. There G. W. Bourne built his namesake, the *George W. Bourne,* which carried 281 Saints to New Orleans in 1851. Jacob Perkins produced the relatively small square-rigger *Hartley,* which transported two Mormon companies to the same port. He also built the medium-sized *Olympus,* carrier for one company in a historic voyage during which some fifty other passengers were converted and baptized into the Mormon Church. In Portland, Maine, Samuel Dyer built the ships *Emblem* and *Tyrian,* used by the Mormons in the 1840s. In Richmond, Maine, the well-known Harrison Springer built the square-rigger *Ellen Maria,* which gave passage to three Mormon companies in the 1850s.[8]

Most renowned of all Yankee shipbuilders was Donald McKay of Boston. Born in Nova Scotia, he was a shipwright's apprentice at sixteen, acquired his own shipyard in East Boston at thirty-four, and went on to achieve world fame as the builder of the finest packet and clipper ships. Two of his craft—the 1,115-ton *Antarctic* and the 1,118-ton *Cornelius Grinnell*—transported four Mormon companies. Another Boston shipbuilder, Paul Curtis, produced two splendid packets that each brought an emigrant company to Boston—the *Enoch Train* of 1,618 tons and the *Wellfleet* of 1,353 tons. More than a decade earlier he had built the square-rigged *Lucas* of only 350 tons, which brought a company of Saints from Sydney, Australia, to San Francisco in 1857. John Taylor at Chelsea and Medford, Massachusetts, built three ships used by the Mormons—the 1,534-ton *George Washington,* the 996-ton *Clara Wheeler,* and the 648-ton *Josiah Bradlee.*

Three New York shipyards turned out a number of ships used in the Mormon trade. Brown & Bell built the *Britannia,* the 1,327-ton *Constitution,* the 611-ton *North America,* which brought the second organized company in September of 1840, and the 895-ton *Siddons.* Jacob Westervelt and his associates built the 1,771-ton *Amazon,* about which Charles Dickens wrote; the *Hudson* of 1,618 tons; and the 1,168-ton *Underwriter.* W. H. Webb built the *Columbia* and also the *Thornton,* the passengers of which formed one of the historic and tragic handcart companies.

Other significant builders of ships that carried Mormon emigrants were William Cramp, who produced the *Bridgewater* and *Isaac Jeanes* at Philadelphia, and George Raynes of Portsmouth, New Hampshire. Raynes and his associates turned out seven full-rigged ships used in the Mormon movement: the 1,137-ton *America*, the 1,049-ton *Empire*, the 595-ton *Isaac Allerton*, the 600-ton *Isaac Newton*—the first vessel to bring the Saints to New Orleans—the 849-ton *Jersey*, the 721-ton *John Cumming*, and the 799-ton *North Atlantic*, each of which carried a Mormon company.

The names of American shipbuilders, shipowners, and shipmasters are thoroughly intertwined with Mormon history. Many of these names were emblazoned on the bows and sterns of the emigrant ships, and they represent a vibrant and exuberant maritime nation. There is a nostalgia, a reawakening link with another past in some of the ship names: *R. K. Page, Swanton, James Pennell, Charles Buck, Cornelius Grinnell, Enoch Train, George W. Bourne, G. W. Kendall, Isaac Jeanes, James Nesmith, John Cumming, Joseph Badger, S. Curling, William Stetson,* and *William Tapscott.* These ships and others bearing the names of the builders or owners symbolized the individual enterprise and skill of the Yankees who bridged the Old and New Worlds. Other ships bore names that were associated in some way with the builders and owners through places, such as the *Kennebec,* or through relationships. Others were named from just a fancy or notion.[9]

Yet not all the vessels were crafted by Americans. Twenty-five of the Mormon emigrant carriers were built in foreign lands, but their builders were less well known. Canadian shipyards launched fifteen of the foreign ships, England produced seven, and Germany, India, and Norway each built one. Only two of the foreign-built ships—the *Golconda* constructed in New Brunswick and the *Zetland* from Nova Scotia—exceeded a thousand tons.

Wherever possible Americans preferred to build their wooden craft from live oak and other hard woods. Maine and Canadian ships built of spruce, hackmatack, and pine were known as "soft wood" vessels. White oak that grew in a narrow strip from Virginia to Mississippi was in great demand for Yankee vessels, and it was from this tough timber that the famous *Constitution* received her nickname "Old Ironsides." Trees with natural crooks were especially prized for use as knees, futtocks, keels, and other angle pieces. After framing with white oak, Yankee shipwrights often used pitch-pine for outside planking and inside lining. The keel and keelsons would be fashioned from massive logs of pitch-pine. Tall, straight pines from North American forests were ideal for masts and spars.

Ships were usually constructed in the open, and exposure to weather helped season the wood. The keel was set out on blocks, then the keel timbers were joined and scarfed together with huge fastening bolts. After the stem and stern posts and their supporting knee and angle pieces were raised upright, the ribs, or frames, were attached with the knees and beams as support for the decks. To these ribs planking was fastened with toenails, or trunnels. These trunnels were wooden pegs usually made of oak and were driven through holes drilled with an auger. The strakes, or planking, varied in thickness, the heaviest known as "wales." These wales braced the ship longitudinally and where there would be severe strain. Many ships had yellow metal or copper bolts throughout. Others had iron bolts above the ballast loadlines. Bottom planking was felted and coppered below the normal water line, and deckhouses were planked with white pine on white oak framing.

All wooden ships had two enemies—dry rot and toredo, or ship worm. As a protection against these scourges, the bottoms were coppered periodically with a yellow metal sheath. American vessels were painted in different ways. Topsides were often black with thin yellow or white lines, although some were brown or yellow.

Shipbuilding comprised many crafts. In addition to shipwrights it employed sail makers, ironmongers, rope makers, trunnel makers, joiners, mast and spar makers, tinsmiths, coppersmiths, painters, block makers, caulkers, pump makers, and ship chandlers.[10]

Although many transient sailing vessels carried Mormon emigrants to America, packet ships accounted for a significant number of Atlantic passages under canvas. These packets were affiliated—often temporarily—with various shipping lines. In the mid-nineteenth century there were fifty sailing packet lines in transatlantic service. Of these lines thirty-six ran to New York, five to Philadelphia, four to New Orleans, three to Boston, one to Baltimore, and one to Charleston.[11] Such packet lines were served by the most skilled, rugged, and hard-bitten seamen afloat.

Packets lived for speed. To meet a timetable—with almost fanatical determination—their officers and crews challenged the wild Atlantic on their own terms. In summer and winter, night and day, fair weather and foul these strong and sturdy square-riggers maximized canvas—often carrying sail when it was impossible for sailors to go aloft to take it in. In a word, packets were built to fight the seas. Their masters were expected to fight time, to keep a schedule. In fact, the stress was so great that the average packet captain was burned out after about five years in the transatlantic trade. Their bucko mates were trained to fight and drive reluctant crews with fists and belaying pins. These tough, hard, and frequently brutal officers believed they had to prove themselves a match for disreputable crews, known as "packet rats," too often supplied by New York and Liverpool crimps through trickery, drugs, and alcohol. These wooden ships were sailed by men of steel, hardened by the world's hardest school of seamanship.

The oldest and most famous of the packet lines was the Black Ball, which began its Liverpool–New York run on schedule in 1818.[12] Black Ball ships were typically painted black with bright bands, and they were easily identified by a large black ball painted or sewn on the fore topsail and a red burgee sporting a black ball. Their deck houses, bulwarks, and boats were often painted green, and later the vessels had painted black ports on a white strake to give the appearance of a man-of-war. Poop and deck houses, lower masts and yards, bowsprit, boom and spencer gaff, and spanker gaff were painted white. The upper masts, spars, and jib booms were black.[13]

In 1835 Captain Charles H. Marshall, one of America's greatest packet masters, became manager of the Black Ball Line. He once had commanded the ship *Britannia*, which transported the first Mormon emigrant company to America. Other Black Ball ships used by the Mormon emigrants and missionaries were the *North America, Columbia, Montezuma,* and *Oxford.* The Black Ball Line survived for sixty years, a pioneer in a fascinating period of the American merchant marine. Its reputation was world-wide, for disciplined and smart passages, but also for tough but able masters. Among its famous captains were John Rathbone, Enoch Cook, and Alfred B. Lowber, all of whom skippered emigrant packets. Yet the Black Ball liners acquired a notoriety which found expression in some old sea chanteys:

> 'Tis larboard and starboard on deck you will sprawl.
> For kicking Jack Williams commands the Black Ball.[14]

Other packet lines played a part in the Mormon migration. It should be mentioned that ships often operated in more than one line at different times over the years as conditions changed. Many were engaged on occasion by transocean and coastal lines, which is evident from the packet lists. For example, the ship *Chaos*, which brought a Mormon company to America in 1841, was included in no less than eight packet rosters during her service: Black Star Line, Taylor & Merrill Line, Samuel Thompson's Line, Slate's Liverpool Line, Packet Line, Dispatch Line, Union Line, and Commercial Line. The ship *Rockaway*, also an early Mormon emigrant carrier, was listed in the Line of Liverpool Packets, Merchant's Line, Corner Line, Crescent City Line, Lincoln's Line, Hurlbut Line, and Brigham line. The ship *Jersey* was likewise affiliated with at least seven packet lines, including the Black Star and Regular lines.[15]

Ships used by Mormon emigrants and missionaries operated in more than forty different packet lines at various times in their service. About sixteen of these vessels were engaged by the Regular Line between Liverpool and American ports. Train's Line, which was distinguished by a large "T" on the fore topsails of its ships, supplied some eleven windships for the

Mormon migration. This line was taken over by Warren & Thayer in 1855. Other lines that listed "Mormon" ships were the New or Red Star Line, Tapscott's Line, Dispatch Line, and Dramatic Line. The Blue Swallowtail Line with its blue and white burgee, the Red Swallowtail Line with its red and white burgee, White Star Line, Black Diamond Line, Black X Line, Cope Line, Red Z Line, and Kermit Line were among those shipping firms that listed vessels utilized by the Saints.[16]

In crossing the Atlantic under sail, seamen spoke of the passages as uphill and downhill. The uphill passage was from Europe to America. Typically, the prevailing winds were westerlies, which meant that emigrant ships encountered headwinds most of the way. The vessel therefore had to buck the wind, tacking much of the time. A packet sailing westward usually took at least ten days longer to reach the United States than the return voyage to Europe. Eastward passages were naturally faster since the ship sailed with the wind and was aided by the Gulf Stream.

Although it was the world's most important commercial highway, the Atlantic was a formidable gauntlet of wind and wave. To many emigrants, the Atlantic crossing was far more dangerous, frightening, and harrowing than crossing the plains in covered wagons. One Danish convert later said that her six weeks at sea were the most miserable weeks of her life, including walking from Nebraska to Utah with a pioneer company. There is no doubt that in the early 1840s emigrants aboard sailing vessels had a hard time. In bad weather hatches were battened down, and one reporter wrote that "men, women, and children screamed all night in terror." William Clayton, who recorded the second emigrant voyage from Liverpool to New York in 1840 aboard ship *North America*, described a storm in the first few days at sea: "The wind blew hard . . . many were sick all night. . . . Such sickness, vomiting, groaning and bad smells I never witnessed before and added to this the closeness of the births almost suffocated us for want of air. . . . On the Friday night a little girl belonging to a family in the second cabin was frightened by the storm and lost her reason." Two days later he wrote, "This night the child which was frightened died."[17]

The Saints knew what to expect when they boarded ship. They were told of the discomforts, santitation problems, disease, storms, lustful sailors, poor food, and the sheer tedium of days at sea. Church leaders often gave detailed instruction on cleanliness, preparation of food, scheduled teaching and study, and the importance of discipline. Emigrant companies were organized into wards with presiding officers, and because of their discipline the Mormons usually fared better than other emigrants.

At that time shipboard conditions were scandalous. Stephen de Vere, a social worker, made a report to the British Emigration Commissioners in 1847 which said in part:

Before the emigrant has been a week at sea he is an altered man. How can it be otherwise? Hundreds of poor people, men, women, and children, of all ages from the drivelling idiot of ninety to the babe just born, huddled together, without light, air, wallowing in filth, and breathing a fetid atmosphere, sick in body, dispirited in heart; the fevered patients lying between the sound, in sleeping places so narrow as to deny them the power of indulging, by a change of position, the natural restlessness of the disease; by their agonized ravings disturbing those around and predisposing them, through the effects of the imagination, to imbibe the contagion; living without food or medicine except as administered by the hand of casual charity; dying without the voice of spiritual consolation, and buried in the deep without the rites of the Church. The food is generally ill-selected, and seldom sufficiently cooked, in consequence of the insufficiency and bad construction of the cooking places. The supply of water, hardly enough for cooking and drinking, does not allow washing, in many ships the filthy beds, teeming with all abomination, are never required to be brought on deck and aired; the narrow space between the sleeping berths and the piles of boxes is never washed or scraped, but breathes up a damp and fetid stench, until the day before arrival at quarantine, when all hands are required to "scrub up", and put on a fair face for the doctor and Government inspector.[18]

In the early years of Mormon emigration, steerage passengers supplied their own food; later, legislation required vessels carrying emigrants to provide a daily ration. Sleeping quarters between decks were of the rudest sort, and overcrowding was common in sailing craft that during the three decades of emigration under canvas never exceeded two thousand tons. As a result of regulations in successive British and American Passenger Acts, conditions improved somewhat over the years, yet sea travel remained relatively primitive during the sailing vessel era. A good example is provided by the accommodations of the ship *Franklin,* which transported 413 Danish Saints from Hamburg to New York in April 1862.

The emigrants were quartered below deck. There were 160 bunks "so wide that three persons could easily have room in one of them side by side." Passengers received their rations, consisting of beef, pork, peas, beans, potatoes, pearl barley, rice, prunes, syrup, vinegar, pepper, coffee, tea, sugar, butter, rye bread, sea biscuits, water, flour, salted herring, salt, and oil for lamps. There were eleven lanterns, six furnished by the ship and five by the emigrants. The Saints also hired an extra cook and appointed two men to assist him. Whether the crowded steerage contributed to the outbreak of disease will never be known for certain, but during the passage measles and chicken pox claimed forty-eight lives, or 11 percent of the company. Most of the victims were children.[19]

Ballou's Pictorial engravings capture scenes of burdened but determined emigrants boarding a Liverpool packet for the long and arduous voyage to America. *Courtesy The Peabody Museum of Salem.*

Overcrowding added to the discomfort. Large emigrant companies—frequently more than 500 persons—had to be quartered between decks in limited space. Huddled together in a rolling and sometimes pitching vessel, these men, women, and children suffered in body and spirit from lack of privacy. Even in the best of ships overcrowding compounded the misery and indignity of seasickness, dysentery, and other afflictions.

During the 1861 passage of the ship *Monarch of the Sea* from Liverpool to New York—the first of two such voyages made by this largest windship used by the Mormons—955 Saints were crammed together on three decks. Since families were berthed amidships where there happened to be a little more space available, the resourceful president of the emigrants found a happy solution. He proposed that betrothed couples be married to ease the overcrowding in the quarters for single passengers, and many marriages were promptly solemnized.[20]

Even when the weather was fair, life on shipboard was not always tranquil. There were the usual petty jealousies, complaints about conditions, cultural differences, friction among emigrants, and conflicts between passengers and crew. An ugly crew of the clipper *Emerald Isle* in 1868 "molested" the young women. When Hans Jensen Hals protested, the deck hands threatened the brethren with physical violence. The captain responded by rattling the irons which he told Hals he had used on uncooperative passengers in the past.[21] On board the ship *Kennebec* in 1852 there were Irish emigrants in addition to 333 Mormons. During the passage to New Orleans the Irish fell short of provisions and stole whatever they could from the Mormons. As a result, the Saints subsisted on half rations for the last four or five days before landing.[22]

Aboard the German square-rigger *Humboldt* during her second voyage with Mormon emigrants in 1866 the food was simple but poor in quality. According to Olof Jensen, a steerage passenger, the diet consisted of soup, potatoes, fish, bread, and hardtack biscuits. Cooking was done in huge iron pots, "so large the cook could get inside." No bread was baked, and the biscuits became "extremely hard and dry." The potatoes were "sour and soggy." Drinking water had been taken from the River Elbe in Germany and stored in wooden barrels. These barrels had been burned black on the inside, causing the water to become "black as coal." Some water had been placed in large iron barrels that rusted and turned it red. "Pigs would object to the food and water," he wrote. Bunks were made of common lumber with space for four across in two tiers.[23]

Even if conditions on shipboard were quite tolerable, the risk of disease was always present. Parents were warned before sailing that the toll was particularly high among children. Principal causes of death were measles, chickenpox, cholera, smallpox, dysentery, and accidents. Since the records of many voyages are incomplete, it is not possible to determine the total number of deaths at sea; however, 84 of the 176 emigrant voyages of sailing craft had at least one death. There were more than 530 fatalities, but details of many voyages are lacking and undoubtedly some deaths were not recorded. Besides the 48 deaths on the voyage of the *Franklin* in 1862, unusually high mortality rates were recorded by the ships listed in Appendix 4. Epidemics that began on shipboard often took an even heavier toll after the passengers had landed. Particularly tragic was the loss of life among the emigrants of the *Jessie Munn* and *Benjamin Adams* in 1854. Cholera broke out during the voyage to New Orleans and followed the Saints to their camp at Westport, Missouri. Some 200 out of 678 died. That they "died in the Lord" was the only comfort.[24]

Burial at sea was commonplace. The funeral service usually consisted of a brief prayer and sometimes consoling remarks before the body encased in its canvas shroud was dropped over the side. On the bark *Carnatic* in 1848, for example, the remains were sewn into canvas with a "great weight of coal" attached to the feet and then consigned to the deep. "The water was so still that the corpse was seen as it sank to a great depth."[25]

The cycle of life was uninterrupted aboard ships—there was birth as well as death. Although records are incomplete, at least 47 emigrant sailing vessels hosted some 110 births. The highest number of births was seven aboard the ship *International* on her 1853 voyage to New Orleans. Some infants and mothers are known to have died following childbirth. It was not unusual to name a baby for a favorite captain—or even for a ship. For example, two infants were born aboard the large square-rigger *General McClellan* in 1864 and christened Jenny McClellan and George McClellan. During the 1856 passage of the ship *Enoch Train* there were four births and two of the children were named after the vessel: Christina Enoch Lyon and Enoch Train Hargraves. The ship *Westmoreland* and her master Captain Robert R. Decan were jointly honored in 1857 when a baby was named Decan Westmoreland Goff.[26]

To the emigrant inexperienced on the water, the fear of the ocean itself often overshadowed all other hardships on shipboard. One cannot view the turbulent Atlantic or the unpacific Pacific in all of their vastness without a feeling of awe and a strange loneliness. The green and gray surface, except for the brighter blue where the Gulf Stream flows, is cold and impersonal, and it produced the emotion expressed in the seaman's prayer: "Save us, O God. Thine ocean is so large, and our little boat is so small."

Yet the ocean was there, and it had to be crossed. Under sail the emigrants placed themselves at the mercy of varying and inconstant winds and uncompromising waves. The sea was not always friendly, and to these travelers no words were more terrifying than "lost at sea." Those words created many specters in the mind, conjured up visions of the restless tyranny of the ocean, the relentless waves beating and tearing a ship apart, the screams of the doomed, and the lonely rendezvous with fate. Coleridge caught the mood of man's lonely struggle with the sea in his "Rime of the Ancient Mariner":

> Alone, alone, all, all alone,
> Alone on a wide, wide sea![27]

The emigrant's fear of the ocean was well founded; in the sailing ship era shipwreck was all too common. At certain times, when the winter gales and summer hurricanes raged, the toll was especially high. The years 1840 and 1841 were particularly bad. During the fourteen months ending December 31, 1841, 557 vessels were reported wrecked—mostly along the Atlantic coast—and 28 more were listed as missing. Some 650 lives were lost. An almost equal number of vessels were casualties in British waters. Western Ocean packets suffered least of all shipping, and many won acclaim by rescuing sinking ships.[28]

The Mormons were fortunate in their choice of vessels. During the three decades under sail their emigrant ships all made safe passages except the bark *Julia Ann*, wrecked in 1855 out of Australia. The Saints and some masters attributed this remarkable safety record to the hand of Providence and the fact that ships were often dedicated and blessed before embarking on an emigrant voyage. Many of these vessels were eventually lost at sea, but not while carrying Mormon passengers. Yet Mormon emigrant ships did not escape the battering of stormy seas. Some reported dismasting, shredded sails, serious leaks, and dismantled rigging during passage.

It is no wonder then that the emigrant was often anxious and apprehensive during the ocean crossing. At night in his bunk he would hear the strange creaking noises of the ship. His quarters were dark and confining; only one or two lanterns swinging near the hatch diffused a dim light. He would hear the crying children, the retching and vomiting of the seasick, the crash of waves on the hull and at times bursting over the deck, the flap of canvas, the wind whistling through the shrouds and rigging, the cursing of scrambling seamen, the impatient shouts of officers, and the muttering and groaning of despairing companions.

The worst fears came near realization more than once. In 1843 the British bark *Yorkshire* encountered a storm so frightening that a mate asked the passengers how they would feel to be shipwrecked like Paul the Apostle. Undaunted, Elder Thomas Bullock promptly responded, "It is very likely we shall be shipwrecked; but the hull of this old vessel has got to carry us safe into New Orleans." As if to spurn his faith, the elements erupted with

Between decks of a sailing packet emigrants ate, slept, and languished—sometimes hatched down in semi-darkness and misery as the ship pitched and rolled through storms. These *Illustrated London News* engravings represent typical conditions for steerage passengers. *Courtesy The Peabody Museum of Salem.*

vivid lightning and a white squall "caught the fore-top-royal sail, which careened the vessel." Then the force of the wind snapped the foremast, mainmast, and mizzenmast with a loud crash. Almost the entire rigging—masts, jib, spanker, and sixteen sails and studding poles—was swept overboard with a great splash. The ship gave a surge and righted herself. The deck was a shambles, and the *Yorkshire* had to hoist a sail on "the stump of the mainmast" attached to the bow. Under this jury rig the bark with her terrified passengers made her way to New Orleans.[29]

Two years later the Yankee ship *Palmyra* ran into a severe storm shortly after leaving Liverpool. As the wind increased, fear gripped the emigrants. The intensity of the gale produced mountainous waves. Below deck boxes, tins, pans, bottles, and all other unsecured objects rolled, clashed, and cracked against each other in a dancing, jumbled confusion. The ship pitched and tossed wildly. Some passengers were bounced from their berths to the floor while others held on with difficulty. For eight days the tempest battered the small square-rigger. There were no fires, no cooking. The emigrants subsisted on biscuits and cold water when they felt like eating. Ann Pitchforth wrote that,

> . . . the waves dashed down the hold into the interior of the vessel, hatchway then closed, all in utter darkness and terror, not knowing whether the vessel was sinking or not; none could tell—all prayed—and awful silence prevailed—sharks and sins presenting themselves, and doubts and fears; one awful hour after another passing, we found we were not yet drowned; some took courage and lit the lamps; we met in prayer, we pleaded the promises of our God—faith prevailed; the winds abated, the sky cleared, the fires were again lit, then the luxury of a cup of tea and a little gruel.[30]

The account of Ann Pitchforth vividly describes the fearful reality of an Atlantic storm, the suffering and sheer terror of the emigrants, and the dangers on shipboard caused by the pitching and rolling of the ship. It is noteworthy that on this crossing the *Palmyra* rescued nine survivors of a sinking vessel who had managed to keep their craft afloat for seventeen days in water up to their waists.

Again and again Mormon missionaries and emigrants—most of whom had previously known only land-locked lives—revealed their fear and awe of the menacing Atlantic. Their references to its furious winds, dense fogs, immense icebergs, huge waves, and diabolical gales arising without warning confirm this body of water as likely the most dangerous in the world. In 1846 Wilford Woodruff, returning to New York aboard the ship *Ashburton*, penned a horror story of nearly twenty days of hurricanes, cold snow, hail, frost, a second mate swept overboard, and sails ripped to ribbons.[31] In 1850 the ship *Argo* was sailing blind in pitch darkness off the coast of Cuba when she narrowly escaped disaster. Suddenly the heavens were brightened by a strange light which showed a huge rock dead ahead. Captain Charles Mills, a veteran mariner, was able to turn the vessel and avoid what had seemed an inevitable collision. The Saints interpreted the light as providential.[32] That same year, as the ship *James Pennell* was nearing the end of her second Mormon emigrant voyage, a sudden gale arose as she approached the mouth of the Mississippi. Soon her main and mizzen masts were broken and part of the rigging was washed overboard. The vessel drifted helplessly for several days. Nearly all of the food and water had been consumed, and the emigrants faced the very real prospect of starvation. Luckily a pilot boat found the crippled ship and towed her to New Orleans.[33]

Storms were not the only source of fear. The ship *Forest Monarch* was becalmed for some days in 1853 on a voyage from Liverpool to New Orleans, creating a shortage of provisions. The passage took 59 days, compared with an average of 54 days.[34] Patience Loader, an emigrant aboard the ship *Horizon*, was anxious when a large shark followed the vessel for what seemed an unusual length of time. She may have thought the fish was an omen.[35] In 1859, during a voyage from South Africa to Boston, the British bark *Alacrity* met with dense fog in the Atlantic. Visibility was so poor that fear of shipwreck caused the Saints aboard to fast and pray for their safety. The master, unable to navigate by observing the sun, moon, or stars, climbed the mast searching for an opening in the fog. Through the lifting mist he saw that his vessel was headed for the Nantucket Shoals off the Massachusetts coast. There was just time for him to change course.[36]

For the success of the Mormon migration to America the shipmasters of their vessels are entitled to no small share of the credit. It can well be said that a ship is no better than her skipper; the Saints certainly benefited from professional seamanship. The reason was partly the great care with which the Mormons engaged their vessels, but it was also true that the master mariners—especially those in the packet and clipper service—were a remarkable class of men who often combined the finest qualities of manhood and leadership. They were hard, tough, competent, and experienced, and they were keenly aware of their responsibility for the security of their ships and the safety of their passengers. Many were of Yankee stock, and most had earned their position on the quarter-deck after years of training before the mast. Independent, enterprising, and courageous, these sea captains were respected—if not always loved—by the Mormons.

The early missionaries had nothing but praise for such mariners as captains Nathaniel B. Palmer of the packet ship *Garrick*, Joseph C. Delano of the packet *Patrick Henry*, Zenas Winsor of the clipper ships *Monsoon* and *Viking*, John Blackburn of the Tasmanian bark *Petrel*, and George Leslie of the British bark *Gazelle*. Captain Thomas D. Scott of the ship *John Brightman* of Calcutta became a generous benefactor of Elder Richard Ballantyne, and Robert Wright of the British snow *Royal Thistle* provided the destitute Ballantyne with passage from Madras to London.

By contrast, at the beginning of his journey from San Pedro to San Francisco Ballantyne was somewhat critical of Captain John Erskine of the brig *Col. Fremont*.[37] A few other missionaries gave their skippers negative appraisals. For example, on his South American mission Parley P. Pratt was outraged by the conduct of Captain C. E. Sampson of the American bark *Henry Kelsey* and the unidentified master of the brig *Dracut*.[38] Yet the missionaries and their shipmasters seemed to get along reasonably well together in most instances.

As for the emigrants, their relationship with the masters was usually good.   In 1844 the American bark *Fanny* carried 210 Saints from Liverpool to New Orleans. According to William Kay, presiding elder of the emigrant company, Captain Thomas Patterson and his crew displayed a "kindness I believe could scarcely be met with; his liberality exceeds all that ever came under our notice. . . . The cabin and its provisions have been at the service of all who stood in need of them, and the captain has with his own hand ministered unto the necessities of all that required it."[39]

The ship *Hartley* made two emigrant voyages. On the first passage to New Orleans Captain S. Cammett was "very kind to the emigrants," and several sailors were converted to the church. The second voyage in 1850, one year later, was a different story. Captain Charles C. Morrill's conduct was described as "shameful." He reportedly made the situation of the Saints "as miserable as possible" and invited women passengers into his cabin.[40]

On a 59-day passage to New Orleans in 1848, Captain William McKenzie of the British bark *Carnatic* developed a warm affection for the Mormon emigrants. He had been particularly thoughtful and considerate throughout the journey, appreciating the Mormons' good order and discipline. The *Millennial Star* noted: "So attached had the kind-hearted captain become to the Saints which he had brought across the mighty deep, that he parted with them in tears, and the crew bestowed three cheers as the emigrants left the vessel."

The voyage of the ship *Berlin* from Liverpool to New Orleans in 1849 resulted in 43 deaths from cholera (28 among the Mormons), which possibly influenced the bitter feelings of the Saints toward Captain Alfred F. Smith. He had ordered some of the bedding, clothing, and property of the victims thrown overboard to reduce contagion. It is possible that their judgment of the master was somewhat biased, but in any case, the Mormons "were highly dissatisfied with Captain Smith's conduct toward them."

No shipmaster was held in higher esteem than Captain David Brown of the Yankee square-rigger *International.* In 1853, during a particularly happy voyage to New Orleans, Captain Brown and most of his crew were converted to the Mormon Church, and he was ordained an elder. Presiding Elder Christopher Arthur described the popular skipper as "a noble, generous-hearted man; and to his honor I can say that no man ever left Liverpool with a company of Saints more beloved by them, or who has been more friendly and social than he has been with us; indeed, words are inadequate to express the fatherly care over us as a people."[41]

Captain George Kerr of the British ship *Golconda* was likewise held in high regard. The *Millennial Star* stated that his conduct "gave great satisfaction to all the company, and before parting a vote of thanks, with three cheers was tendered him." The following year, 1854, Captain Arthur M. Fales, master and part-owner of the American ship *Germanicus,* was given this tribute by Elder Richard Cook, president of the 220 Mormon emigrants, after a 69-day passage to New Orleans: "Captain Fales is a very agreeable gentleman to travel with, and seeks to make the passengers comfortable."[42]

On the first of three "Mormon" voyages the American ship *John J. Boyd* was skippered by Captain Thomas Austin. It was very stormy crossing. Elder Charles Savage, a missionary returning with the emigrant company, wrote: "Our captain got superstitious on account of the long passage, and ordered that there should be no singing on board; the mate said that all ships that had preachers on board were *always* sure of a bad passage; however, the Lord heard our prayers, and in His own due time we arrived at our destination." It took the ship 66 days to reach New York.[43]

In early 1856 the large square-rigged *Enoch Train* brought 534 Saints to Boston. Her master was Captain Henry P. Rich. The voyage was relatively pleasant, and Captain Rich and his officers "were very kind to the emigrants."[44] In the Pacific at about the same time, Captain S. F. Sargent of the small bark *Jenny Ford* composed several hymns that were sung by the Australian Mormons emigrating to San Francisco. Apparently a religious man, Captain Sargent was kind and hospitable to his passengers, who honored him with a testimonal before the end of the voyage.[45]

Captain Sanders Curling of Thomaston, Maine, part-owner of the Yankee square-rigger *S. Curling,* won great praise from the Saints on his second Mormon emigrant voyage to New York. During this 1856 passage two babies were born and named for the master, Dan Curling Dee and Claudia Curling Reynolds. Elder Dan Jones, president of the 707 Mormons on board and one of the church's most colorful leaders, developed a close friendship with Captain Curling, and the two spent hours spinning yarns together as they paced the quarterdeck "scrutinizing the horizon."

In a letter to Franklin D. Richards, Elder Jones praised the master's conduct as "generous, courteous, and philanthropic." The seaman was especially diligent in caring for the sick and allowed the Saints the "freedom of his commodious and splendid ship." He was not only humane but exhibited a parental concern over his passengers. "At home among the stars, born in a storm, cradled on the ocean, few things escaped his eagle eye, with such a one, hours have I spent with a pleasure known only to weather-beaten old tars. May he moor his barque, yes, his *fleet* in Zion's snug harbour, ere the equinoctial gales of life beset him."[46] Such a tribute could only come from one who appreciated professional seamanship, for Jones himself had a seafaring background.

A year later the large square-rigged *George Washington* carried a company of 817 Saints from Liverpool to New York. She was skippered by Captain Josiah S. Comings (sometimes spelled Cummings), who, upon receiving a complimentary note from the Mormon leaders, responded as follows: "I am free to acknowledge that on no previous voyage have my passengers conducted themselves so orderly and peaceably as those in your charge; cleanliness, morality, sobriety, reciprocation of favors and general good behavior were pre-eminently conspicuous in their conduct and character."[47]

Another well-known packet master was Captain G. D. S. Trask, who commanded two square-riggers that brought three companies of Mormons to New York—the *Manchester* and *General McClellan*. The Saints held him in high esteem, and when a baby was born on shipboard in 1862, the parents honored him in naming the child Henry John Trask Adamson. Captain Trask presented the parents with a congratulatory letter accompanied by a chart of the Atlantic, designating the latitude and longitude where the child was born. The emigrants praised the captain for his "courtesy and uniform kindness" and presented him with a testimonial expressing their feelings.[48]

No master was more *dis*liked by the Saints than Captain D. Schilling of the German ship *Athena* (*Athenia* in some records), which carried 484 Scandinavian Saints from Hamburg to New York in 1862. Although an able mariner, the master harbored antagonism and contempt for his passengers. When Ola N. Liljenquist, the Swedish president of the Mormon company, protested that the water and food were unfit, Captain Schilling informed him that he had brought emigrants across the ocean for twenty-five years and that he was the sole authority on shipboard. He further emphasized his point by producing handcuffs and irons he had used on complaining passengers. Liljenquist wrote in his journal that "One Sunday afternoon, after we had concluded our afternoon services, I suppose through jealousy and not having any influence with the Saints, he threat-

As advertised in this rare poster, the 1,736-ton clipper ship *Emerald Isle* was noted for fast passages. Three Mormon companies crossed the Atlantic in this vessel; the third voyage—and least pleasant for the Saints—was one of the last made under sail (1868). *Courtesy National Maritime Museum, San Francisco.*

ened to throw me overboard and I suppose he would have carried out his purpose had he dared to."[49] During this unhappy voyage 38 passengers died of measles and other ailments.

In 1864 the full-rigged *Hudson* made an unusually slow passage to New York. Captain Isaiah Pratt, master of this large windship, did "much to alleviate the fatigue of the journey," during which measles took the lives of nine children. In like manner, Captain Henry P. Hovey of the *Amazon*, one of the largest and most famous packet ships, "studied the comfort and happiness of all passengers and made every requisite exertion to ensure the health, comfort and safety of the company." Captain Thomas William Freeman of the ship *Belle Wood* did his utmost to make the voyage pleasant and comfortable for more than 600 Mormon emigrants in 1865.[50]

Little is known about Captain Charles Sisson's treatment of the Saints who crossed the Atlantic in 1865 aboard his ship *Bridgewater.* He was a famous clipper and packet ship skipper and is also remembered for a quaint story. Before departing on one of his long voyages, he ordered his young daughter to remain in the yard. He warned her that if she left without permission he would punish her. Shortly before he was to board his ship, the little girl was missing, and he had to leave without inflicting punishment. A year later, when he returned, he took the disobedient child over his knee and dispensed a good spanking.[51] It is likely that he also ran his ship with a firm hand.

In 1868 the *Emerald Isle* left Liverpool carrying 876 Mormons, including the last Scandinavians to cross the Atlantic in a sailing vessel. This clipper ship had transported two previous emigrant companies. The earlier voyages had been made under Captain George B. Cornish, a well-known mariner who apparently got along well with the Saints. However, a Captain Gillespie commanded the ship on this third crossing. According to the *Millennial Star*, no other emigrating company was known to have been so mistreated by the ship's officers and crew, and it became necessary for presiding elder Hans Jensen Hals to protest and remind the captain of the contractual and legal rights of the emigrants. On one occasion a mate attacked a woman passenger. When a Mormon came to her rescue and chastised the mate, the crew threatened violence until the master restored order. Not only were the Saints treated harshly, but bad drinking water caused much sickness. Measles also broke out among the children; 37 passengers died on shipboard, and 38 were taken ashore ill. It was felt that the drinking water contributed to the high death rate, and the Saints— rightly or wrongly—placed much of the blame for their troubles on Captain Gillespie.

The last sailing ship to leave Liverpool with Mormon emigrants was the full-rigged, three-decked *Constitution*. Skippered by Captain William

Hatten, she sailed shortly after the *Emerald Isle*, and it was a happy voyage. The morale of the 457 Saints was excellent, and the master was highly praised for the "interest he manifested towards the passengers and the many liberties extended to them." The health of the company was almost universally good, and there were no deaths during the passage. Captain Hatten was popular, and he went out of his way to help the Saints celebrate July twenty-fourth.[52] Even though the *Constitution* had sailed from Liverpool four days later, she arrived at New York nine days ahead of the *Emerald Isle*.

Among the smallest sailing vessels used by Mormon emigrants was the British bark *Albert*, which in October 1865 sailed from Melbourne, Australia, with a Mormon company on a voyage to San Francisco of about 100 days. Built in Massachusetts, this bark was later sold to Australian owners. *Courtesy The Peabody Museum of Salem.*

No ship is more prominent in Mormon history than the 445-ton *Brooklyn*, which brought the first Saints to California around the Horn in 1846. This painting by an unknown American artist probably dates from the late nineteenth century. *Courtesy M. H. de Young Memorial Museum, San Francisco, and Hirschl & Adler Gallery, New York City.*

Four

A Saga of Sail

During the 1840s some 8,600 Mormons emigrated over water to Zion. There were 52 voyages of organized companies—51 across the Atlantic and one from the east to the west coast of America, the historic journey of the ship *Brooklyn* around Cape Horn. All of these passages were made in sailing craft, 45 in full-rigged ships and seven in barks. Forty-eight different vessels were used, four of which made two voyages each.

The sailing vessels were comparatively small, ranging from 330 tons for the British bark *Caroline* to 1,283 tons for the British square-rigger *Zetland* and averaging 663 tons. Of the 52 passages, 39 were made under the American flag and 13 under the British ensign. Liverpool was the port of embarkation for 48 voyages, Bristol for two, and New York for the ship *Brooklyn*. Of the ports of debarkation New Orleans accounted for 43, New York five, Quebec two, and San Francisco one. The ports for one voyage could not be ascertained—that of the bark *Caroline* in 1841.

Passages during this decade were slow and tedious. From Liverpool to New Orleans the fastest time was 37 days and the slowest 71 days, the average 54 days. From Liverpool to New York the sailing time was much shorter, ranging from 29 to 44 days and averaging 35. The two voyages from Bristol to Quebec—about which little else is known—required 63 and 75 days. The longest sea passage made by Mormon emigrants was the 177-day voyage of the ship *Brooklyn* to San Francisco. (See Appendix 2 for vessel types, Appendix 5 for ports of embarkation and debarkation, and Appendix 6 for passage times.)

In the early years of Mormon emigration few voyages were documented in detail. One exception was the second company's crossing in 1840 aboard the Black Ball packet ship *North America*. William Clayton, an English convert, kept a journal of the 34-day passage from Liverpool to New York.

[69]

His pen described the reality of ocean travel in such episodes as the near wreck of the 611-ton square-rigger on a rock, a severe gale that caused general seasickness and terrified the passengers, the rigging blown away in a storm, the sanitation problems and stench between decks, a fire in the galley, women flirting with the sailors, the friction between Captain Alfred B. Lowber and the Saints, and the deaths of six children.[1]

The 68-day voyage of the British ship *Emerald* in late 1842 was particularly wearisome to the Saints. After leaving Liverpool the 250 emigrating Mormons grew restless and dissatisfied. Parley P. Pratt, the Mormon apostle who presided over the company, wrote this account of the crossing: "We had a tedious passage of ten weeks, and some difficulties, murmurings and rebellions; but the Saints on board were called together, and chastened and reproved sharply, which brought them to repentance. We then humbled ourselves and called on the Lord, and he sent a fair wind, and brought us into port in time to save us from starvation." The vessel reached New Orleans early in January 1843.[2]

Another notable passage began on January 16, 1843. On that date the Yankee square-rigger *Swanton* eased out of the Liverpool harbor bound for New Orleans with 212 Mormon passengers aboard. It was the first of two such voyages. Apostle Lorenzo Snow presided over the Saints, and his first task was to organize the company. He appointed elders M. Auley and Robert Reed as his counselors and then divided the emigrants into two groups. Twelve officers were designated "to attend to the comfort and cleanliness of the Saints." At six every morning the clanging of a bell awakened the emigrants, and they set about doing their assigned tasks. Every night at seven o'clock a prayer meeting was held, and twice on Sunday and every Tuesday and Thursday nights the Saints attended a "preaching" service. "Peace and health prevailed among the people, though some were disposed to murmur a little. Much of the power of God was manifested in the restoration of the sick by anointing with oil, and through the prayer of faith."

One of these healing experiences involved Captain Davenport's steward, a highly respected and popular young German who had suddenly fallen ill. His sickness grew worse until it seemed that death was inevitable. The captain was in despair, and the ship's officers and crew all gave up hope of the young man's recovery. Then a Mormon woman, a "Sister Martin," went to the master and urged him to allow Apostle Snow to administer to the steward according to the Mormon custom. Captain Davenport replied that it would be useless, but Sister Martin persisted. Finally the seaman gave his consent. Lorenzo Snow entered the cabin and found the captain in tears. He told the Mormon that it was too late. Without answering Snow seated himself beside the dying man. He prayed silently for a few

Sporting the emblem of the Black Ball Line on her fore-topsail, the *North America* transported the second company from Liverpool to America in 1840. *Courtesy The Peabody Museum of Salem.*

moments, then "he laid his hands on the head of the young man, prayed, and in the name of Jesus Christ rebuked the disease and commanded him to be made whole. Very soon after, to the joy and astonishment of all, he was seen walking the deck, praising and glorifying God for his restoration. The officers and sailors acknowledged the miraculous power of God, and on landing at New Orleans several of them were baptized."[3]

Of all Mormon sea journeys, the voyage of the ship *Brooklyn* was unique. She carried an emigrant company from New York to California, then a possession of Mexico. This company was recruited by Elder Samuel Brannan, a native of Maine, and a printer by trade, at the time the Mormons were being driven out of Illinois. These emigrants were mostly farmers, mechanics, and tradesmen from the eastern states. The company consisted of 70 men, 68 women, and 100 children, Mormons but for a few exceptions.

The square-rigger was a tired merchantman of 445 tons, built twelve years earlier but still seaworthy. Her master, a principal owner, was Captain Abel W. Richardson, a competent seaman who was a New Yorker about forty-eight years old. He fully realized that time was running out for his ship. Competition for passengers and cargo was intense, and the larger and newer vessels were winning an increasing share of the shipping business.

He was willing, therefore, to sign a charter party with the Mormons on attractive terms.

Under the direction of the captain and Elder Brannan preparations were made for a long voyage. Carpenters added bunks and cubicles between decks. A dining area was furnished with a long rude table and backless benches which would also serve for meetings, recreation, sewing, and court sessions. Rules of conduct and a plan of work assignments were drawn up, and two black cooks were hired. Cargo was loaded on board, including a large supply of farm implements, tools, three flouring mills, a printing press, firearms, powder and ball, provisions for life both on shipboard and ashore, and a library.

On February 4, 1846, a cool winter afternoon, the *Brooklyn* eased away from her East River berth and slowly moved beyond the Battery, glided through the Narrows, passed between Staten and Coney islands, and plowed into the Atlantic. On this day the Mormons at Nauvoo were coincidentally beginning their great trek to the Rocky Mountains.

Swaying and rolling with the ocean swells, the square-rigger headed southward. During the 177-day passage the vessel lay becalmed for a long time in the tropics. She encountered severe gales in both the Atlantic and Pacific oceans, and passengers were "hatched down" between decks as the waves crashed over the ship with the water at times splashing into the staterooms. The noise of the tempest was mingled with the cries of frightened children, the comforting voices of parents, and the groans of the sick. Between decks there were only two dim and swinging lamps in the passageway, and women and children had to be lashed to their berths in the darkness. Furniture and other movable objects were flung about, creating further hazard. Her experiences led one woman to say, "Of all the memories of my life, not one is so bitter as that dreary six months' voyage, in an emigrant ship, round the Horn."[4] One storm was so terrifying that the captain gave up hope of survival. He was surprised when the Mormons assured him that all would be well and it was so.

The *Brooklyn* doubled Cape Horn without great hardship, but later she was blown almost back to that point by a gale off Chile. The ship made two anchorages before reaching California. She visited Juan Fernandez Island for five days. It was here that Alexander Selkirk lived whose adventures had inspired the classic story *Robinson Crusoe*. It was also here that Laura Goodwin was buried. Of the ten passengers who died she was the only one not buried at sea. The second anchorage was at Honolulu, where the emigrants remained ten days.

During this historic voyage two children were born and named Atlantic and Pacific. Four backsliders were excommunicated from the church for improprieties. On July 31 the *Brooklyn* dropped anchor in the San Francisco Bay. Here the emigrants found the American flag flying over Yerba Buena. The passengers were set ashore in a small boat between Clay and Washington streets, and for a brief time San Francisco was largely a Mormon town.[5]

The first decade of emigration closed with the sailing of the 1,283-ton British ship *Zetland* from Liverpool—the largest vessel used by the Saints to that time. Built less than a year earlier by "Bluenose" shipwrights of Nova Scotia, this beautiful square-rigger moved down the Mersey on November 10, 1849, with about 250 Saints aboard. It was her second "Mormon" voyage that year. The first had an unhappy sequel to a 63-day passage when cholera broke out among the emigrants shortly after their landing at New Orleans, but this second journey of 44 days ended on a happy note with the arrival at New Orleans on Christmas Eve.[6]

During the 1850s the number of Mormon emigrants crossing the oceans more than doubled compared with the prior ten years—a total of about 21,200. These emigrants came in 78 identified voyages—all but one in sailing craft, that one exception the Cunard steamship *Niagara*, sailing in 1852 between Liverpool and Boston with about twenty Saints. Of the passages made under canvas, square-riggers accounted for 69, barks 6, and brigs two. Sixty-seven different sailing vessels were used, ten of which made more than one "Mormon" voyage.

The windships in this period were considerably bigger and roomier and could accommodate many more emigrants. They ranged from the 183-ton brig *G. W. Kendall* that carried a small company in the Pacific to the commodious 1,775-ton ship *Horizon* that carried 856 emigrants across the Atlantic. The average was 977 tons, compared with 663 tons during the 1840s. Similarly, emigrant companies now averaged 266 persons compared with 157 in the first decade. Of the 77 passages under sail, 65 originated in Liverpool; five in Sydney and Newcastle; two each in Melbourne, Port Elizabeth, and Calcutta; and one in Tahiti. Thirty-eight voyages terminated at New Orleans, sixteen at New York, seven at Philadelphia, seven at Boston, four at San Francisco, three at San Pedro, one at Honolulu, and one in the wreck of the *Julia Ann* at the Scilly Islands. Of these voyages 69 were under the American flag.

As can be seen in Appendix 6, passage times did not improve, even with the larger vessels. The average voyage between Liverpool and New Orleans was still 54 days and ranged from 36 to 70 days, almost the same as in the ten years prior. From Liverpool to New York passages actually took longer, averaging 39 days against 35 days. The fastest time was 28 days, the slowest 66. It is significant, however, that the emigrant ships made better time from Liverpool to Boston and Philadelphia, averaging 33 days to Boston and 38 days to Philadelphia against the 39 days to New York.

There were some unusually long voyages during the 1850s: from Sydney to San Francisco required 94 days, from Melbourne to San Francisco 81 days, from Newcastle in Australia to San Pedro 83 days, from Sydney to San Pedro 80 and 103 days, from Calcutta to San Francisco 112 days, and from Port Elizabeth in South Africa to Boston 55 and 71 days.

Most of these emigrant voyages fell into a routine pattern. Events that landsmen would consider extraordinary became ordinary and the unusual commonplace. Birth, disease, death, and burial in the deep were expected and accepted with brief notes in logs and journals—when they were recorded at all. Shipboard life was marked by a succession of long days on the silent water, fickle spates of bad weather, stresses on patience and humor, dull periods of housekeeping and cleaning, and contrived programs of instruction and religious services to promote not only spirituality but also discipline and harmony. But there were exceptions.

On March 4, 1851, the 744-ton ship *Olympus* of Kennebunk, Maine, left Liverpool bound for New Orleans with a company of 245 Mormons. After three weeks of tranquil and pleasant sailing, broken only by bouts of seasickness and the violence of a young lad who went berserk with "evil spirits" and had to be exorcised, Captain Horace A. Wilson walked the deck peering at the sky. He suddenly ordered all watches to shorten sail. When a passenger asked why he gave such an order in fair weather, he replied, "Don't you see that cloud yonder." The questioner said he did. "Well, when that strikes our ship we will have no need for so much canvas."

The cloud grew larger. The sailors aloft hauled down the outrigged sails and were close reefing the main topsail as the squall struck. The ship reeled drunkenly, trembled, shook, and rocked. The squall gained in fury, and the wind carried the foremast overboard and seriously sprang the mainmast at its deck wedges and housing. Several men were nearly caught in the sails and flung overboard. The mast was now hanging over the side, and it was necessary to cut loose the stays with axes to free the ship. With the wind at hurricane force the ship was "thrown on her beam ends and became unmanageable." Two men aloft trying to furl the sails were in a precarious position, and both were blown from the rigging but miraculously dropped in the belly of the sail rather than the churning water. The captain could only exclaim, "My God, how did they get there!"

All passengers were ordered below, except for two men who volunteered to assist the crew. The hatches were battened down, and the emigrants huddled together in the darkness as waves crashed over the decks and sent water down the hatchways into the hold. After the sails were furled and set to stand the storm, orders were given to man the pumps. There was water in the hold about four feet deep. Hour after hour the men pumped frantically with no apparent headway, and the storm continued without a lull.

With a string of oaths, Captain Wilson summoned his officers for a consultation, then ordered his second mate to go to Elder William Howell, who presided over the Saints. He said, "You go to the captain of the Mormons and tell him from Captain Wilson that if the God of the Mormons can do anything to save the ship and the people, they had better be calling on Him to do so, for we are now sinking at the rate of a foot every hour; and if the storm continues we shall all be at the bottom of the ocean before daylight."

Elder Howell was in his bunk when he received the message. He responded with these words: "Very well. You may tell Captain Wilson that we are not going to the bottom of the ocean, for we embarked from Liverpool on a voyage for New Orleans, and we will arrive safely in that port. Our God will protect us."

The scene below decks was confusion compounded. Trunks and boxes were rolling, sliding, and striking each other. The passengers were crying, praying and moaning. Elder Howell dressed quickly and called about twelve men to join him in prayer. He asked one after another to pray, and finally he prayed himself. Wilson G. Nowers recorded this eyewitness account:

> While he was still engaged in prayer, I noticed a material change in the motion of the ship; for instead of her rolling and pitching as she had been doing, she seemed to tremble as one suffering from the effects of a severe cold. Varied thoughts passed through my mind; I could not entertain the idea that the vessel was sinking, nor could I realize that the storm had so suddenly abated. At the close of the prayer of President Howell, all responded with a hearty Amen, and we arose from our position. President Howell then remarked, "You may all retire to your beds." I returned to the deck to find that the storm had miraculously ceased; the wind had gone down, and the waves were stilled immediately round about the ship, while in the distance the billows were still raging.

The Mormons and Captain Wilson attributed their deliverance to Providence, and the experience rekindled religious fervor aboard. After repairs were made and a jury mast rigged, the master gave the Saints permission to hold religious services. The emigrants bathed, shaved, and attired themselves in clean clothing. They preached enthusiastically to the non-Mormons on board, improvised from a large barrel a baptismal font which could be mounted from a ladder on deck, and proceeded to baptize and confer the gift of the Holy Ghost by the laying on of hands. Sometime later a platform suspended by ropes was lowered into the ocean and baptisms were performed in that contrivance. During the voyage of 54 days, fifty converts were baptized, including one just before embarkation and one after arrival at New Orleans.[7]

Less dramatic was the voyage of the Yankee ship *Jersey*. Her passage from Liverpool to New Orleans is significant largely because Frederick Piercy, an artist, described the details of shipboard life. His account was published in James Linforth's *Route from Liverpool to Great Salt Lake Valley*. Piercy embarked on the 849-ton square-rigger at Liverpool on February 5, 1853. He found a berth in the second cabin, which accommodated eight persons. He met Captain John Day of Salem, Massachusetts, whom he pictured as "a short, fat, fussy old fellow in spectacles, and, like most fat people with abundant corporations, he seemed to be tolerably good tempered." His opinion of the first mate was less flattering, however: "He was a more angular body, all sharp points and corners. It was evident it would not do to run against him. His teeth that remained were long and pointed, his complexion, hair and eyebrows were dark, and he had the largest and lightest grey eyes I ever saw—they were absolutely luminous. He was an uncomfortable fellow to look at."

Piercy thought the crew were a "picturesque looking set of fellows," and hoped their courage and daring in a storm would match their "taking God's name in vain." He spoke well of the English and Welsh steerage passengers and found their confusion of tongues "quite amusing until you were personally interested in what was said." He was impressed with how well they got along and particularly with their cooperation and helpfulness to other emigrants. He did learn that Captain Day was not the "good tempered" man he had originally assumed when he saw the master fly into a rage upon finding a couple of stowaways—a man and a woman—and give the man a punch on the head and a black eye before sending the two ashore.

After the *Jersey* was towed down the River Mersey and past the Rock Lighthouse and Fort, her sails were unfurled and filled. His thoughts were mixed—regret at leaving his native England and loved ones and fear and anxiety in facing the perils of the sea and the dangers of a strange and wild country. As the ship entered the ocean and the land faded in the distance, he heard the voices of men and women singing, "Yes, my native land, I love thee."

Soon the deck was deserted—and for good reason. Almost everyone was seasick. He found his cabin companions huddled together, one holding a basin, another on his hands and knees in evident misery, and others dashing to the rail and then back to their berths. Then the ocean swells caused the vessel to roll and pitch so that tin cans, boxes, and other things moved and danced about the cabin.

The next day some 314 emigrants were given their rules and regulations. They were divided into districts, each under the direction of a president. Married couples were located in the center of the ship. Single passengers were placed at the two extremities, the men at the bow and the women at the stern. The district presidents and their counselors had to see that "the ship was cleaned out every morning, that all *lights* except *ship lights* were put out at eight o'clock at night, and never on any account to permit a naked or uncovered light to be in the ship." No immorality was tolerated, and each district met nightly for prayer and necessary instruction. There were also daily meetings in council to discuss conditions in the districts and receive counsel and direction.

Scrupulous cleanliness was enforced, even to the extent of frequent fumigation and sprinkling with lime. On warm days all passengers, including the sick, were brought on deck into the open air and sunshine. Apparently these disciplinary measures were successful, for there was only one death—a very old woman. During the voyage the emigrants generally enjoyed good health. Such was the routine on ship board, and Piercy concluded that "the little world behaved itself remarkably well. After a few days all became used to the motion of the ship. Sickness disappeared, and was only remembered to be laughed at. Merry groups assembled on the deck, and, sitting in the sunshine, told stories, sang songs, and cracked jokes by the hour together, and generally with a propriety most unexceptional."

It was a happy voyage. The weather was "charming" and grew warmer as winter was left behind and the vessel glided smoothly into the sunshine of the Gulf of Mexico. The *Jersey* sailed past Haiti and Cuba and anchored at the mouth of the Mississippi River. A tugboat towed her into New Orleans, 44 days out of Liverpool.[8]

Among the most memorable windship voyages was that of the *International*. With 425 Saints on board this Yankee square-rigger of 1,003 tons sailed from Liverpool on February 28, 1853. Captain David Brown commanded the vessel. Elder Christopher Arthur and his two counselors, John Lyon and Richard Waddington, presided over the emigrants, who were divided in turn into eight wards, each with its own presidency. From the outset there was mutual respect and close rapport between the ship's company and the Mormons, and during this voyage the missionaries baptized forty-eight converts, including Captain Brown, his two mates, and eighteen sailors. Although the passage to New Orleans took 54 days and was marred by several delaying gales and seven deaths, the health of the emigrants was surprisingly good; seven babies were born, and five couples were married.

On April 6 the emigrants and ship's officers and crew celebrated the anniversary of the founding of the Mormon Church. The festivities commenced with an assembly on the forecastle and the firing of six musket rounds. Then the participants marched to the poop deck. A pageant was performed with the presidency and twelve young men robed in white.

Twelve young women in light-colored dresses then appeared carrying white scrolls inscribed amid ribbons and white rosettes with the words "Utah's rights." They were followed by twelve older men, each carrying a Bible and a Book of Mormon. The Saints received the sacrament of the Lord's Supper, and four marriages were solemnized. For three hours the celebration continued, with songs, recitations, speeches, and finally dancing. This same good feeling remained for the rest of the voyage.[9]

It is remarkable that over half a century, Mormon emigrants experienced only one sea disaster, the wreck of the American bark *Julia Ann*. This 372-ton windship had made a voyage with Mormon passengers in 1854, but the following year—on November 7—the *Julia Ann* sailed out of the Sydney harbor once more, bound for San Francisco. Among her fifty-six passengers were twenty-eight Mormons, including elders James Graham and John S. Eldredge, who were returning from their missionary service in Australia. The shipmaster was Captain Benjamin F. Pond, half-owner of the small vessel. Elder John Penfield, Sr., presided over the Saints.

Early in the voyage the *Julia Ann* encountered heavy seas and strong winds, causing much seasickness on board. Captain Pond charted a course between Mopea and the Scilly Islands, and all went well until October 3. On that day a watch was placed on the foretop, and the vessel was logged at 11½ knots an hour. Suddenly the sea took on a broken appearance, and about an hour later the small bark struck a coral reef head-on with a tremendous crash. The impact swung her around broadside to the reef, and the sea broke completely over the stricken vessel at every swell.

Captain Pond immediately ordered all passengers to the after cabin, and the rush to the cabin was one of panic and confusion. Several mothers snatched their children from their beds and carried them undressed in their arms. A sailor with great presence of mind struck a light and calmed the people by assuring them that even though the ship would be lost their lives could be saved since they were near the reef.

Another sailor managed with the aid of the spanker boom to swim to the reef with a rope. With the rope attached to the reef, many were able to make their escape from the vessel. Five Mormons drowned, however, two women and three children. John McCarthy, one of the survivors, described the tragedies:

> I saw mothers nursing their babes in the midst of falling masts and broken spars, while the breakers were rolling twenty feet high over the wreck. One lady—sister Harris—preparatory to leaving the ship with her two children, the eldest of which was two years old, tied the youngest, a babe six weeks old to her breast; the vessel immediately afterwards broke in two across the main hatch, and the waters rushing in, engulfed herself and child amid the struggling waves and timbers of the wreck.

The other woman, "a sister Humphrey," had three children. As John McCarthy wrote,

When the vessel struck she told her friends to protect her children and convey them safely to Great Salt Lake City, for her earthly career was run. Shortly afterwards she, with one of her children, was swept by a sea into the foaming surf, and they were seen no more. There was also a young mother of seventeen, who manifested true courage during the dreadful scene; her husband took their child and lashed it to his back, and struggled to the reef on a rope, with his wife close behind him, and the three were saved unhurt.[10]

One incident reveals the character of Captain Pond. While the crew was putting the passengers ashore, the second mate was carrying a bag containing $8,000. The master ordered him to leave the money and carry a little girl ashore instead. The mate did so. The money was lost, but a child was saved.

Most of the passengers reached the reef; their bodies were lacerated by the coral. A few more were swept ashore on pieces of wreckage when the vessel broke up. When dawn came, the survivors were heartened by the outline of the Scilly Islands some twelve miles away. It was evident that the bark had struck on a reef southwest of the islands and that their true position was about sixteen miles from the place indicated on the chart.

Immediately the crew and passengers began building a raft from the wreckage. For two days they remained on the reef under a burning tropical sun without food or water. On the third day their raft brought them to an uninhabited island where the only living creatures were rats, seafowl, shellfish, turtles, and fish. By scraping holes in the sand, the castaways obtained water that had been made reasonably potable by the sand's filtration. A fire was kindled with the aid of a magnifying glass, and they prepared a meal of roasted shell fish.

Captain Pond took charge of the survivors, directing them to live as a brotherhood and to hunt and fish together for their common sustenance. For seven weeks the stranded group worked harmoniously together living off the land; once they caught a 300-pound turtle for food. In the meantime the ship's carpenter built a quarter boat, which was launched with some difficulty with the captain and nine men aboard. After a precarious 4-day voyage across the reef and through the squalls the men reached Bora Bora, where the people received them with great kindness. Captain Pond went on to Huahine, where he chartered the 94-ton schooner *Emma Packer*. This vessel took the survivors off the island and brought them to Tahiti, where they were well treated. In May 1856 some of the Saints continued their passage to San Francisco aboard the brig *G. W. Kendall*, arriving June 27 after a 52-day voyage.[11]

As the clipper ship *Charles Buck* was towed by a steam tug out of the Liverpool harbor and down the Mersey, Captain William W. Smalley of St. George, Maine, had mixed feelings about his 403 Mormon passengers. For some reason he seemed hostile to the emigrants and on occasion showed his irritation. Yet he provided Richard Ballantyne, president of the emigrant company, a first-class single cabin and invited him to share the lounge and meals with him and his wife.

The *Charles Buck* sailed January 17, 1855, and Elder Ballantyne busied himself in organizing the Saints into four wards. He was determined that there would be order and discipline in the company, and he imparted a series of rules and instruction. There would be no grumbling. Women were not to flirt with the sailors, and guards would be posted to prevent any sexual improprieties. He gave particular attention to sanitation, cooking, and religious observances. Nor did he neglect the sick. He anointed the afflicted with oil and administered a blessing, but if the spirit did not heal he resorted to more mundane remedies. His medical prescriptions included castor oil, vinegar, loaf sugar, paregoric, carbonate of soda, treacle, barley water, peppermint, laudanum, composition tea, and various mixtures and elixirs of such ingredients. When a young girl injured her leg he and Captain Smalley sutured an eight-inch gash.

There were other accidents. One day a seven-year-old boy was playing near the rigging when a strong breeze suddenly tightened the lines, and the youngster was caught by a rope and thrown into the ocean. While horrified parents and passengers crowded the rail, a boatload of sailors was lowered, and the men rowed frantically to rescue the boy. It was too late. The child surfaced momentarily but then disappeared forever. Later another accident cost the life of a sailor, who fell overboard and drowned near the mouth of the Mississippi.

On one occasion Captain Smalley called the emigrants on deck—several hundred of them—asking them to crowd the rail. The reason soon became clear. For some time he had observed a mysterious craft stalking his ship. Fearing piracy, the master felt that a show of numbers might discourage any hostile act. The ploy worked. If buccaneers did man the unidentified ship —and a few of this diminishing breed might well have remained in the Caribbean—they obviously had second thoughts. To everyone's relief, the suspicious vessel abruptly turned away and soon disappeared.

This 56-day passage ended at New Orleans on March 14. The emigrants had suffered from food shortages and friction with non-Mormon passengers as well as accidents. Richard Ballantyne recorded two excommunications, a birth, and four deaths.[12]

It was almost noon on November 27, 1855. Two Mormon elders, William H. Walker and Leonard I. Smith, boarded the 169-ton brig *Unity* anchored at Algoa Bay, Port Elizabeth, South Africa. The missionaries were going home after more than two and a half years preaching Mormonism to South Africans with good success. In fact, fifteen of their converts were accompanying them to London and from there to America. The following day the small vessel sailed out of Port Elizabeth. This voyage was unusual because the brig's owners were John Stock, Thomas Parker, and Charles Roper—three Mormon converts.

During the first few days the passengers experienced the usual seasickness. For more than two months the Saints were on the water, the monotony broken by the birth of a baby girl, a brief visit on the island of St. Helena, crossing the equator on Christmas Day, and battling several days of rough weather. These emigrants—the first to gather from South Africa—landed at London on January 29.[13]

In the 1850s two voyages exceeded 100 days each. On May 29, 1855, the Yankee ship *Frank Johnson* sailed from Calcutta with a small company of Saints. No details of the passage are known, except that the square-rigger encountered strong headwinds and anchored off Singapore on June 27. The *Daily Alta California* of September 18, 1855, reported her arrival at San Francisco. In 1857 the 350-ton square-rigger *Lucas* carried 69 Mormons from Sydney to San Pedro, California, in a 103-day passage, but information on this voyage is also meager.[14]

More than 20,000 Mormons emigrated across the Atlantic and Pacific oceans aboard sailing vessels during the 1860s. Another 3,900 emigrated from Liverpool to New York in steamships in the closing years of the decade. These ten years were the high-water mark of Mormon overseas migration, for at least 24,600 Saints traveled by ship to Zion in that period, under both canvas and steam.

There were 46 sailing vessel passages from 1860 through mid-1868. Of these voyages 40 were made by ships, five by barks, and one by a brig. Eighteen vessels had made more than one voyage with Mormon companies. Of the sailing passages 25 originated at Liverpool, one at Le Havre, one at Melbourne, eight at Hamburg, five at Port Elizabeth, and six at London. All voyages terminated at New York with three exceptions—one at San Francisco and two at Boston. Thirty of the voyages were under the American flag, ten under the British, five under the German, and one under the Norwegian.

In the 1860s Mormon companies were significantly larger, averaging 424 emigrants compared with 266 in the prior decade, in companies ranging from seven to 974 persons. The largest company was carried by the largest ship, *Monarch of the Sea*, a square-rigger of 1,979 tons, in 1864,

Largest of the emigrant sailing ships, the *Monarch of the Sea* (top) transported the two largest Mormon companies crossing the Atlantic under canvas. *Courtesy The Mariners Museum, Newport News, Virginia.* In 1863 Charles Dickens, the "Uncommercial Traveller," boarded the emigrant ship *Amazon* (bottom). He found the Mormons "strikingly different from all other people in like circumstances whom I have ever seen." *Courtesy The Peabody Museum of Salem.*

The smallest vessel used in the sixties was the 256-ton British bark *Echo*. The average for all vessels in that period was 1,137 tons compared with 977 tons in the 1850s.

Although sailing vessels were bigger and presumed to be faster, passage times were not materially improved. From Liverpool to New York the passages ranged from 28 to 55 days during the sixties, averaging 38 days against 39 days in the fifties and 35 days in the forties. Two voyages from Port Elizabeth to Boston took 62 and 68 days. In the previous decade two comparable voyages had required 55 and 71 days.

During the sixties Mormon companies were typically well ordered, but shipboard conditions were much improved over earlier voyages, and the ships were more commodious if not always more comfortable. Among these better vessels was the 1,525-ton *William Tapscott*. This American square-rigger carried more Mormons across the Atlantic than any other single sailing vessel. In three voyages from Liverpool to New York she transported 2,262 Saints—725 in 1859, 730 in 1860, and 807 in 1862. The first and last passages were uneventful, but stormy weather and an outbreak of small-pox caused considerable distress for the 1860 emigrants and resulted in ten deaths during the 35 days at sea. The ship was held in quarantine in New York until physicians came aboard and vaccinated the remaining passengers.[15]

Another fine and exceptionally strong ship was the *Monarch of the Sea*. This 1,979-ton three decker, which some describe as a clipper, brought from Liverpool to New York the two largest Mormon companies of any sailing craft—955 Saints in 1861 and 974 in 1864. The total of 1,929 emigrants was the third highest under sail, and these Atlantic crossings took 34 and 36 days. The *Monarch of the Sea* sailed the oceans for more than twenty-five years before she was reported lost.[16]

In 1863 the 1,311-ton American ship *John J. Boyd* made her third voyage between Liverpool and New York with a Mormon company on board. This company of 767 passengers brought the total number of Saints this square-rigger carried to about 1,981—the second highest of the sailing ships. It was a 29-day passage, and the emigrants reported that both the food and sanitary conditions were commendable. Her two previous "Mormon" voyages were made in 1855 and 1862.

Few emigrant vessels attracted more public notice than the ship *Amazon*. Not only was she a famous packet, but also one of the finest products of American shipwrights. She was rated at 1,771 tons, sharp-modeled, powerful, and sported a female figurehead below her bowsprit. What added to the *Amazon*'s fame was a visit of Charles Dickens and other prominent individuals to see what a Mormon emigrant ship was like before she sailed from London. Dickens met her owner and master, Captain Henry P.

Hovey, and wrote a generally favorable and warm sketch of the Mormons entitled "Bound for the Great Salt Lake," included in his *The Uncommercial Traveller*. The square-rigger sailed down the River Thames June 4, 1863, and arrived at New York 44 days later—much slower than the *Amazon*'s average time westward of 28 days. Although there were headwinds and the death of a child, it was a successful passage.

Some of the larger sailing vessels built in Maine were called "Down Easters" or "Cape Horners." These sturdy wooden square-riggers were noted for their toughness, and many of them proved themselves in the treacherous passage around Cape Horn. Among these ships was the 1,518-ton *General McClellan*, and during her service of more than thirty-one years she would make 14 passages to California. On May 21, 1864, this powerful windship sailed from Liverpool under the command of the able Captain G. D. S. Trask with 802 Mormon passengers aboard. About two weeks out of port a severe gale rocked the emigrants in their quarters between decks. Mary Roberts Roskelly, a young Welsh convert, described how her brother John was tossed about among the boxes and trunks:

> I remember well how some people were crying, some praying and some singing all night as long as the storm lasted. We got John to bed and the girls went to bed on one side while the married folks had their bed on the other side of the room. When we were all settled as best we could for the rocking of the ship and the seasickness among us, there came an extra swell of the sea. The ship rocked slowly, then lurched, which landed John, bed and all down on the floor among the buckets and shoes, etc. and rolled him under the bunks.

His mother feared he would somehow roll out of the ship, but his father assured her that John would roll back—and he did. After 33 days the *General McClellan* brought her passengers safely to the New York harbor.[17]

On April 12, 1865, a small two-masted sailing craft set her canvas and moved slowly out of Algoa Bay from Port Elizabeth, South Africa. She was the 276-ton brig *Mexicana*, flying the British ensign and carrying forty-seven Latter-day Saints on a 67-day voyage to New York. The emigrants formed a well-organized company and conscientiously established strict rules of decorum, hygiene, worship, and study. Religious services and prayers were faithfully held. Guard duty was scheduled to discourage moral laxity, and a school for children was established. Yet, in spite of all sanitation measures, one problem was never solved—bedbugs. These pests tormented the Saints in their sleep, and one day school even had to be dismissed.

The tedium of ocean travel was broken on occasion. One day Captain William Sanderson and a mate caught two albatrosses and let them loose

In 1862 the German ship *Athena* carried 484 Scandinavians between Hamburg and New York. Thirty-eight died on board, one of the highest death tolls in Mormon emigration. *Courtesy Bernhard Havighorst; original in Haus Seefahrt, Bremen-Grohn.*

on deck, and the children were excited. Then there was a disciplinary matter, which presiding elder Miner G. Atwood recorded in his journal: "Samuel Francom was a very bad boy; we were obliged to tie him up to the ship's mast." The boy promised to be good and was released, but the next day Samuel was again tied up "because he would not obey." Apparently the Francom family were troublesome, for about two weeks later John Francom called Elder Adolphus H. Noon a liar and was likewise tied up for several hours. Then came a death. George Kershaw had been sick for some days and grew steadily worse. Although the elders anointed and administered to him, he died on June 6. Funeral services were held and the body, sewn into a shroud of canvas with a bag of sand at the feet, was consigned to the deep. He left a wife and six children. Twelve days later the *Mexicana* dropped anchor in New York harbor.[18]

From 1862 to mid-1866 seven vessels made eight emigrant passages from Hamburg to New York, mostly with Scandinavian Saints. Four ships flew the German flag—the *Athena, Electric, Franklin,* and *Humboldt.* All but the latter were built in America but sold to German owners during the Civil War. The British ship *Kenilworth* was also American-built. It was not uncommon at that time for Yankee shipowners to sell their vessels to foreign buyers to protect them from Confederate raiders. The remaining vessels were the American ship *B. S. Kimball* and the small Norwegian bark *Cavour*. By and large the emigrants did not fare very well on these passages. Mistreatment and heavy loss of life characterized the voyage of the *Athena*, and death rates seemed abnormally high on most of the others crossings. However, the deaths apparently stemmed more from diseases that were particularly hard on children than from shipboard conditions.

Ocean travel under sail was largely over after 1868. The steamship era for Mormon emigrants had arrived. There was, however, one exception, and that was the voyage of the American barkentine *Malay*. This 812-ton two-decker sailed from Sydney on February 21, 1879, with a small company of Saints. Except for the arrival notice in the *Daily Alta California* in San Francisco on May 11, 1879, no details of the company are known, but with this long Pacific voyage the saga of sail ended.[19]

Yet as this era comes to an end certain conclusions are warranted. In general, it can be said that the Mormon emigration under sail was a success. The Saints showed a remarkable ability to cope with strange and demoralizing situations. Although shipboard conditions grew more tolerable over the years, the result of legislation and competition, the sea journey was still in many cases a test of faith. Lives were sometimes altered. Some converts became disillusioned and claimed that at sea the church was not the same as on land—no doubt partly their reaction to the firm discipline and insistence on model deportment and cleanliness. A few apostatized or were excommunicated; however, the great majority remained staunch and faithful.

To many emigrants the crowded life on a ship for weeks on end was a shock. Even under British law, which allowed three adult passengers for each five tons of registered tonnage, that provision was not a generous space allocation. A 1,000-ton vessel, for example, could carry 600 adults, a goodly number in confined quarters. Overcrowding also created sanitation problems, such as inadequate toilet and bathing facilities. For this reason emigrants preferred American ships that had two heads, or water closets, on each side of the deck. Even then these enclosures could smell like cesspools.

Sanitation required constant policing. Emigrants were expected to clean their living quarters daily and air their bedding twice weekly, and most ships were given a thorough scrubbing every week or so. Yet even the closest supervision could not eradicate all odors and pests. From time to time ships would burn gas to fill steerage areas with smoke, a kind of fumigating process. Yet pests could survive. For example, Charles W. Penrose awakened on a voyage one morning to find that a rat had given birth in his shoe. Lice could be persistent, and more than one emigrant company formed a delousing committee. Food and water were occasionally contaminated, and diarrhea and stomach ailments developed.

Under sail, life on shipboard was reduced almost to a primitive state, but in time the church gained a reputation for skilled management of its emigration. There were mistakes and miscalculations, but on the whole Mormon emigrants were better prepared, more secure, and seemed to adjust more readily to the hardships at sea than did others who made the same voyages without organized planning.

One of four German ships that carried Mormons from Hamburg to New York, the square-rigged *Humboldt* brought two companies across the Atlantic in 1862 and 1866. Shortly after the second passage the vessel was lost at sea. *Courtesy Museum Für Hamburgische Geschichte.*

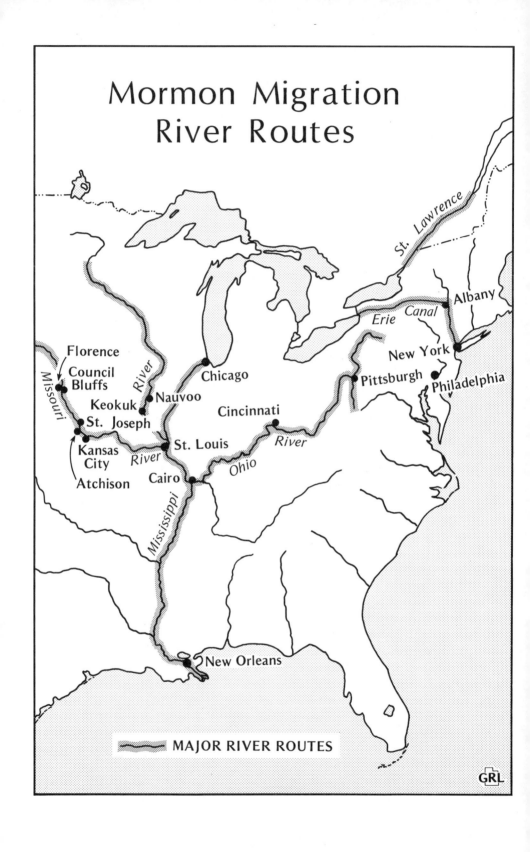

Mormon Migration
River Routes

St. Lawrence

Erie Canal

Albany

New York

Pittsburgh

Philadelphia

Florence

Council Bluffs

Missouri River

Chicago

Keokuk

Nauvoo

Cincinnati

St. Joseph

River

St. Louis

River

Kansas City

Ohio

Atchison

Cairo

Mississippi

New Orleans

MAJOR RIVER ROUTES

GRL

Five

Queens of the Rivers

It was the summer of 1831. The wooden side-wheeler *Chieftain* maneuvered gently against the landing at St. Louis, the sprawling and bustling frontier city that lived for and by the nourishing trade on the Mississippi and Missouri rivers. This small riverboat of only 116 tons was typical of those in her day that threaded their courses among the treacherous bends and tricky sandbars of this mighty waterway. She was built with a cabin above her one deck, and her draft was shallow—barely five feet. Her stern was round, and she carried a billethead on her bow. There were no masts. Instead, twin stacks belched gusts of smoke and steam into the sky, and a fuel-hungry and noisy power plant drove her oversized paddles through the swirling muddy waters.

At the wharf the *Chieftain* discharged about sixty Mormon passengers, the first organized company of Latter-day Saints to gather in the West. These emigrants were the Colesville Branch of the Mormon Church from Broome County, New York, and were traveling to Independence, Missouri. They had come a long way, about 1,200 miles. Part of the journey had been on water, a lake sloop from Buffalo, New York, to Fairport, Ohio, and then the river trip aboard the steamboat. Their trek was almost over, but it was the forerunner of a remarkable migration and gathering that would continue on the rivers of America for more than forty years.[1]

From that beginning Mormon emigrants increasingly moved over the great network of America's waterways. At first the movement was solely from state to state—a pageant of driven people from New York, Pennsylvania, Ohio, Indiana, Missouri, and Illinois. Then in 1840 and the succeeding years the influx of European Saints added a new dimension, when after weeks on the sea these newcomers in growing numbers landed in Quebec, New York, Philadelphia, Boston, and New Orleans to continue their

[89]

From 1840 to 1855 more than eighty Mormon emigrant companies landed at New Orleans, where thousands of passengers were unloaded from ocean packets for transshipment by steamboat up the Mississippi and Missouri rivers. *Courtesy National Maritime Museum, Greenwich.*

journey on the rivers. In those early years railroads were in their infancy, and steamboats offered the best means of entering the heartland of the continent. Unfortunately, details of these river trips are often sparse, although many of the steamboats have been identified.

Of the various watercourses four were most frequently traveled—the Hudson, Ohio, Missouri, and Mississippi. By far the most important to the Mormons was the Mississippi, the largest river in North America and certainly one of the greatest trade waterways in the world. Appropriately called the "Father of Waters," this expanding yellow stream on its southern course was almost a living thing, bringing its fertile silt to rich farming areas, but also death and disaster with its raging floods unleashed periodically on helpless settlements. It had borne the bobbing canoes of Indians, the rafts and boats of explorers and pioneers, and finally the chugging steamers of traders in an industrial age.

From 1840 into early 1855 most Mormon emigrants to the New World traveled up the Mississippi and Missouri river system under steam to such river ports as Nauvoo, St. Louis, Council Bluffs, Keokuk, Atchison, and Florence. Of the first 93 Mormon companies 81 landed at New Orleans; in those years some 18,500 Saints crossed the oceans, and out of that total about 17,600 disembarked at the Louisiana city. Unlike any port of entry the European had imagined, the "Paris of the Bayous" was romantic, colorful, and exciting after the tedious weeks at sea, offering a balm to the weary and homesick.

At that time New Orleans was the fourth ranking world port. A city of watery environs, it fought constantly against its own high water table and a sometimes rampaging Mississippi that threatened to overflow the levees. It was located about 110 miles from the Gulf of Mexico and was the hub of an economy built on slavery, water traffic, and the cotton trade. It had a polyglot population. Among its inhabitants were the French, Spanish, Italian, German, Anglo-Saxon, Indian, and African. The latter were particularly numerous. In 1850, for example, Louisiana contained some 240,000 black slaves and about 270,000 free residents.[2] However, the culture of New Orleans was predominantly French, and its spirit of "live and let live" unmistakably Parisian.

This dry spot in a wet terrain was a vital scene. By 1840 New Orleans was the busiest American seaport outside of New York and certainly one of the wealthiest cities in the United States, supporting more than 100,000 people. Some of these people lived with luxury and elegance in beautiful residences along Bourbon and Royal streets. Others lived with poverty and squalor in rude shacks on the outskirts. The aristocracy enjoyed their opera, chamber music, and theater. The Africans sang and danced their nostalgic rhythms to the thump of drums, and sailors on shore leave reveled in the boisterous singing and dancing provided by the saloons and brothels. The French Quarter could supply almost anything.

A wide-eyed emigrant soon realized that New Orleans was two cities—one for the free and the "haves" and the other for the slave and "have nots." As he strolled in Lafayette Square, he could see finely-dressed ladies twirling their parasols, handsomely-groomed gentry wearing top hats, delighted children playing under the watchful gaze of black nannies, and fancy carriages and stylish horsemen passing slow-moving carts and burdened slaves. Further on he would find the promenade replaced by shabby derelicts, drunken seamen, beckoning prostitutes, and toiling blacks.

The sightseeing traveler was already aware of the wharves stretching for miles along the river bank, a thriving area where hundreds of steamboats and ocean-going vessels were moored or sailing in and out of the port. From Chartres Street, noted for its fashionable shops, he would come to the Place d'Armes fronting the St. Louis Cathedral with its twin towers and central steeple, the Cabildo, used as a city hall, and the Arsenal. Other imposing churches and public buildings would impress the visitor with their striking architecture, and he would observe that Canal Street was becoming the commercial heart of the city with a string of shops, stores, banks, and warehouses attracting ambitious merchants and speculators.

Yet the commercial and cultural tapestry of New Orleans did not conceal the dirt nor protect its inhabitants from the sweltering heat, oppressive humidity, or—most of all—disease. Unsanitary conditions and mosquito-breeding marshes and bayous produced recurring epidemics of cholera, yellow fever, and other ills. Over a period of forty-three years ending in 1860, more than 28,000 deaths from yellow fever alone were recorded, and cholera took its toll of Mormons passing through the city and traveling up the Mississippi. In brief, New Orleans was a city of many facets—a cultural oasis, a thriving business capital, and a pesthole. Still, it was something of a miracle, struggling against numerous obstacles and somehow surviving in splendor.[3]

Shortly after the War of 1812 the first steamboats began navigating the Mississippi, supplying a much-needed transfusion of lifeblood to the nation's river commerce. It can well be said that from this time the Father of Waters became the Mother of Steamboats.[4] These early vessels evolved from the wide and flat keelboat and were designed to cope with the many shallows, submerged snags, treacherous sandbars, and ever-shifting channels of the river. Only a very shallow-draft vessel would do, and it was necessary to locate the engine and boilers on deck rather than in a hold as with steamships. The beamy, shallow-draft Mississippi steamboat differed considerably from the deeper-draft Hudson River and Long Island Sound steamers, which were more akin to the ocean steamship and operated in safer waters. The Mississippi craft was developed by Captain Henry Miller Shreve and other experienced boatman and owed little to Robert Fulton, whose creations plied the eastern waters.

The Mississippi steamer was—at least initially—crude, underpowered, imperfectly engined, noisy, and unattractive. She had none of the sleek grace and arresting beauty of a sailing vessel or even a steamship. Some early steamboats were rigged with sails fore-and-aft in the hope that the wind would aid the laboring engine. Others employed muscular keelboat crewmen who could pole the craft over shoals and shallows.

If emigrants landing at New Orleans suffered any illusion that the water hazards were over, they would soon be disappointed. Mississippi steamers could offer cheap transportation and many other things, but not safety. Their record was not reassuring to the jaded traveler. Between 1810 and 1850 more than 4,000 people were killed or injured in steamboat disasters, and 576 boats were lost on western rivers. More accidents were attributed to striking snags than any other cause. Fire, collision, ice, and explosion also took their toll. Exploding boilers, collapsing flues, and bursting steam pipes were particularly destructive. *DeBow's Review* for 1848 reported 233 explosions on steamboats up to that year. These accidents killed from 1,015 to 2,563 persons, depending on the source—in either case the greatest loss of life from any cause.[5] While some explosions resulted from ignorance and carelessness, many were traceable to irresponsible racing —a popular but dangerous sport in those years.

Because of the high loss rate, western river steamers had an average life of only about four or five years.[6] Mindful of the mortality rate from snags, explosions, and other hazards, owners often built their steamboats as cheaply as possible, with crude and sometimes imperfect engines and boilers. Typically the Mississippi steamer was a side-wheeler, shallow-hulled, wide-beamed, multi-tiered, and distinguished by tall twin stacks with ornamental crowns. Her head was usually plain, and it has been said that she was so ugly many thought her beautiful. In the early years stern-wheel steamboats were less common on the Mississippi, but after the Civil War they were more prevalent—particularly on the Missouri River.

As Mormon emigrants discovered, steamboat accommodations ranged from steerage to cabin class. The poor were deck passengers and crowded below without food, bed, or plumbing facilities. The well-to-do cabin passengers traveled in comfort, if not luxury, on the boiler deck but not near the boiler. By and large, the Mormons could only afford the lowest fares and were quartered accordingly.

Humanity of every description and motivation was moved up and down the great river aboard steamboats. Herman Melville recorded his impressions of this traffic:

Natives of all sorts, and foreigners; men of business and men of pleasure; parlor men and backwoodsmen; farm-hunters and fame-hunters,
heiress-hunters, gold-hunters, buffalo-hunters, bee hunters, happiness-
hunters, truth-hunters, and still keener hunters after all these hunters.
Fine ladies in slippers, and moccasined squaws; Northern speculators
and Eastern philosophers; English, Irish, German, Scotch, Danes; Santa
Fe traders in striped blankets, and Broadway bucks in cravats of cloth
of gold; fine-looking Kentucky boatmen, and Japanese-looking Mississippi cotton planters; Quakers in full drab, and United States soldiers in
full regimentals; slaves, black, mulatto, quadroon; modish young Spanish Creoles, and old-fashioned French Jews, Mormons and Papists . . .
teetotalers and convivialists; deacons and blacklegs; hardshell Baptists
and clay-eaters; grinning negroes, and Sioux chiefs solemn as high
priests. In short, a piebald parliament, an Ararcharsis Gloots congress of
all kinds of that multiform pilgrim species, man.[7]

After landing at New Orleans the Mormon emigrants lost little time in
beginning their trip up the Mississippi. They settled themselves and their
baggage aboard the steamer, heard the steam whistle signal departure, and
watched the big paddles whip and churn the water. They could see the
wharves slipping behind them, and a new adventure lay ahead. The
paddle-wheeler drove herself against the current and moved upstream
about six miles an hour. The journey could take from one to two weeks,
depending on river conditions. The steamboat would usually replenish its
fuel twice daily. Farmers along the riverbank eager to clear their fields of
trees added to their incomes by supplying wood to passing steamers. There
were few wharves along the river because of varying water levels, but in
larger towns and cities wharf boats were used to make a landing. The
success of the trip depended largely on the pilot, whom Mark Twain
immortalized in his writings. To him the river was a textbook, technical
and complex. It had to be studied endlessly; for he had to know the changing channels, the deceptive bends, dangerous snags, and inevitable sandbars.
This knowledge came only from years of experience on the river.

Perhaps no words picture more descriptively a Mississippi steamboat
voyage than those of Lafcadio Hearn, a colorful essayist and newspaper-
man:

There is no perceptible motion of the river vessel; it is like the movement of a balloon, so steady that not we, but the world seems to move.
Under the stars the river seems to unroll its endlessness like an immea-
surable ribbon of silver purple. There is a noiseless ripple in it as of
watered silk. There is a heavy smell of nature, of luxuriant verdure;
the feminine outline of the hills, dotted with the chrome yellow of
window lights, are blue black; the vast arch of stars blossoms overhead;
there is no sound save the colossal breathing of the laboring engines.

Frederick Piercy landed at New Orleans from the ship *Jersey*. He sketched this view of the levee and a Mississippi side-wheeler, then boarded a "panting, steaming leviathan" and proceeded up the "father of waters." *Courtesy Church Archives, Church of Jesus Christ of Latter-day Saints.*

The stream widens; the banks lessen; the heavens seem to grow deeper, the stars whiter, the blue bluer. Under the night it is all a blue world, as in a planet illuminated by a colored sun.

The calls of the passing boats, sonorous as the music of vast silver trumpets, ring out clear but echoless—there are now no hills to give back a ghostly answer. Days are born in gold and die in rose color; and the stream widens, widens, broadens towards the eternity of the sea under the eternity of the sky.[8]

During the 1840–1855 period 81 organized Mormon companies ascended the Mississippi and Missouri rivers. The number of steamboats used is not known, since some were not identified by name. Others are known to have made more than one passage with Saints aboard, and certain emigrant companies were divided and transported in two or more steamers. However, at least 45 steamboats have been identified, and all but one were side-wheelers—that one being the *F. X. Aubrey*, a stern-wheeler.

These steamers varied widely in capacity. The smallest was the 60-ton *Maid of Iowa* owned by Joseph Smith. Her dimensions were 115 x 18.3 x 3 feet, the shallowest draft of all the vessels. The largest was the 1,024-ton *John Simonds*. Her dimensions were 295 x 40.5 x 8 feet. The median tonnage of all these steamboats was about 300 tons.[9]

On March 27, 1842, a Sunday, from two to three thousand Latter-day Saints assembled at the landing in Nauvoo, Illinois. In the distance they could see the 95-ton *Ariel* steaming up the Mississippi. Her deck was crowded with 170 Mormon converts from England who had not anticipated such a welcome. As the little steamboat neared the landing, her passengers were singing a hymn above the noise of the throbbing engines. Among those greeting the newcomers were President Joseph Smith, Brigham Young, Willard Richards, and William Clayton. The latter wept when he recognized friends from the Manchester Branch, over which he had presided. Lyman Wight, leader of the emigrant company, reported to the Mormon Prophet that the *Ariel* carried "about three thousand dollars worth of goods for the Temple and Nauvoo House." After a round of handshaking, embraces, and tears, the English Saints were taken to various homes along with their luggage and hospitably accommodated.[10]

Emigrants from several sailing vessels continued their journey from New Orleans to Nauvoo aboard the 220-ton *Amaranth*. The first of these companies disembarked from the ship *Hope* on April 1, 1842. About sixty Mormons took passage on the *Amaranth*, and another 150 boarded the *Louisa*, a smaller steamer of 152 tons. A year later emigrants from the ship *Swanton* boarded the *Amaranth* at New Orleans but encountered a delay on the way to Nauvoo, waiting for the river to open. In May 1843 this steamboat received the Mormons from the ship *Claiborne* at New Orleans and also picked up the Saints at St. Louis who had crossed the ocean aboard the bark *Yorkshire* and had traveled there on the *Dove*, a 168-tonner. With these two companies the *Amaranth* went on to Nauvoo.[11]

The *Alex. Scott* was a popular Mississippi steamboat in the 1840s. At 487 tons a relatively large vessel in her day, she carried at least three Mormon emigrant companies upstream from New Orleans. In November 1842 this steamboat transported the Saints transferred from the ship *Sidney*. Progress up the river was rapid until the steamer reached the mouth of the Ohio. There she ran aground and was held fast for three days. After resuming her passage the vessel was again held up—this time for three weeks ninety miles from St. Louis because of low water. According to the Church Emigration record, the *Alex. Scott* made at least two other passages with Mormon companies. On March 19, 1851, Saints landed from the ship *Ellen*, steamed out of New Orleans aboard this steamboat, and made "a good passage" to St. Louis, arriving a week later on March 26. On April 9 of that year the ship *Ellen Maria* transferred most of her Mormon passengers to the *Alex. Scott*, which carried them to St. Louis. They arrived April 16 after a 7-day journey. On the trip a woman fell overboard and drowned while drawing a bucket of water; such accidents were not unusual. This fine side-wheeler had only one deck, a transom stern, a cabin above a plain head, and plied the Mississippi for about twelve years before being dismantled—as indicated in her registrations. In 1851 Mormons paid $2.50 for each adult, including all baggage, and half fare for children.

After a long and difficult voyage aboard the ship *Emerald*, a Mormon company landed at New Orleans early in 1843. There Apostle Parley P. Pratt chartered the 248-ton side-wheeler *Goddess of Liberty* and continued the journey up the Mississippi to St. Louis, which took about a week. Eighty miles from St. Louis Elder Pratt, fearing the Missouri mobs, took his family ashore at Chester, Illinois. The rest of the Saints landed at St. Louis but could go no farther because of ice on the river. In the spring, after the ice had cleared, Captain Dan Jones came down from Nauvoo and brought these Mormons up to that city aboard the *Maid of Iowa*.[12]

One of two side-wheelers owned by Mormon leaders, the *Nauvoo*—formerly *Des Moines*—played a part in a little-known episode in church history. This small upper Mississippi riverboat had been used by Lt. Robert E. Lee of the United States Army Corps of Engineers in a survey to improve navigation around the St. Louis harbor, which was threatened by snags and other obstacles. When Congress refused to appropriate more funds for this purpose, Lee—twenty years before he assumed command of the Confederate Army—put the *Des Moines*, two keelboats, and other items up for public auction. Interested in acquiring a steamboat for use in transporting church members and merchandise to Nauvoo, Joseph Smith and other prominent Mormon businessmen made a bid for the vessel and keelboats. The purchase was made with a note of $4,866.38 dated September 10, 1840, payable in eight months. Signers of the note were Peter Haws, Henry W. Miller, George Miller, Hyrum Smith, and Joseph Smith. The steamboat was remodeled and renamed the *Nauvoo*, but apparently was never registered by the new owners. The 1838 registration of the *Des Moines* indicated that she had been built at Pittsburgh, Pennsylvania, that year, possibly an error since she may have been in operation a year earlier. The document showed that she was 93 tons, had a cabin above her one deck, a plain head, no masts, a double rudder, and dimensions of 123 x 20.3 x 4.2 feet.

The *Nauvoo* had a brief career under her Mormon owners. It is known that she freighted lead from mines in Galena to St. Louis and that Joseph Smith made two trips on the vessel "to keep out of the way of the officers of the law." It also appears that an interest in the paddle-wheeler and keelboats had been sold to outsiders. Within a short time the *Nauvoo* was wrecked by striking rocks and sandbars outside the usual navigation channels. Suit was brought against the pilots. Involved litigation developed that continued for several years, even after the deaths of Joseph and Hyrum Smith. The *Nauvoo* eventually passed to other owners and was converted to a barge.[13]

Of the Mormon-owned steamboats the 60-ton *Maid of Iowa* had the
most active service, short though it was. This small craft was built in 1842
by Captain Dan Jones and Levi Moffit at Augusta, Iowa. Her registration
states that she had a cabin above her one deck, a plain head, no masts, and
a transom stern. No doubt twin chimneys jutted skyward amidships, or
slightly forward, noisily belching forth fumes. The *Maid of Iowa* began
trading on the Mississippi. It was while she was carrying cargoes and
passengers into Nauvoo that Captain Dan Jones learned about the Mormon
Church and was baptized early in 1843. He became a close friend of Joseph
Smith and a year later would be with the Mormon Prophet in prison at
Carthage jail until just before his murder. Joseph Smith would tell him
that he would live to fulfill a mission in his native Wales. Jones did indeed
go to Wales to become one of the church's most effective missionaries.

In the spring of 1843 Joseph Smith acquired Levi Moffit's half interest
in the steamboat, giving two notes for $1,375. Afterwards he bought the
remaining ownership share of Dan Jones. The *Maid of Iowa*'s registration
of May 2, 1844, listed as sole owner "Joseph Smith of Nauvoo Illinois in
trust for the Church of Jesus Christ of Latter day Saints."

In the Nauvoo period the little side-wheeler carried Mormons from
New Orleans to Nauvoo. Joseph and Hyrum Smith both preached from
her deck. She ferried passengers between Montrose and Nauvoo, the two
Mormon settlements on opposite sides of the river. She freighted corn and
wheat for the temple builders. She played a role in patrolling the rivers
in 1843 trying to rescue Joseph Smith from a Missouri sheriff. Captain
Jones, with some armed Mormons, sought to intercept any riverboat carrying the kidnapped leader illegally to Missouri. The *Maid of Iowa* was sometimes used to take groups on pleasure cruises, and at one time Joseph
Smith concealed himself on the steamboat to avoid capture by his enemies.
In 1845, after their Prophet's murder, the church leaders arranged the
sale of the vessel. A year later the *Maid of Iowa* was reported lost.[14]

After the ship *Palmyra* docked at New Orleans, most of the Mormon
passengers started up the Mississippi on April 18, 1845, aboard the 319-ton
steamboat *Julia Chouteau*. It was a "miserable passage of 9 days" to St.
Louis. On April 28 the remaining Saints followed aboard the *Galena*,
a 135-ton side-wheeler. Some of the Mormons remained in St. Louis to
earn enough for their passage to Nauvoo.[15]

After the Saints left Nauvoo in early 1846, the Missouri River became
a vital waterway for the migrating church. In small and large groups
Mormons traveled up that river to Council Bluffs, Winter Quarters, and
other points. An example was the Allen Compton family, who had been
driven from Hancock County, Illinois. Their home was burned, their pos-

sessions lost. On May 2, 1846, the small *St. Croix*, a one-decked wooden side-wheeler out of St. Louis, carried this family to Council Bluffs, Iowa.[16]

A spiraling staircase of water and mud flowing some 3,000 miles from the Rocky Mountains to the Mississippi, the Missouri River was the most traveled passageway beyond St. Louis to the American West. Its nickname "Big Muddy" was well deserved. As the Missouri carved its course through the high country, it gathered sand, gravel, and silt in large amounts which were deposited in the Mississippi and eventually even the Gulf of Mexico. It was a broad, dangerous, and changeable stream. Indians, fur trappers, venturesome traders, explorers, pioneers, and steamboaters would all agree on one fact: the Big Muddy was a navigator's nightmare. A riverboat pilot had to be ever alert for tree trunks, snags, debris, fickle currents, treacherous sandbars, rocks, and the plain cussedness of the river itself.

Yet for all its orneriness and awesomeness, the Missouri had been navigated by steamboats in increasing numbers since 1819. Paddle-wheelers traveled upstream as far as 2,600 miles to Fort Benton, and carcasses of the steamers that failed were not an uncommon sight. It was an era of adventure, excitement, and exhilaration—and it opened the West. This spirit was rhapsodized by Whittier in these lines from "On Receiving an Eagle's Quill from Lake Superior," quoted by Albert D. Richardson in 1867:

> Behind the squaw's light birch canoe,
>   The steamer rocks and raves;
> And city lots are staked for sale
>   Above old Indian graves.

> I hear the tread of pioneers
>   Of nations yet to be—
> The first low wash of waves where soon
>   Shall roll a human sea.

On April 23, 1848, the entire company of Mormons from the bark *Carnatic* boarded the new 570-ton side-wheeler *Mameluke* and proceeded up the Mississippi from New Orleans. It was a pleasant trip of seven days to St. Louis. A year later this fine steamboat would be destroyed by fire. At St. Louis these Saints together with emigrants from other parts of the United States—numbering in all about 150—arranged passage up the Missouri River with Captain H. R. Patterson, skipper of the 129-ton *Mustang*. Each adult paid a $5.00 fare, including 100 pounds of baggage. The one-decked steamer left May 9 and arrived about the middle of the month at Winter Quarters, Nebraska. During the passage there was a tragedy when a "Sister Kerr" from Scotland fell overboard and drowned on a dark night. Her body was never recovered.[17]

Among the largest riverboats on the Mississippi River was the 688-ton side-wheeler *Grand Turk*, which carried at least two Mormon companies from New Orleans to St. Louis. *Courtesy Missouri Historical Society (Neg. River 159).*

Cholera sometimes broke out among steamboat passengers, as it did on the side-wheeler *Iowa*. This 455-ton steamer left New Orleans April 5, 1849, with Mormon emigrants from the ship *Zetland* and some other travelers. There was an epidemic of cholera in New Orleans, and soon some of the passengers came down with the disease. Seven died before arrival at Memphis and were buried on Island "82." Then the pilot and another crew member died. On April 12 the vessel docked at St. Louis with some passengers still sick, three others having died the previous night.[18]

On April 11, 1849, a company of 108 Saints sailed from St. Louis aboard the side-wheeler *Mandan* of 204 tons. Among the passengers were apostles Erastus Snow, Ezra T. Benson, and Amasa M. Lyman. It took five days to reach Covington, a distance of 140 miles. According to the Journal History, Church Archives, the steamer "ran on a rock and was so injured as to render her unsafe. The captain told the passengers that he would go no further till his boat was repaired. Consequently the company after choosing Bro. John Scott Captain took their effects on shore, struck up their tents on the bank of the Missouri River to wait the return of the boat. Bro. Amasa M. Lyman went back with her to see that her officers complied with their contract." Apparently the steamboat returned and took the Saints to Council Bluffs. The *Mandan* was reported among the twenty-three steamboats burned in the great fire at St. Louis on May 17, 1849.[19]

Among the steamboats used by the Mormons was the popular 688-ton side-wheeler *Grand Turk*. At least two companies of Saints traveled from New Orleans to St. Louis aboard this river craft. On April 11, 1849, the emigrants from the ship *Henry Ware* went up the Mississippi aboard the *Grand Turk*, which was likely skippered by her owner and master, Captain Newman Robirds. On May 31, 1854, some of the Mormons arriving at New Orleans on the ship *Marshfield* took this famed two-decker to St. Louis, where they landed about the middle of June. The steamboat was destroyed in a fire at New Orleans in 1854.[20]

One of the steamboat disasters involving Mormons occurred April 25, 1849. On that date the steamer *Dacotah* (or *Dahcota*) with forty Latter-day Saints on board, including George P. Dykes, struck a snag and sank in the Missouri River in Nebraska. One child was smothered in the panic, and the Saints lost their luggage. "Teams were sent to their aid from Kanesville, Iowa," according to the Journal History.[21]

After crossing the Atlantic safely aboard the ship *Buena Vista*, about 249 Saints landed at New Orleans April 19, 1849, during a cholera epidemic. The Mormons proceeded up the Mississippi aboard the *Highland Mary*, a 159-ton side-wheeler owned by George W. Atchison, Sr., and skippered by Captain George W. Atchison, Jr. Cholera broke out among the passengers traveling up the river, and by the time the steamboat docked at Council Bluffs on the Missouri River on May 17, sixty Welsh Saints had died, making this one of the Mormons' most tragic river trips.[22]

In the 1850s steamboats plying the Mississippi and Missouri rivers were bigger, better, and more comfortable than their counterparts of the previous decade. For example, in the forties the steamboats used by migrating Mormons on these rivers averaged only some 235 tons, with a median size of about 195 tons. In contrast, the average size steamboat used in the fifties was about 410 tons, with a 310-ton median. It is also significant that very few of these vessels in the forties exceeded 200 feet in length, while in the following decade fewer than half the steamboats were under 200 feet.[23]

Yet steamboat traffic on the Mississippi would crest during the 1850s and then decline. The principal reason was the changing pattern of overseas emigration. In 1855 the Mormons, as an example, shifted their port of debarkation from New Orleans to New York and other eastern ports, to take advantage of the service which resulted from the rapid expansion of the railroads westward, but for a time the river played a vital role.

In late 1850 the Mormon emigrants from the ship *Joseph Badger* arrived at New Orleans and then traveled to St. Louis aboard the 260-ton side-wheeler *El Paso*, landing in early December. There the Saints remained temporarily to work and earn enough to continue their journey to Utah. The *El Paso* was newly constructed and was owned and commanded by Captain Thomas H. Brierly of St. Louis, a well-known riverman.[24]

The year 1851 was particularly active for Mormon steamboat voyages. Saints from the ship *George W. Bourne* were transported from New Orleans to St. Louis aboard the 499-ton side-wheeler *Concordia*, commanded by Captain William H. Cable. It was a 7-day passage and, according to Elder William Gibson, cost the Saints "10s. 5d. each adult; children under twelve and over two years old, half price; infants and baggage, free; distance twelve hundred miles to St. Louis."[25] Emigrants from the ship *Olympus* transferred at New Orleans to the *Atlantic*, a 667-ton side-wheeler owned and skippered by Captain J. H. Oglesby. The steamer arrived at St. Louis May 8 and some passengers were quarantined because of a case of cholera. This company together with some Saints from New England and St. Louis resumed their journey aboard the 248-ton side-wheeler *Statesman*, of which Captain James Gormley was master. The *Frontier Guardian* of May 30, 1851, reported the arrival of the *Statesman* at Kanesville (Council Bluffs), Iowa, thirteen days out of St. Louis. The article mentioned that fifty out of fifty-two passengers who were not Mormons were baptized into the church during the voyage of the *Olympus* before landing at New Orleans and that a similar situation had developed on the *Statesman*. After her arrival the cooks and deck hands left the steamboat to join the Mormons as teamsters on the trek across the plains to Utah.[26] Another steamboat from St. Louis arrived at Kanesville the same month with 200 English Saints from the ship *Ellen*. This side-wheeler was the *Sacramento*, a 221-tonner commanded by Captain Richard McGuire of St. Louis. A young girl, Elizabeth Bladen, died of tuberculosis coming up the Missouri. The large company from the ship *Ellen Maria* arrived at Council Bluffs aboard the side-wheeler *Robert Campbell* on May 21. This steamboat of 269 tons was skippered by Captain William Edds and operated out of St. Louis.[27]

The following year—1852—brought the worst maritime disaster of the Mormon migration. It originated with the transporting of the Mormon emigrants who had arrived at New Orleans aboard the ship *Kennebec*. On March 14 these Saints took passage up the Mississippi on board the steamboat *Pride of the West*, a 321-ton side-wheeler commanded by her owner, Captain Daniel B. Hunt. After the steamboat arrived at St. Louis, some of the emigrants decided to remain in that city for a time. Others arranged passage up the Missouri River on the *Saluda*, a side-wheeler of 223 tons which was six years old and somewhat dilapidated. Her machinery was tired and worn. Two years earlier the *Saluda* had struck a snag and sunk. Her master and owner, Captain Francis T. Belt, had bought her for a bargain price after she had been raised and repaired. He had visions of a very profitable operation, and on this trip he had about 175 passengers, including some 90 Mormons.

It was a bad time to travel up the Missouri, but the side-wheeler left St. Louis March 30. She made slow progress and did not reach Lexington, Missouri, until April 4. As she drew abreast of the town, Captain Belt decided to skirt a point of land ahead—particularly since the Big Muddy was sweeping its current against the town. The torrent was ice-laden, carrying debris with its yellow flow. The swollen stream was typical of the spring floods. Firing hard against the tide, the *Saluda* drove into the swirling water again and again. Each time she was forced back. Her double boilers and engines were no match for the angry river that thrust chunks of ice against her bow and hull. Finally Captain Belt retreated and eased his craft into the landing at Lexington. There he had the paddles broken by floating ice repaired.

On the morning of April 9, possibly goaded by the complaints of some cold and frustrated passengers, Captain Belt resolved to get the balky *Saluda* under way. By this time the ice had ceased running, and the river seemed more navigable. He ordered the fireboxes filled and the steam pressure increased. All would probably have gone well, except that the engineers had carelessly permitted the boilers to get dry and red hot. When the engines started, the pumps forced cold water into the boilers. As the paddles revolved the second or third time, the boilers exploded with a thunderous noise. The explosion, heard all over the area, completely wrecked the

Saluda. The hull disintegrated. Timbers, splinters, pieces of boilers, engine parts, fragmented chimneys, bales, freight, and bodies were propelled skyward. A blossom of steam, smoke, and flying objects filled the air. Captain Belt's body landed half way up a steep embankment. A demolished 600-pound safe, a watchdog, and second clerk Jonathan F. Blackburn were blown into the sky and came down 200 yards upstream. Two pilots were flung into the water and disappeared. In ten minutes the shattered steamboat had sunk. Ironically, it was Good Friday.

The horror of the scene stunned the town, but rescuers soon went into action. Twenty-six mangled bodies were recovered. As many more were found with arms and legs missing. Other bodies were terribly scalded. Mutilated corpses were even found in the streets of Lexington. Several passengers had been hurled into the middle of the river, and some were found high up the bluff. A man on shore was dismembered by a piece of the boiler flue, another killed by a broken timber. A brick house nearby collapsed from a chunk of iron. Parents and children searched frantically among the dead and wounded. It was a screaming, bloody nightmare. Shock and grief were everywhere. One survivor lost his wife and seven children. A woman lost her husband and three children. Since all of the steamboat records were destroyed, it was impossible to determine the number who perished, but it was estimated that about 100 were killed and many others wounded. It is believed that between twenty-five and thirty Mormons were killed. This steamboat disaster was the worst of any on the Big Muddy—and the greatest accidental cause of death during the entire Mormon migration.

A short distance from the *Saluda* was the steamboat *Isabel*, which had arrived at Lexington the night before. In disbelief her passengers witnessed the catastrophe and saw the bodies and wreckage flying in all directions. They tried to recover the corpses floating around them, without much success. Immediately after the accident the master of the *Isabel* generously offered free passage to Council Bluffs, with provisions, to any of the survivors. Many accepted his offer and within a few hours of the disaster were on their way up the Missouri.

Others, including the wounded and their relatives, remained behind. The people of Lexington and surrounding areas promptly organized to provide relief to the survivors. Committees were formed to raise funds, to bury the dead, to care for the injured, and to find homes for the orphans. The kind and generous treatment given the surviving Mormon and other passengers of the *Saluda* has never been forgotten and should ever be a credit to Lexington. Many of the orphan children were adopted by its citizens and lived their lives in that Missouri town—far from England and Utah.[28]

About a year after the *Saluda* tragedy, Mormon emigrants from the
ship *Jersey* docked at New Orleans. Elder John Brown met the newcomers
and arranged passage for them on the large steamboat *John Simonds*. Built
the year before by Captain Newman Robirds, this 1,024-ton cargo carrier
was engaged in the cotton trade and was the biggest steamer used by the
Mormons on the western rivers. She was a side-wheeler built of wood with
six boilers and 10-foot stroke engines driving fumes through her twin chimneys. For their passage adults paid $2.25 each, children between three and
fourteen half fare, and those under three went free of charge. In late March
1853 the paddle riverboat ascended the Mississippi to St. Louis. There the
Saints changed to another steam packet and continued to Keokuk, Iowa,
which was a "prosperous voyage lasting a few days only." It is noteworthy
that the *John Simonds* ran on the Mississippi for ten years, and then during
the Civil War was deliberately scuttled by the Confederates to block a river
channel against Union traffic.[29]

About the same time, another company of Saints from the ship *Golconda* landed at New Orleans. These emigrants were transferred to the
682-ton wooden steam-packet *Illinois*, possibly commanded by Captain
David T. Smithers. This side-wheeler transported the company to St. Louis
and shortly afterwards continued up the Missouri to Keokuk, Iowa. This
steamboat operated on the western rivers for more than a decade and
apparently was used during the Civil War.[30]

During 1854 five popular steamboats were among those utilized by the
Mormons. The 598-ton steamer *L. M. Kennett*, for example, carried emigrants from the ship *Benjamin Adams* from New Orleans to St. Louis,
arriving April 3. This steamboat's registration indicates she was a fairly
typical Mississippi paddle vessel—one deck, no masts, transom stern, light
tuck, no figurehead, and full built. Her managing owner was Captain John
N. Boffinger of St. Louis, who was also skipper. After landing at St. Louis
the emigrants were joined by other Saints who had crossed the Atlantic
aboard the ship *Jessie Munn*, and both companies continued up the Big
Muddy to Kansas City, Missouri, on another steamboat.[31]

The 593-ton *James Robb*, owned and commanded by Captain Hercule
Carroll of St. Louis, followed up the Mississippi a few weeks later with the
Saints who had arrived at New Orleans on the ship *Marshfield*. Part of
that company made the river trip soon afterwards aboard the *Grand Turk*.
At St. Louis the emigrants transferred to another unnamed riverboat and
went on to Kansas City, Missouri. A year later the *James Robb* was
snagged and lost.

The fourth of these noted steamboats was the 593-ton side-wheeler
Josiah Lawrence. Owned and skippered by Captain Norman Cutter, this
paddle steamer carried the emigrants from the ship *John M. Wood* from

New Orleans to St. Louis in early May. Some time later these Saints made their way to Kansas City, where they outfitted for the trek across the plains.

On June 13, 1854, the Saints from the ship *Germanicus* started up the Mississippi from New Orleans aboard the large side-wheeler *Uncle Sam.* At 903 tons this single-decked steamboat was the second biggest vessel to transport Mormon emigrants on the western rivers. The fare was $3.50 for each adult, including luggage, and half fare for children under fourteen. At St. Louis part of the company remained until the next season, and the others went on to the Mormon encampment near Kansas City. The *Uncle Sam* plied the rivers for more than fourteen years. She often carried about 100 passengers in the cabins and 500 on deck as well as 400 tons of freight. No doubt most of the Mormons were quartered on deck.[32]

During the early months of 1855 Mormon travel on the Mississippi was unusually heavy. Emigrants from the ship *Clara Wheeler* landed at New Orleans on January 11 and were soon on their way up the Mississippi aboard the 607-ton steamer *Oceana*, probably skippered by Captain G. W. Boyd. According to the *Millennial Star*, "Nearly one-half of the company had not the means wherewith to pay their passage to St. Louis; but the more well-to-do Saints who had more money than they needed themselves, were influenced to lend to those who had none, and thus all who desired to continue the journey were enabled to do so." About a month later the *Oceana* carried the Saints from the ship *James Nesmith* from New Orleans to St. Louis, arriving March 7. On the trip up-river seven Mormons died. About a third of the company went on to Weston, Missouri, and remained in that area until they could finance their trek to the Great Salt Lake Valley.[33]

On March 1, 1855, after landing at New Orleans from the ship *Rockaway*, within twenty-four hours the Mormon emigrants were steaming up-river aboard the 198-ton steamer *Saranak*, which was partly owned and skippered by Captain R. A. Reilly. Ten days later the vessel ran upon a snag about sixty-five miles below Cairo, Illinois. To free the steamboat, it was necessary to unload and then reload most of the cargo. The river trip took 16 days to St. Louis, where some of the Saints remained to earn enough money for the rest of their journey to Utah.

On March 12, 1855, about 175 of the Mormon emigrants from the ship *James Nesmith* resumed their passage from St. Louis to Atchison, Kansas, aboard the steamboat *Clara.* It was a trip bedeviled by delay and disease. At Leavenworth low water compelled the steamer to lay up for a time, during which another Mormon company arrived. There twenty Saints died of cholera, and on the way to Atchison nine more deaths were recorded. This 351-ton side-wheeler was skippered and partly owned by Captain Joshua Cheever. A year later the *Clara* was sunk by ice at St. Louis.

QUEENS OF THE RIVERS

On March 14, 1855, the last Mormon emigrant company landed at New Orleans. These Saints—about 400 of them—had crossed the Atlantic under the leadership of Richard Ballantyne aboard the square-rigger *Charles Buck*. It had been a long and at times hectic voyage, but two days later the entire company boarded the 482-ton steamboat *Michigan*. The fare from New Orleans to St. Louis was $3.50 for each adult, with half fare for children under fourteen. The emigrants received generous donations from other Saints to help defray the cost of their passage. It was not a pleasant river trip. As the steamboat left New Orleans, John Eccleson fell overboard and drowned. Four children died during the voyage. Another man fell overboard and perished. The master, a Captain Sheble, was hostile to the Saints, and Richard Ballantyne described his conduct as "disgraceful in the extreme." The company arrived at St. Louis on March 27—after a passage of 11 days.

In size and length the Hudson could not compare with the Mississippi and Missouri rivers, yet in grandeur and beauty its 315 miles were unsurpassed. The Hudson might be a midget, but it was also many other things— a valuable water source, a sewer, a ship channel, a trout stream, a playground, and a commercial highway. It has been called the "Rhine of America" because of stretches that resembled the shores of its German counterpart. Its diverse and changing landscape were both charming and seductive. As one ascended this artery, a panorama of perpetual enchantment unfolded along its course—cliffs, heights, vistas, forests, foliage, wilderness, pools, and marshes. There was also the restless hand of man and his creations, not always enhancing the handiwork of nature but nevertheless adding an emphasis to the river's life-giving importance.

The Hudson was more than one river winding through the heartland of New York state. It was a collection of tributaries, streams, and man-made canals that swelled its widening flow from the Tear-of-the-Clouds high in the Adirondack Mountains to the Manhattan estuary. The native Indians described the Hudson as The-Water-That-Flows-Two-Ways, and properly so. As the ocean tide rushed up the estuary and river channel twice daily it reversed the natural current entering the Atlantic and created the illusion that the river ran north. Then, as the tide receded, the flow south to the sea was reasserted. As a result, the Hudson became a mixture of salt and fresh water.

The Hudson is a navigable river, as its explorer Henry Hudson proved in 1609. Large vessels can sail up the watercourse to Albany, and smaller craft can continue on to Troy. This navigation capacity inspired one of the great early American engineering triumphs, the Erie Canal. This manmade waterway was completed in 1825 and wedded the waters of the Hudson with Lake Erie, linking the two with 363 miles of constructed canal.

It was a boon to travelers and freighters, for it assured water transportation from New York City to the Great Lakes region. It not only brought industry and prosperity to upper New York state but was also a key to the opening of the West to a flood of immigration.

No less important in opening the West was the Ohio River. This great watercourse wound and twisted southward from Pittsburgh, Pennsylvania, where the Allegheny and Monongahela rivers met, and emptied into the Mississippi River at Cairo, Illinois. Today it flows through some of the richest farm lands and industrial areas in the United States; however, Indians and early pioneers paddled their canoes and small boats down this river in their westward travels, and emigrants from Europe were transported in paddle-wheel steamers over the waterway to Mississippi and Missouri river ports.

When the first organized company of converts crossed the Atlantic on board the ship *Britannia* in 1840, they made their way from New York to Pittsburgh, where they engaged passage on the small side-wheeler *William Penn*, a 105-ton one-decker, and sailed April 3, arriving at Montrose, Iowa, on April 16, 1841.[34]

The Mormon company that crossed the Atlantic in the ship *North America* was the second to arrive in America, landing at New York City October 12, 1840. The following day the emigrants started up the Hudson aboard the 168-ton side-wheeler *Congress*; one of the company, H. C. Greenhalgh, died during the three-day passage to Albany. At some point—probably Albany—the Saints transferred to the 162-ton steamer *Chautauque* and continued their journey through the Erie Canal to Buffalo. William Clayton recorded that this leg of the trip went "pretty well" except for the emigrants being "short of provisions." At Buffalo the company took the lake steamer *Illinois*, a 755-ton side-wheeler with apparently also a screw propeller and a draft of about 13 feet. Skippered by Captain Blake, the *Illinois* left on October 26, arriving at Detroit on the thirty-first and at Chicago on November 4. This steamer is said to have carried more settlers to Wisconsin and Illinois than any other vessel on the Great Lakes.[35]

In 1855, after the Mormons began traveling westward by rail and had ceased to arrive at New Orleans, four sailing ships docked on the Delaware at Philadelphia and four others at New York. Many of these emigrants traveled by rail to Pittsburgh and then sailed down the Ohio to the Mormon encampments on the Missouri. The Saints from the ship *Siddons* took an unnamed steamboat from Pittsburgh to St. Louis, arriving May 7, but an infant died on the way. The next day some of these emigrants continued on to Atchison, Kansas, on board the 297-ton side-wheeler *Golden State*, which was partly owned and commanded by Captain Joseph M. Calhoon. About two weeks earlier the *Golden State* had brought a large Mormon company to Atchison, where the emigrants made a temporary camp. The *Squatter Sovereign*, an Atchison newspaper dated May 1, 1855, described this transient settlement: "The camp of the emigrants just back of town presents a city-like appearance, their tents leaving streets, alleys, etc., between them. The health of the emigrants is good, with but little or no sickness among them."

Other emigrants from the ship *Siddons* boarded the 310-ton steamboat *Polar Star*, partly owned and skippered by Captain Thomas F. Brierly of St. Louis, and the stern-wheel paddle steamboat *F. X. Aubrey* of 247 tons, commanded by Captain Ambrose Reeder or Captain Grant Marsh. These steamboats left St. Louis in early May. Both were popular packets on the run up the Missouri River.[36]

In May of 1855 about 600 emigrants from the ships *Chimborazo* and *S. Curling* met at Pittsburgh and boarded the "excellent and commodious steamboat *Amazon*," a 410-ton side-wheeler. Under the leadership of Elder Edward Stevenson these Saints traveled down the Ohio River to the Mississippi, arriving at St. Louis June 2. About half of the company continued on to Atchison with the *Amazon* on June 8. This steamboat's registration shows Captain William B. Haslett of Pittsburgh as the master and managing owner. Another 140 Mormons transferred to the 228-ton side-wheeler *Ben Bolt* on June 4 and continued their journey from St. Louis to Atchison. On a subsequent passage still another body of emigrants took the *Ben Bolt* at St. Louis and arrived at Atchison June 19. Captain James F. Boyd was the registered master and principal owner.

After the ship *Juventa* arrived at Philadelphia May 5, 1855, her Mormon passengers traveled to Pittsburgh by rail. There they divided into two groups. About 150 sailed down the Ohio to St. Louis on the 282-ton steamboat *Washington City*. Captain George W. Ebert was the master and principal owner of this steamer. Another 200 made the same trip aboard the *Equinox*, a 297-ton side-wheeler partly owned and skippered by Captain B. F. Hutcheson. At Atchison many Saints became ill—probably with cholera—and some died, including Elder James F. Bell, who had presided over the Malta Mission.

The names of a number of steamboats which transported Mormon emigrants have been obscured by time and sparse records. One such vessel, the *Omaha*, is believed to have carried groups of Saints up the Missouri on more than one occasion. Yet little is known of this 307-ton steamer except that she plied the western rivers for nearly a decade and then was sunk by ice. Unfortunately, even less is known about her Mormon passengers and their destinations.[37]

The steamboat era was drawing to a close. Fewer and fewer Mormons employed this means of transportation as the railroads penetrated deeper

Florence, Nebraska—known earlier as Winter Quarters—was an important staging area for Mormon wagon trains to Utah. This sketch by George Simons pictures the landing of Mormons from the steamboat *Omaha* at this frontier settlement. *Courtesy Free Public Library, Council Bluffs, Iowa.*

into the West. Several significant river trips were made in the late fifties and sixties, however. In May 1859, for example, after the ship *William Tapscott* landed her Mormon passengers at New York, the emigrant company journeyed westward on a route no other company had taken. These Saints steamed up the Hudson River to Albany, went on to Windsor, Canada, and then crossed over to Detroit. From there they traveled by train to St. Joseph, Missouri, and boarded the steamboat *St. Mary* on May 21. Four days later this 295-ton vessel discharged her passengers at Florence, Nebraska. The *St. Mary* was commanded by Captain M. Morrison, and later that year she was snagged and lost above St. Joseph.[38]

On June 20, 1860, the ship *William Tapscott* landed another large Mormon company at Castle Garden in New York City. The next day they boarded one of the largest and most famous steamboats on the Hudson River, the 1,332-ton side-wheeler *Isaac Newton*, probably the biggest riverboat used by Mormon emigrants. In fact, in her early years she was advertised as the largest steamboat in the New and Old Worlds. She was over 300 feet long, spun paddle wheels that were 39 feet high, and had a 4-foot dip, giving her a speed of about twenty miles an hour. This steamer, which would be destroyed by an explosion in 1863, brought the Saints to Albany on June 22. From that point the emigrants traveled to Rochester, Niagara Falls, Windsor, Detroit, Chicago, Quincy, and St. Joseph, Missouri. At the latter town thirteen sick passengers were hospitalized, but by the next day they had recovered sufficiently to take a steamboat up the river to Florence, Nebraska.[39]

In late May of 1862 emigrants from the German ship *Franklin* landed at New York and then made their way to St. Joseph. There the company crowded aboard the 350-ton, one-decked side-wheeler *West Wind*. They found the accommodations insufficient for so many passengers, and the two days on the Missouri to Florence were cramped and unpleasant. Two years later this steamboat would be destroyed by fire, and the emigrant company was sadly historic in that between Hamburg and Salt Lake City 62 of the 413 passengers died.[40]

After the brig *Mexicana* landed her company of some 45 South African emigrants at New York in June 1865, the Saints traveled by rail to St. Joseph, arriving June 27. They then boarded the side-wheeler *Colorado* and continued up the Missouri to Wyoming, Nebraska, landing June 30 at that gathering place for their trek across the plains.[41]

From then on into the seventies steamboats played only an occasional role in the Mormon migration—a chapter of history forever closed.

Six

Engines of the Sea

Time was overtaking the windship. The age-old reliance on sail was receding, and a new force was driving water craft through the resisting and inconstant waves and against the onslaughts of stormy weather. The Industrial Revolution had harnessed steam, and its effect was indeed revolutionary. The change was not only in the mode of propulsion, but also in the construction of the ships themselves. Wooden ships were giving way to iron, and iron would soon give way to steel. Much of the beauty of the full-rigged packet and clipper ships sailing with the wind, the white-winged and stately tall-masted creations, would gradually—but not quite—disappear from the seas. Now there were new creations—not as beautiful, not as spectacular in the early years. Some would term them mechanical monsters of iron and steel, of clamor and smoke, speeding over the oceans. Yet these new vessels were an improvement, drastically changing water transportation. In time these steamships would become more beautiful, cleaner, and quieter.

It has also been said that the age of sail was one of wooden ships and iron men and that the age of steam was one of iron ships and wooden men. Perhaps so, for certainly there were no tougher or more durable seamen than the old canvasbacks. Under steam a new type of master and sailor evolved, bred to different conditions and technology—which could be just as trying and demanding in another sense. These men of the ocean liners may not have been as colorful, but their qualifications were no less. Engineering and mechanical skills assumed added importance, and seamanship took on a new dimension.

It should be remembered that steam power was well developed by the middle of the nineteenth century, and by 1840 the number of steam vessels was increasing at a rapid rate. By 1860 a total of 1,945 steamships had

[113]

In 1852 a score of Mormons sailed to Boston aboard the wooden Cunard paddle-wheeler *Niagara* in thirteen days—the fastest Atlantic crossing up to that time. This vessel was the only steamship used in the Mormon transatlantic passages before 1867. *Courtesy Stewart Bale Ltd., Liverpool.*

been built in the United Kingdom alone. It is also a fact that by 1850 most of the British steam merchant marine was of iron instead of wood and that the screw-driven steamer was replacing the paddle-wheeler.[1] Yet steam was slow in supplanting sail. Steamship passenger fares were high, and few emigrants could afford the cost. For years, therefore, the Mormons utilized steamships only for the connecting runs in the Baltic and North seas and along the coasts. Between 1840 and 1867 the Saints crossed the Atlantic in but one steamship—the Cunard paddle-wheeler *Niagara*. This 1,825-ton wooden steamer sailed from Liverpool on March 6, 1852, with about 20 Mormons, including Apostle John Taylor. She docked at Boston 13 days later—the fastest passage of Mormon emigrants to that date and about a third of the average passage time of a sailing ship.[2]

The next steamship crossing of a Mormon company was not made until June 21, 1867, when the Guion liner *Manhattan* sailed from Liverpool with 482 converts aboard to arrive at New York July 4. It was the first of six such voyages made by this 2,869-ton steamer, which carried a total of 1,308 Saints to America. After that 1867 passage, three voyages were made under sail in 1868 and then no more windship journeys until 1879, when the barkentine *Malay* carried an emigrant company from Australia to San Francisco.

Of the 21 transocean steamships used in the Mormon emigration, 20 have been definitely identified. Seventeen were foreign built—9 in England, 7 in Scotland, and one in Ireland. Only three of the steamships were built in the United States—the 2,143-ton *Nevada* (not to be confused with her larger British namesake), *City of Sydney*, and *Alameda*. These ships were turned out by J. Simonson of Brooklyn, New York; J. Roach & Son of Chester, Pennsylvania; and Cramp & Sons, also of Chester. Palmer's Ship-building & Iron Co. at Jarrow-on-Tyne and Newcastle produced at least nine of the British-built steamers—principally those used in the Guion Line. In Scotland John Elder of Glasgow built the *Alaska* and *Arizona*; Caird & Co. of Greenock, the *City of Berlin*; and Robert Steele & Co. of Greenock, the *Niagara*. (See Appendix 3 for a complete list of builders and locations.)

The emigrant steamships ranged widely in size. The smallest was the *Wonga Wonga* of 1,002 tons, and the largest was the *Alaska* of 6,392 tons. Each decade the steamers grew larger. During the 1860s the median tonnage was 2,869, which compares with 3,132 tons in the seventies and 3,238 in the eighties. (See Appendix 2 for more complete information on ship tonnages.)

Of the 157 Atlantic and Pacific passages made by the 21 steamships, 149 were from Liverpool to New York. One was made from Liverpool to Boston and another to Philadelphia. Passage times to these eastern seaports ranged from 8 to 17 days with a median of 12 days. In the Pacific, three voyages were made from Sydney to San Francisco and two from Auckland to San Francisco, with passage times ranging from 24 to 33 days.

From 1840 through 1890 these 21 steamships transported an estimated 41,000 of the more than 91,000 Mormon passengers to America, or 45 percent. In fact, almost a third of all emigrating Saints crossed the Atlantic in three Guion Line steamers: the *Wyoming*, which carried 10,473 Mormons in 38 voyages, the *Nevada*, which carried about 9,600 in 35 voyages, and the *Wisconsin*, which brought some 8,900 in 33 voyages. The latter vessel also provided passage to the largest single Mormon company, 976 emigrants in July of 1873.

Fewer than a dozen shipping lines supplied steamship passage for Mormon emigrants. Of these transocean shippers the Cunard Line was the earliest and most famous. It began operation in 1840, the creation of that great pioneer of water transportation, Samuel Cunard. This shipping company outlasted all of its competition and still survives. Its founder was from Halifax, Nova Scotia, and was described as a "bright, tight little man with keen eyes, firm lips, and happy manners." He was then the most successful shipper in North America. For twenty-five years his sailing packets had carried mail in the Maritime Provinces. At a time when Americans were slow to recognize that the era of sail was passing, this able

Telegraphic Address : " ATALANTA, LIVERPOOL."

GUION LINE

ROYAL & UNITED STATES MAIL   STEAMERS TO NEW YORK.

Ship.	Captain.	Tons.	Ship.	Captain.	Tons.	Ship.	Captain.	Tons.
ALASKA	MURRAY	6900	NEVADA	DOUGLAS	3600	WYOMING	RIGBY	3720
ARIZONA	BROOKS	6000	WISCONSIN	BENTLEY	3700	ABYSSINIA	PRICE	3500

Intended Sailings from LIVERPOOL to NEW YORK

1886		1887		1887	
ALASKA	Dec. 4th	WYOMING	Jan. 15th	WYOMING	Feb. 19th
WYOMING	Dec. 11th	ARIZONA	Jan. 22nd	ARIZONA	Feb. 26th
ARIZONA	Dec. 18th	NEVADA	Jan. 29th	NEVADA	Mar. 5th
NEVADA	Dec. 25th	WISCONSIN	Feb. 5th	WISCONSIN	Mar. 12th
WISCONSIN	Jan. 1st (1887)	ALASKA	Feb. 12th	ALASKA	Mar. 19th
ALASKA	Jan. 8th				

CALLING AT QUEENSTOWN ON THE FOLLOWING DAY.

The Steamers of this Line have always sailed the safest route to New York as a proof of this they have not lost a single passenger by accident for 30 years, they are all built in water-tight compartments, and are furnished with every requisite to make the passage across the Atlantic both safe and agreeable, having Bath-room, Smoking-room on deck), Drawing-room, Piano and Library ; also experienced Surgeon, Stewardess, and Caterer on each Steamer. The State-rooms are all on the upper deck, thus insuring those greatest of all luxuries at sea, perfect ventilation and light.

SALOON PASSAGE from LIVERPOOL OR QUEENSTOWN, 10 Pounds to 25 Pounds each berth, according to the size, situation, and accommodation of the State-room occupied; all having the same privileges in the Saloon. Children under 12 years, Half-fare ; Infants Free.

A Deposit of half the full fare is required to secure a Cabin Berth, the balance to be paid the day before sailing.

RETURN TICKETS ISSUED AT REDUCED RATES.

These rates include a Liberal Table and Stewards' Fees, but without Wines or Liquors, which can be obtained on board.

Passengers booked through at Low Rates, to all parts of the UNITED STATES, CANADA, MANITOBA, also via San Francisco to AUSTRALIA, CHINA, JAPAN, and INDIA.

LUGGAGE (of which 20 cubic feet for each Adult is allowed free) will go on board with the Passengers in the Tender that leaves the Landing Stage for the Steamer on the day of sailing.

NEW ZEALAND passengers booked by the New Zealand Shipping Company's fast Royal Mail Steamers from London. Full particulars, fares, vacant berths, &c. on application to GUION & CO., or any of their Agents.

FASTEST PASSAGES.

S.S. ALASKA   -   6 days 18 hours 37 minutes.
S.S. ARIZONA -   -   7 „   3   „   38   „

For Passage, Plans of Saloon and further information, apply to

GUION & CO.,

Drury Buildings, 21, Water Street, LIVERPOOL.
5, Waterloo Place, Pall Mall, LONDON, S.W.
And A. M. UNDERHILL & CO., 29 Broadway, NEW YORK.

A. H. GROVES, 5, Rue Scribe, PARIS.

No shipping company was more important to Mormon emigration than the Guion Line. Twelve steamships flying the Guion flag transported more than 40,000 converts across the Atlantic. *Courtesy Church Archives, Church of Jesus Christ of Latter-day Saints.*

and shrewd Canadian envisioned the potential of transatlantic steamship service. He went to England and persuaded the British government to award him a mail subsidy for a steamship line. It was a marriage of mutual convenience, and soon Cunard steamships were running on the Atlantic.[3]

Although only the Cunard paddle-wheeler *Niagara* carried Mormon emigrants across the Atlantic (in 1852), the *Abyssinia* served in the Cunard fleet until 1880 and then was sold to the Guion Line. Under the Guion flag this ship carried a company of 416 Saints from Liverpool to New York in 1882. However, Cunard liners were often used by missionaries and no doubt individual emigrants for many years, including the *Africa*, *Etna*, and *Scotia*. While the Cunard ships with their red and black funnels flying the line's blue burgee and white star—and later a golden lion on red—became a fixture in the Atlantic trade, it was the Guion Line that provided most of the Saints' steamship passages.

No shipping company, therefore, was more important to the Mormon migration than the Guion Line, known officially as the Liverpool & Great Western Steamship Company Limited. In fact, this line far overshadowed all other transporters of Mormon emigrants—both sail and steam. Twelve of the 21 steamships used by the Saints operated under the Guion flag—a blue flag with a black star inside a white diamond. These Guion ships, with their distinctive black funnels topped with a broad red band and rigged with auxiliary sails, carried some 40,500 Latter-day Saints from Liverpool to New York—about 98 percent of all Mormon steamship passengers. (See Appendix 8 for data on steamship lines.)

The Guion Line was developed by the American-born Stephen Barker Guion. As a young man, he became a partner in Williams & Guion, managing owners of the old Black Star Line of sailing packets from New York to Liverpool. In 1851 he established a branch office in Liverpool under the trade style Guion & Co. Business soon prospered, largely because of the growing stream of European emigrants to America. During the summer months Guion ships would carry as many as a thousand emigrants a week across the Atlantic.

When the Civil War disrupted American commerce, ships flying the Stars and Stripes retreated from the packet trade. Some Yankee vessels were sold to owners in the United Kingdom, and British flag tonnage—particularly steamships—expanded into the westbound emigrant traffic. In the war years steerage passengers began to desert sail and turned increasingly to steam for ocean travel. At that time Williams & Guion arranged to supply the Cunard and National steamships with emigrants instead of transporting them in their own ships. Later the firm organized the Liverpool & Great Western Steamship Company to replace sailing packets with steamers. In August 1866 the *Manhattan*—the first steamship under

In 1867 Mormon emigrants made their first Atlantic crossing aboard a Guion Line steamship, the *Manhattan*. This screw-driven steamer, a sister ship of the *Minnesota* and *Colorado*, made five additional such voyages. *Courtesy National Maritime Museum, San Francisco.*

Guion's Black Star flag—made her maiden voyage to New York. For nearly three decades Guion liners flying the British ensign survived Atlantic gales and disasters at sea carrying steerage and cabin passengers between Liverpool and New York. There was, however, one financial storm the Guion Line could not weather—bankruptcy in 1894.[4]

Yet, while Guion was still operating, a close—though informal—relationship developed between the shipping line and the Mormons, one that would last for more than a quarter of a century. It was initiated with the *Manhattan* voyage in 1867. With that experience church leaders recognized that higher-priced steamship fares could be justified in faster voyages and increased safety and comfort of the emigrants. It was also evident that steamships were carrying a growing proportion of the total overseas immigration into the United States. In 1868, after sending three companies on sailing packets, British Mission president Franklin D. Richards negotiated an agreement with Guion to transport the remaining emigrants for that year.[5]

It was a timely agreement for Guion, which was making the transition from sail to steam. Guion found in the Mormon market an opportunity for steady emigrant business. To solidify its position, the line offered several inducements. Guion agreed to pay Mormon agents a 7½ percent commission on fares. It also offered free cabin passage to twelve returning elders for each 300 emigrants, and additional missionaries above that ratio could have cabin passage for steerage fare. On occasion Guion was willing to hire Mormons as crew members in exchange for free passage. Such savings were significant, especially since in 1878 the church had started to pay the return passage of its missionaries.[6]

Although Mormon agents continued to search for bargains with other lines, Guion was able to meet the competition. Therefore, rather than make a change, the Mormons accepted Guion's concessions. Fares over the years ranged from about £3 to at least £6; eventually the line guaranteed the Mormons the lowest shipping cartel rates. As a result of this understanding, together with the brokers' commissions applied to fares, Mormon emigrants could pay as much as one third less than regular steerage passengers.

Perhaps the most important inducement was Guion's passenger agent, George Ramsden. Anthon H. Lund described him as a "brusque and gruff" personality but "always as gentle as a lamb" to the Mormons. He respected and seemed to like the Latter-day Saints and was proud that Franklin D. Richards had struck an agreement with him on the basis of a handshake. He defended the Mormons before shipowners and pressured railroads to grant the emigrants discounts. When the American Secretary of State, William Evarts, began what was almost a personal vendetta against the Saints and tried to discourage their immigration, Ramsden persisted in transporting the Mormons.

Once when a consul was posting a notice that Mormons would not be accepted at American ports, Ramsden appeared in a "towering rage" and ordered the consul "to pull down the notice. The latter said he was acting on orders from the government. Ramsden replied that the government had nothing to do with his ships, and that he did not ask a passenger what his religion was. His strong stand saved our emigration from being stopped."[7] Later Stephen Guion met with Evarts and made certain that Mormon emigration would not be interrupted.

Other shipping firms were concerned about the special chartering arrangements for the emigrants, particularly as there were some incidents of non-Mormon relatives and friends coming aboard as converts. This naturally caused embarrassment to both Guion and the church, and shipping and mission officials tightened their supervision to avoid criticism.

Over the years other steamship lines played relatively a minor role in the Mormon gathering. Most prominent of these shippers was the Inman Line. Inman ships were easily recognized by their black funnels with a white band, flying not only the British ensign but also the line's red flag with a black diamond enclosed in a white square. In 1884 the Inman *City of Berlin* brought 93 Mormon emigrants to New York. Several other steamers of this line, including the *City of Antwerp* and *City of Baltimore*, provided transportation for Mormon missionaries. Another British shipping company was the California, New Zealand & Australian Mail Steamship Co., which supplied the small *Wonga Wonga* for one emigrant passage in the Pacific.[8]

Four American lines operated steamships used by the Saints, each of which made one voyage with an emigrant company. For example, the American Steamship Company listed the *British King*, which carried Mormon emigrants across the Atlantic to Philadelphia in 1886. In the Pacific the *Alameda* and *Australia* of the Oceanic Steamship Line, the *City of Sydney* of the Pacific Mail Steamship Company, and the side-wheeler *Nevada* of the United States, New Zealand and Australia Mail Steamship Co. all transported Mormon converts.[9]

Although steamships reduced the passage time on the Western Ocean to about two weeks, and later less, an Atlantic crossing—even with the best of steam—was no pleasure cruise. It is true that British and American legislation had improved shipboard conditions for passengers, yet steerage accommodations were still crowded, noisy, and generally miserable. The poor could afford only the barest necessities, and these passengers usually slept on canvas bunks six feet long and eighteen inches wide. Straw mattresses often could be obtained at extra cost and would be thrown overboard before the ship docked at New York. Between decks hundreds of emigrants of diverse backgrounds and tongues were confined with a demoralizing lack of privacy, and the scourge of seasickness produced a huddled collection of humanity retching, heaving, moaning, crying, and befouling the air and living space. Their discomforts were usually compounded by their location —on the lower decks near the machinery. Here the vibration of the engines and motion of the ship were greater than the cabin passengers experienced. During storms the steamer's pitching, rolling, and plunging was enough to churn the strongest stomach and test the stoutest heart.[10]

Famous travelers in the early steamship period had few kind words about the Atlantic passage. Charles Dickens, even as a cabin passenger, was disenchanted with his voyage on the Cunard liner *Britannia*, which he described as "a British smoke-box." He wrote that his cabin was an "utterly impracticable, thoroughly hopeless, and profoundly preposterous box" and that stowing his wife's luggage in it was as feasible as "a giraffe could be persuaded . . . into a flower pot." His displeasure was evidenced by his decision to return to England in a sailing ship.[11]

Robert Louis Stevenson was critical not only of the accommodations for less affluent passengers but the class distinctions as well. While he found a few more conveniences in second cabin than in steerage, the major difference he noted was that "in steerage there are males and females; in the second cabin, ladies and gentlemen." Neither was he impressed with the emigrants on board the steamer *Devonia*. "We were a company of the rejected," he wrote, "the drunken, the incompetent, the weak, the prodigal, all who had been unable to prevail against circumstances in the one land, were now fleeing pitifully to another; and though one or two might still succeed, all had already failed." It was not a happy voyage for him. He concluded that "the steerage conquered me; I conformed more and more to the type of the place, not only in manner but at heart, growing hostile to the officers and cabin passengers who looked down upon me. It seemed no disgrace to be confounded with my company; for I may as well declare at once I found their manners as gentle and becoming as those of any other class."[12]

For the crew, especially in the engine room, it was yet another world. Richard Henry Dana, author of *Two Years Before the Mast*, gave this picture of the stokehole of the *Persia*: "In these deep and unknown regions . . . in the glare of the opening and closing furnace door, live and toil a body of grim, blackened and oily men. . . . When down among them on the brick and iron floors . . . I lost all sense of being at sea."[13]

Steamship crews increasingly represented a wide range of skills, from marine engineers to stokers, from able seamen to stewards, and from mechanics to chefs. As steamer service developed, the ratio of crew to passengers increased. Steamships became floating hotels and pleasure palaces—particularly for the rich and prominent travelers.

For the wealthy, steamship travel was a world of its own. Steamship lines competed to supply the best in grace and comfort for their preferred voyagers. On the sea palatial living became a reality, and most of the passenger space on the ocean liners was reserved for those with means and prestige. First class travelers luxuriated in comfortable—if not plush—staterooms, delighted in the best cuisine served by elegant stewards, and enjoyed the personal blandishments of ships' officers. Such Grand Saloon denizens could have virtually all of the amenities of the greatest land hotels. Their world was remote and isolated, and it is understandable that these passengers were often oblivious of the hundreds of emigrants jammed into limited space in the lower decks and the toil and dirt of the engine room crew who kept the ship moving. In time steerage passage would be upgraded to tourist or more dignified descriptions, but for many years emigrants were the lifeblood of most steamship lines.

The different worlds aboard the steamship—hard worlds and dream worlds—were facets of an awesome machine, a monumental engineering triumph. It was the greatest and most complex moving object invented by man and itself an epic in history. The steamship was first fashioned with paddle wheels and wooden hulls. Screw propellers replaced the churning

Most Mormon voyages—especially after 1855—terminated at New York. In this Currier & Ives lithograph of Manhattan in 1876, Castle Garden is the circular structure in the lower left-hand corner between the Hudson and East rivers. *Courtesy The New-York Historical Society.*

paddles, and hulls became iron and soon steel. Then twin screws were developed which enabled a ship to continue if one propeller failed. Twin screws led shipbuilders to abandon sails as an auxiliary source of power, and sails were generally eliminated after 1889.[14]

With the disappearance of sails, the silhouette of the modern steamer changed. Function became the governing principle. The beautifully curved clipper bows and the bowsprit gave way to the knife-edged straight stem. Tall smokestacks and tiered superstructures were built up from the hull, and eventually the ocean liner would become a trim and attractive creation.[15]

Yet, with all her improvements over the decades, the steamship remained vulnerable to the wrathful ocean. Man had never tamed the elements. Violent storms would still send crockery flying from the tables, luggage whipping around a stateroom, and seasick passengers lunging for the rail. Atlantic gales, Pacific typhoons, giant waves, deceptive icebergs, and fog would still take their toll. Although built to be safer, faster, and bigger, steamships were no less mortal than their builders. Myths of a vessel's unsinkability were shattered time and time again—most dramatically, of course, by the *Titanic* disaster in 1912. It is interesting that no Mormon emigrant company suffered loss from shipwreck while crossing the Atlantic or Pacific aboard a steamship. However, of the 20 steamers identified as having transported Mormon emigrants, six were eventually lost at sea—either from natural or man-made causes.[16]

After 1855, before emigrants from Europe were allowed to land at New York, authorities intercepted the arriving ships at the Narrows—a small passage leading from the Atlantic Ocean to New York Harbor. There they sorted out the sick and infectious and sent them to a special hospital. The remaining ship-weary passengers were loaded on barges for processing at Castle Garden, a receiving station at the lower tip of Manhattan Island. Castle Garden was a former theater, a large circular building decorated on the inside with paintings, with a seating capacity of upwards of 8,000 persons.[17]

This processing terminal was prepared for the benefit of the emigrants. Castle Garden was intended to be a source of helpful information and assistance to the new arrivals. One passenger wrote: "I am told that all emigrants arriving at New York land here, where they may remain free of charge for about five days. There are no beds here for emigrants to lie upon; but they are at liberty to lie upon the benches and floor of the building, which the majority of the emigrants do."

Although swindlers and confidence men were naturally forbidden to enter the premises, in practice Castle Garden became an ideal place for all kinds of cheats and crooks with their clever schemes to victimize the newcomers. The predators stalked the unwary emigrants, trying to separate

them from their money. The fact that New York City was only a transfer
point for many emigrants bound for other destinations encouraged dishonest operators to pose as travel agents. It was often difficult for a stranger,
particularly one with a limited knowledge of English, to determine who
legitimately represented the rail, coach, and steamboat transit systems.
Mormon leaders early recognized the problem of the exposure of their converts to the unscrupulous element and established their own agents at all
major ports of embarkation and debarkation. Profiting from years of
experience and an effective organization, these church representatives
smoothly arranged transportation from Castle Garden and protected and
sheltered their people from dishonest operators.

For the Mormon emigrants the transocean steamship was yet another
beginning—one of increased speed, safety, and convenience.

Formerly a fort and then a concert hall in New York's Battery area, Castle Garden was
opened as an immigrant landing depot in 1855. Millions of new arrivals were processed
here until 1890. *Courtesy The Peabody Museum of Salem.*

Seven

Greyhounds of Steam

Their names were not romantic, except to those who dreamed of adventure in American cities and states. Most names were indeed American and carried an aura of opportunity. With such geography emblazoned on their bows, the awesome machines with throbbing engines plowed through the water with cargoes of hopeful converts searching for their Zion. One after another these steamships deposited new life and blood on American shores.

Of the Mormons who emigrated under steam, some 3,900 crossed the Atlantic in 11 voyages prior to 1870. During the next decade—the seventies —about 16,500 in 59 steamer passages came to America, and the remaining years through 1890 saw approximately 20,700 arriving in 87 transocean trips aboard steamships.

After the earliest steamship crossings of the *Niagara* in 1852 and the *Manhattan* in 1867, the names of other steam vessels were entered in Mormon chronicles. The third steamer to transport Mormon emigrants was the 2,869-ton Guion liner *Minnesota*. She was built with an iron hull, single screw, inverted engines, two masts, and one funnel. Her sister ships were the *Manhattan* and *Colorado*. The *Minnesota* made 11 Mormon passages, bringing 3,907 Saints from Liverpool to New York. Her first began on June 30, 1868, and her last, July 8, 1874. These passages averaged a brisk 12.5 days. Captain James Price commanded the vessel on the first crossing, and his conduct was described as "gentlemanly, kind and upright."[1] During this voyage the Saints did considerable dancing and singing, held meetings twice on Sunday—once on deck in the open air—and gave a special concert celebrating July Fourth. Only a few incidents were recorded on the other passages. In 1871 an aged woman convert died and was buried at sea, and in 1872 two babies were born during one crossing. The following voyage was marked by a violent storm that smashed the bulkhead

[125]

and brought a cascade of water three feet deep into the lower decks.[2]

The *Colorado* was the fourth transatlantic steamship used by the Saints. This Guion liner was brig-rigged but at 2,927 tons was built slightly larger than her sister *Minnesota*. The *Colorado* carried five companies to New York, totaling about 1,150 Mormons. Under the leadership of Elder William B. Preston the first emigrants sailed from Liverpool on July 14, 1868. Captain Robert Charles Cutting was the shipmaster. The vessel steamed down the Mersey in the afternoon, with "the sun shining brightly, the sky without a cloud and no sadness appearing on a single countenance except on those who returned to shore after bidding their friends farewell." The fifth voyage began on July 12, 1871, from Liverpool, the steamship under the command of Captain Thomas F. Freeman and the Saints under the direction of Elder Hamilton G. Park. The five passages averaged 13 days and were uneventful. Less than a year later the *Colorado* collided with another vessel in the River Mersey and sank with a loss of six lives.[3]

In the summer of 1874 the British steamship *Idaho* carrying 806 Mormons to New York encountered a frightening Atlantic storm. During the severest turbulence the vessel's captain commented "that there were too many 'Mormons' on board for the ship to be harmed; he had carried companies for 18 years and had never heard of a ship carrying 'Mormons' being lost." This 3,132-ton Guion liner, from September 7, 1870, to the fall of 1877, transported six emigrant companies totaling 3,057 Saints from Liverpool to America. The *Idaho* and her sister ship *Nevada* were the first two Guion straight-stem steamers. The *Idaho* was a single-screw, iron-hull steamship with two masts, one funnel, and inverted engines. Her rated speed was 11 knots, and the average time of the six crossings was 12.8 days. In 1878 the *Idaho* was wrecked off Ireland with no loss of life.[4]

The steamship *Nevada* transported approximately 9,600 Mormon emigrants to America (a number surpassed only by the *Wyoming*). This 3,125-ton British steamer plied the seas for almost three decades, and during nineteen years brought 35 companies of Saints from Liverpool to New York. One of the first Guion straight-stemmed vessels, the *Nevada* was built with an iron hull, single screw, two masts brig-rigged, one funnel, three decks, inverted engines, and a rated speed of 11 knots. In 1881 compound engines were installed and the steamer's tonnage increased to 3,617. This great work horse was scrapped in 1896, after having been sold and renamed.[5]

The first of the *Nevada*'s 35 Mormon passages began on September 14, 1870, and the last in November 1889. These transatlantic crossings averaged 11.5 days. Captains John Douglas and William Forsyth skippered the *Nevada* during many of the Mormon voyages. Among her prominent passengers over the years were Lot Smith, the famous Mormon frontiersman

Three Guion Line steamships carried a third of all Mormon emigrants to America. The *Wyoming* (top) made at least 38 voyages and brought more than 10,000 Latter-day Saints across the Atlantic—more than any other ship. The *Nevada* (center) made 35 known passages with 9,600 Mormon passengers, and the *Wisconsin* carried some 8,900 Saints in 33 crossings. *Courtesy The Peabody Museum of Salem* (Wyoming) *and The Mariners Museum, Newport News, Virginia* (Nevada *and* Wisconsin).

and colonizer; Apostle Erastus Snow; Anthon H. Lund, George Reynolds, and James E. Talmage—all later general authorities of the church; David McKay, father of President David O. McKay; and Niels C. Sonne, forebear of two general authorities. Most passages were uneventful, but several unusual episodes were noted. For example, Elder Joseph E. Hyde, a returning missionary, died, and his body was packed in ice to take to Utah. A number of children and a few other adults died and were buried at sea, and two babies born on the voyage were named William Nevada Webster and Nevada Atlantic Larsen.[6]

Despite the popularity of the *Nevada*, no ship carried as many Mormons to America under either sail or steam as the Guion liner *Wyoming*. Over nearly twenty years this British flag steamer made 38 voyages carrying a total of 10,473 Latter-day Saints from Liverpool to New York, in companies ranging from 10 to 775 emigrants. The first passage began May 10, 1871, the last on September 20, 1890. The average time was a quite reasonable 10.8 days. Among her passengers to cross the Atlantic were Elder Joseph F. Smith, released as head of the British Mission, later president of the church; Elder David K. Udall, who would become a colonizer in Arizona; and Elder Charles W. Nibley, a Scotsman who served as president of the British Mission and would become Presiding Bishop of the church and a counselor in the First Presidency. These voyages were not eventful, except that the vessel was almost wrecked near Sable Island, about 700 miles from New York, during an 1873 voyage, and there were the occasional deaths and burials at sea. The 3,283-ton *Wyoming* was similar to other Guion liners of her day; sporting an iron hull, single screw, two masts, one funnel, three decks and a speed of 11½ knots. She was a sister ship of the *Wisconsin* and one of the earliest steamers with compound engines. Her tonnage was later increased to 3,700, and she was scrapped in 1893.[7]

From the standpoint of number of emigrants transported across the Atlantic, the third most important vessel in the Mormon migration was the Guion steamship *Wisconsin*. Only her sister ship *Wyoming* and the *Nevada* carried more Saints to the New World. The 3,238-ton *Wisconsin*, which had the same features as the *Wyoming*, brought 33 companies of from seven to 976 Saints (the largest in Mormon history), totaling some 8,900 Mormons. Her first company sailed from Liverpool on July 31, 1872, and her last left on October 11, 1890—the final company of that year. Passage times to New York averaged 11 days.[8]

For more than eighteen years the *Wisconsin* provided safe passage, crossing the Atlantic with few incidents. The Church Emigration record indicates that the emigrant companies were well ordered and generally harmonious. For example, in 1873 the largest company of 976 Saints reported: "One little child died on the voyage and one was born. Great unity prevailed among the Saints which made it possible for good order to prevail among so large a company." When 714 Mormons from various countries made their crossing in 1877, the "officers of the Guion steamship line remarked that they had never seen a company organized with such precision." On the next voyage the Saints assembled on board the *Wisconsin* and, while awaiting departure, sang "Cheer, Saints, Cheer, We Are Bound for Peaceful Zion" to the accompaniment of a brass band. Music provided considerable entertainment during these voyages, and in 1880 "a fine string band . . . gave selections frequently." That same year the arrival of 727 British and Scandinavian Saints at New York caused some congestion at customs. Elder William C. Staines, the church agent, came on board, but the company was so large that the emigrants could not all be processed that day. As a result, they had to spend the night under the huge dome of Castle Garden. The following day the company was accommodated in seventeen special railroad cars in two sections and journeyed on to Utah.[9]

Among the many passengers of the *Wisconsin* were a Norwegian widow, Anna Widtsoe, and her two sons. The boys—John and Osborne—both rose to eminence in the church. John A. Widtsoe became a noted scientist, educator, writer, and church apostle. He told the story of his mother's journey from Norway to Utah: "The ship after bumping for sixty hours over the shallow North Sea, landed safely in Hull. Then the emigrants and their baggage were taken by rail from Hull to Liverpool, over England's smudgy midlands district. There, in Liverpool, for the first time did the widow see an apostle of the Lord (John Henry Smith). He was as she had expected, a kindly man, but she looked at him with joy as she recalled the authority of the Priesthood committed to him. There the party was augmented by emigrants from Denmark, Sweden, and England. The party embarked on the *S. S. Wisconsin* on October 27, 1883, and reached New York after a rough but otherwise uneventful voyage on November 7, 1883. The next day the long railroad trip from New York to Logan, Utah, was begun."[10]

During the seventies the Guion Line added two larger, but not much faster, steamships to its transatlantic service—the 4,332-ton *Dakota* and her sister ship *Montana* of 4,321 tons. Both were produced by Palmer's Shipbuilding & Iron Co. on the Tyne in England and had similar characteristics: iron hull, single screw, compound engines, two masts, one funnel, length of 400 feet and speed of 17 knots intended but in reality less. These ships were built to accommodate 200 saloon and 1,200 steerage passengers, the saloon space later being reduced. Their maiden voyages were delayed until 1875, but their lives were short. The *Dakota* was wrecked off Anglesey, Wales, in May 1877 with no loss of life. The *Montana* was stranded

Icebergs were among the perils of the Atlantic run. In November 1879 the Guion liner *Arizona*, with a group of Mormons on board, struck an iceberg which crushed her bow. The damaged vessel was able to limp into Newfoundland for temporary repairs. *Courtesy Naval Photographic Center, Department of the Navy.*

three years later, also on the Welsh Coast, and was a total loss. Although both vessels were considered failures, the *Dakota* carried 120 Saints from Liverpool to New York in October 1875, a 10-day passage. The vessel was commanded by Captain William Forsyth, who had previously skippered the *Nevada*. The *Montana* transported two Mormon companies. The first consisted of 20 Mormons who crossed the Atlantic in a 12-day passage during January 1876. A second company of 221 Saints made a 10-day crossing in June 1878.[11]

A still larger Guion liner was the 5,147-ton *Arizona*, built in 1879 by John Elder & Co. at Glasgow, Scotland. Over the next decade this historic steamship carried nine Mormon companies from Liverpool to New York, ranging upwards of 531 Saints and aggregating more than 1,250. The first company sailed in October 1879 and the last in May 1889. These nine passages averaged 9.3 days—the fastest time of any Guion vessel to that date. In fact, the *Arizona* once held the transatlantic speed record.[12]

A few months after the first Mormon crossing this Guion steamer made world news and achieved dubious fame. On November 7, 1879, steaming at full speed off the Grand Banks, she struck a huge iceberg head-on, telescoping twenty-five feet of her bow. Four Mormon missionaries were among the passengers on their way to Liverpool.

"You can't imagine the appalling suddenness of the thing," reported a passenger.

At one moment nothing was further from our thoughts than an accident. Then came that awful crash and those on their feet in the smoking room were either flung to the deck or thrown into a struggling heap on a settee at the forward end of the room. The throb of the engine stopped almost instantly and there was a moment of deathly stillness. Then a hubbub of voices arose and we heard the hysterical screaming of a woman from the saloon. A moment later there was a rush for the deck, not a rush for the boats, you understand, but a wild scramble to get on deck to see what had happened. Dad and I were among the first to reach the door. A glance forward told the story. The *Arizona*'s bow, or what was left of it, was literally buried in a huge iceberg which towered sixty or seventy feet above us. Tons of shattered ice from the face of the berg lay on the turtle deck and made it impossible to see much of the bow. Captain Jones had been below when the ship struck and as he reached the bridge above he called out, "My God, where were your eyes?"[13]

Fortunately the ship was able to limp into the harbor at Saint John's, Newfoundland, without loss of life. Her gashed and crumpled nose had opened a slice all the way to the collision bulkhead; but William H. Guion, head of the Guion Line and a passenger on the *Arizona*, was equal to the occasion. With a showman's flair he arranged that the battered nose be replaced with an improvised wooden bow, after which the *Arizona* sped back to Liverpool for more permanent repairs. Her captain's license was suspended for his foolhardiness in driving his ship at full speed in an area of floating icebergs. For many mariners this incident confirmed their feeling that icebergs were the cause of the disappearance of many Atlantic vessels "missing without a trace."[14]

The accident also was evidence of the seaworthiness of the four-decked *Arizona*, which was reputed to be among the best transocean steamships, and contributed to her popularity and patronage in the years ahead. In any case, she was a sound ship and the first Atlantic liner with a compound three-crank engine. She also had four masts, two funnels, an iron hull, a single screw, a rated speed of 16 knots, a length of 464 feet, and accommodations for 140 first class, 70 second class, and 140 third class passengers. During her forty-seven years' service, until she was scrapped in 1926, the *Arizona* ran in both the Atlantic and Pacific oceans. In 1898 she was acquired by the United States government, converted to a troopship, renamed *Hancock,* and used during the Spanish-American War and World War I.[15]

Five other Atlantic steamships played lesser parts in the Mormon migration. For example, the 3,253-ton *Abyssinia,* carrying a company of 416 Saints, including 28 returning missionaries, sailed from Liverpool on October 21, 1882, arriving at New York November 3—an uneventful 13-day crossing. This British single-screw steamer with her three bark-rigged masts, one funnel, and accommodations for 200 first and 1,050 steerage passengers traded in both Atlantic and Pacific waters. A heavy fuel consumer, she operated in the Cunard Line for ten years and then in the Guion Line from 1880 to 1884—the time of this Mormon voyage. In 1891, after twenty-one years' service, the *Abyssinia* was destroyed by fire in mid-Atlantic, but all on board were saved by a passing German liner.[16]

With a length of eleven times her beam, making the 488-foot *City of Berlin* one of the longest ships afloat, this 5,491-ton Inman liner was the second largest vessel used by Mormon emigrants. On October 23, 1884, this British steamship sailed from Liverpool with 93 Saints aboard and arrived at New York 10 days later. Captain S. J. Kennedy was shipmaster, and Elder Carl August Ek presided over the emigrant company. The *City of Berlin* was built with an iron hull, single screw, one funnel, three masts, compound engines, a speed of 16 knots, 36 furnaces, 12 boilers, and a capacity for 202 cabin and 1,500 steerage passengers. Her greatest shortcoming was her enormous appetite for fuel—she consumed 120 tons of coal daily. Some years after this voyage the *City of Berlin* was sold to the United States government, renamed *Meade,* and used as a troop transport and training ship. She was scrapped in 1921 after forty-six years of service, but has found a place historically as the first transatlantic liner equipped with electric lights.[17]

Another silhouette appeared on the Atlantic horizon, the Guion liner *Alaska.* She was the largest—6,392 tons—and the longest—500 feet—vessel to carry Mormon emigrants in the nineteenth century. This fine single-screw steamer was also the fastest transocean ship of her day. In 1882 she won the Atlantic Blue Ribbon for her record crossing from Liverpool to New York in seven days, six hours, and forty-three minutes. On July 10, 1886, the four-decked *Alaska* sailed with her only company of Mormons from Liverpool, 23 Icelandic emigrants, arriving eight days later at New York—the fastest crossing of any Mormon group. This steamship was built in 1881 by John Elder & Co. at Glasgow, Scotland, with an iron hull, four masts, two funnels, and a rated speed of 17 knots. In 1894 the *Alaska* made the last sailing of the Guion Line. She was broken up in 1902.[18]

In the early 1880s shipbuilders turned from iron to steel—a stronger, lighter, and less brittle material. With steel construction steamships gained some added storage capacity and speed. The first steel vessel to carry Mormon emigrants was the *British King*. This single-screw, 3,412-ton ship operated in the American Line, which advertised itself as "the only trans-atlantic line sailing under the American flag." However, the *British King* was built at Belfast, Ireland, in 1881 and hailed out of Liverpool. She had a length of 410 feet, four bark-rigged masts, one funnel, three decks, compound engines, and a rated speed of 12 knots. On October 13, 1886, this liner sailed from Liverpool with 307 Saints under the leadership of Joshua Greenwood. The shipmaster was Captain J. Kelly (also Kelley). After a 14-day passage the emigrants landed at Philadelphia. It had been almost thirty years since a Mormon company had disembarked at The Quaker City.[19]

On April 27, 1889, a company of 26 Saints sailed from Amsterdam. Little is known about this voyage, except that Elder Martinus Krumperman was in charge of the emigrants. It seems likely that the company traveled to New York, possibly on a Dutch steamship.[20]

On the other side of the world Mormon emigration was sporadic. On June 4, 1871, the first company of Saints to emigrate by steamship from Australia sailed out of Sydney harbor on board the 1,002-ton, single-screw British steamer *Wonga Wonga*. It was a small company in the charge of Elder Edwin S. Kearsley. Shipmaster was a Captain Stewart. About 30 or 40 more Mormon emigrants had expected to leave at that time but were not able to sell their property before the sailing date. On July 8 the *Daily Alta California* reported the arrival in San Francisco of the "Br Stmr Wonga Wonga, Stewart, 37 days, 6 hrs. from Sydney via Fiji 25 days, and Honolulu 11 days and 2 hours." This small steamer was listed in the California, New Zealand & Australian Steamship Co. and hailed out of Sydney. She was scrapped in 1880 after twenty-six years of service.[21]

Another company of 11 New Zealand Saints—the first from that country—sailed from Auckland aboard the United States flag steamship *Nevada*. No record can be found of her arrival in California, but it is believed that the vessel reached San Francisco in late January 1872. The *Nevada* was built in Brooklyn, New York, in 1867. She had side-wheel paddles, beam engines, two masts, two funnels, a straight stem, and a wooden hull. This 2,143-ton three-decker ran between Sydney and San Francisco from 1871 to 1873, and then was purchased by the Pacific Mail Steamship Co.[22]

The *Daily Alta California* of April 8, 1871, described the opening of the New Zealand and Australia service and the steamer *Nevada* under the command of a veteran mariner, Captain J. H. Blethen. The article reported:

The *Nevada* is now lying at Mission-street wharf, and has just been thoroughly overhauled. She is, as so many of our readers know, in all

respects a first-class vessel . . . constructed of live oak, heavily planked.
. . . She has two masts and is brig-rigged . . . can make 15 knots, and
will probably average 260 or 270 miles a day . . . and is regarded as
the fastest vessel on the coast.

On deck are twenty beautiful state-rooms . . . all double, with doors
on either side, and patent ventilators in the top. . . . Right aft is the
ladies' sitting-room, well fitted up, private and ventilated. . . . The
gentlemens' smoking-room . . . is fitted up with a degree of comfort
seldom ever found aboard of ships. On the main deck is the grand
saloon, 90 feet long by 28 feet broad, 8 feet under the beams. On either
side of the saloon is a row of state-rooms, opening on the deck, accom-
modating eighty passengers, ventilated, and in every respect the same
as the rooms upon the upper deck, with two bridal chambers in the
forward part of the saloon.

The most prominent steamship used in the Pacific Mormon migration
was the 1,938-ton *Australia*. Built of iron with a round stern, plain head,
and three decks, this dauntless lady of the sea was constructed at Glasgow,
Scotland, in 1875, flew the British flag until she was acquired in her last
years by the Oceanic Steamship Co. Inc. of San Francisco, and was again
resold in 1898. Her black hull and silhouette of four masts and single funnel
were familiar to many Mormon missionaries and emigrants for more than
two decades. On June 17, 1880, Elder Fred J. May, returning president of
the Australian Mission, and a small group of Saints sailed from Sydney
aboard the *Australia*. Five days later the steamer stopped at Auckland,
New Zealand, and took aboard another small Mormon company in the
charge of President Thomas A. Shreeve. The *Daily Alta California* for July
15, 1880, reported the arrival in San Francisco of the British steamer
Australia under the command of Captain Cargill, "27 days from Sydney . . .
via Honolulu 3 days."[23] How many more emigrants crossed the Pacific in
this ship individually or in small unorganized groups over the years is not
definitely known.

Another company of Saints sailed from Auckland, New Zealand, on
April 26, 1881. These 27 Mormons were passengers of the American
steamship *City of Sydney* and were placed in charge of Elder George Batt,
a returning missionary. Captain Dearborn was master of the vessel. The
3,016-ton steamer arrived at San Francisco on May 17—a 20-day passage.
This single-screw liner of the Pacific Mail Steamship Co. was built at
Chester, Pennsylvania, in 1875. She had four decks, an iron hull, three
masts bark-rigged, one funnel, a straight stem, and compound engines.
In 1915 the *City of Sydney* was sold, engines removed, rigged as a six-
masted barkentine, and fifteen years later scrapped.[24]

The 3,158-ton American steamship *Alameda,* also built at Chester in 1883, was owned by the Oceanic Steamship Company, and in 1888 transported at least one group of Mormon emigrants across the Pacific Ocean. She was a single-screw craft with an iron hull, two masts, one funnel, triple-expansion engines, and a rated speed of 15 knots. Her size was later increased to 3,709 tons and her hull lengthened from 314 to 327 feet. From 1885 to 1901 she ran between San Francisco and Sydney. In 1910 the aging lady was sold to the Alaska Steamship Co. It was about April 18, 1888, when the *Alameda* apparently left Sydney with a small company of Australian Saints. On April 23 the steamer sailed from Auckland with a few more emigrants. These Australian and New Zealand Mormons were under the leadership of Elder John L. Blythe, who was returning from three years in Australia, during which time he had baptized about 20 converts. The *Daily Alta California* of May 13, 1888, reported the arrival in San Francisco of the *Alameda* under the command of Captain Morse, "24 days, 13 hours from Sydney, via Honolulu 7 days; pass and mdse, to J. D. Spreckels & Bros."[25]

During their 157 steamship voyages the Mormon emigrants were in the care of no fewer than 34 masters. Of these masters Captain Charles Leonard Rigby transported 23 companies in three ships: the *Wyoming,* *Wisconsin,* and *Nevada.* Captain Edward Bentley skippered 15 Mormon passages, mostly in the *Wisconsin.* Captain William Forsyth commanded five different vessels, which carried 14 emigrant companies: the *Idaho,* *Dakota, Manhattan, Nevada,* and *Wisconsin.* Captains James Price, John Preston Morrall, and Thomas Jones each carried 11 companies in Guion ships. Captain Samuel Brooks made eight Mormon passages commanding the *Arizona.* (See Appendix 11 for a complete list of masters of two or more Mormon emigrant voyages.)

As this sea epoch drew to a close, it marked the passing of sail and the triumph of the engine. Yet it was also just a beginning, for ahead the oceans would be challenged by gigantic liners—floating palaces—and speedier transocean runs. For the Mormons the year 1890 was a pivot point. The migration changed dramatically, and it would never again be the same.

Eight

Ebb Tide

By 1890 the Mormon migration had peaked and was declining sharply. In half a century more than 85,000 overseas converts had emigrated to the United States. Most of these emigrants—some 55,000—were from the United Kingdom, and about 20,000 were from Scandinavia.[1] The remainder came primarily from Germany, Switzerland, Holland, France, Italy, Australia, New Zealand, and South Africa.

During these years mighty forces were reshaping and shrinking the world. Among the most important was the emergence of the steam engine. Its development was ushering out an era that had relied upon animal power on land and wind power on the sea. Born of a fruitful marriage of science and capital, a new machine age was flourishing; and the resulting innovations in transportation—the railroads, steamboats, and steamships—were accelerating travel. The American continent from 1870 was bound by ribbons of steel, and the oceans and inland waterways were being bridged and increasingly tamed by steam craft.

It was a time of great change. People were on the move as never before, and the Mormon enterprise had become a movement in the most literal sense. Latter-day Saint emigrants, while only a small minority among the millions of foreign-born entering the United States, were not typical. Called a "peculiar" people, Mormon emigrants were not driven by a dream of El Dorado or political paradise. Religion brought them to America, and most of these converts expected little else but struggle and sacrifice in the wild country of their "gathering." Inevitably some faltered, defected, and turned to more worldly interests. Yet the majority carried on and contributed substantially to the settlement of the American West.

As we have seen, the Saints differed from other emigrants in more than motivation. They traveled in tightly-knit and self-governing companies.

[137]

Their organization was an effective ecclesiastical pyramid. Their ships were selectively chartered, and accommodations and provisions were pre-arranged. They also benefited from the assistance of church agents at various port cities, financial aid for the needy through the Perpetual Emigrating Fund, and the detailed scheduling and planning of church leaders.

Perhaps a more significant difference, however, was the underlying religious discipline. The spiritual consciousness of the Saints was demonstrated at the very outset. Before sailing, the ship was dedicated and rules of behavior and cleanliness were adopted. The sexes were separated except in the case of married couples. During the voyage morning and evening prayers were held, and regular meetings for religious worship and instruction were conducted. Quarters were scrubbed and often sprinkled with lime. Bedding was aired, and passengers were required to spend periods on deck. Meals were carefully planned and prepared. The sick were given medication and care and—most certainly—anointed with consecrated oil and blessed. In brief, the line between the temporal and spiritual well-being of the Saints was often indistinguishable.

It was this discipline that caught the eye of Victorian novelist Charles Dickens when he visited a Mormon company aboard the ship *Amazon*. In *The Uncommercial Traveller* he penned this description of the emigrants:

> I go out on the poop-deck, for air, and surveying the emigrants on the deck below. . . . But nobody is in ill-temper, nobody is the worse for drink, nobody swears an oath or uses a coarse word, nobody appears depressed, nobody is weeping, and down upon the deck in every corner . . . people, in every unsuitable attitude for writing, are writing letters. . . . . And these people are so strikingly different from all other people in like circumstances whom I have ever seen. . . . The most of these came aboard yesterday evening. They came from various parts of England in small parties that had never seen one another before. Yet they had not been a couple of hours on board, when they established their own police, made their own regulations, and set their own watches at all the hatchways. Before nine o'clock, the ship was as orderly and as quiet as a man-of-war. . . .
> I afterwards learned that a Despatch was sent home by the captain before he struck out into the wide Atlantic, highly extolling the behavior of these Emigrants, and the perfect order and propriety of all their social arrangements.[2]

Shipmasters and shipping lines appreciated the order and behavior of Mormon emigrants, and many were eager to have them as passengers. In 1854 a select committee of the House of Commons studying emigration under the Passenger Acts reported that no vessels "could be depended upon for comfort and security in the same degree as those under the Mormon agent's care."[3]

No doubt effective logistical management was the principal reason for the unusual success of Mormon voyages. Of the 333 identified transocean passages, 176 under sail and 157 under steam, there was only one failure—in 1855, when the bark *Julia Ann* was wrecked in the Pacific with the loss of five lives. On the rivers the Mormon experience was also fortunate. Although there were minor accidents, the only real disaster was the explosion of the steamboat *Saluda* on the Missouri River, which killed or injured upwards of a hundred Saints.

The Mormon safety record is in sharp contrast to that of other emigrants. For example, although the number of emigrants lost at sea has not been definitely determined, it is known that between 1847 and 1853 at least 59 emigrant ships were lost during Atlantic crossings.[4] *The Latter-day Saints' Millennial Star*, the church publication in Britain, reminded the members of the importance of traveling in organized companies: "At different times in 1854, and with different ships, 34 members of the Church had embarked for New Orleans; some of these were lost at sea, which proved a warning to others not to embark on a voyage across the Atlantic in any but regularly organized companies of Saints."[5]

However, despite their emphasis on sanitation and hygiene, the Saints suffered greatly from disease and seasickness. It is not certainly known that the Mormon mortality rate from disease was abnormally high, but if it was, the presence of many children in Mormon companies must have contributed disproportionately to the death rate. During the long voyages under canvas, measles, cholera, and dysentery—the most prevalent diseases—could sweep through a ship with devastating effect, and the children were the least likely to survive. Of the 24 voyages with more than five deaths, all were made by sailing ships (see Appendix 4). Conversely, deaths during steamship crossings were relatively few, undoubtedly attributable to the faster passages and improved conditions.

No scourge of the sea traveler was more universal than seasickness, which recognized no class, title, race, or creed. To the emigrants seasickness was a living death. Their misery was such that every other alternative doom—tempest, shipwreck, or even piracy—seemed insignificant. They might well pray to die, but few did. Many lyrical sufferers wrote of their bouts. One declared, "It seems like an eternity of spasmodic suffering—talk of amputation! Mental anxiety—chronic disease—why what is the whole catalogue of human ills compared to this attic salt—this bilious dissolution—this sea emetic?" Another described how he was embraced by this affliction: "How pure and sweet the air would be at sea, if it were not for the repeated vomiting of bile, whose effluvia are extremely volatile and settle down at once in the curtains, floor, ceiling, paint, sofa and beds of the cabins."[6]

Yet all things pass away—even seasickness, much to the everlasting gratitude of sea voyagers.

For both missionaries and emigrants the Mormon migration spanned the two epochs of sail and steam navigation, but it was a mixed period of transition. Between 1840 and into 1868 the Atlantic and Pacific crossings, with one exception, were all made in sailing vessels. However, during these same years Saints from the European continent traveled over the North Sea in steamships. These voyages were usually rough and often violent. Then, too, after their arrival in the United States the emigrants were transshipped on steamboats up the Hudson, Ohio, Mississippi, and Missouri rivers. From the landing ports on these rivers, after 1847, the Mormons continued their journey across the plains. By 1870 railroads had largely displaced the riverboats and ox and mule teams, and the movement of the Saints—on both land and water—was almost entirely under steam power.

It is doubtful that any epoch was more colorful, exciting, or arduous than the golden years of sail. In the nineteenth century the slow and clumsy merchantman faced a formidable rival in the packet ship. The packet added a new dimension of speed and regularity for the ocean traveler and in her time was the racehorse of the Atlantic run. Her tall and stately masts, white clouds of canvas, and clean lines became a familiar silhouette at sea. Then, for a brief period, sailed perhaps the finest creation of all—the clipper ship. This lovely lady was even sharper and speedier than the packet. Although built more for freight than for passenger service, these beautiful ships with their curved bows and romantic names—*Emerald Isle, Monsoon*, and *Viking*—found a place in Mormon history.[7]

As another type of square-rigger was developed, the clipper ship became less competitive. This new ship was built in Maine and called a "Down Easter" or "Cape Horner." Strong, full-bodied, and heavily sparred, she was designed with increased cargo and passenger capacity and the sturdiness to weather the severe storms of Cape Horn. Several of these fine ships transported Mormon emigrants, among them the *General McClellan* and *St. Mark*, but they were latecomers in the era of Mormon emigration under canvas.[8]

During the sailing ship period Mormon emigrants voyaged over the oceans in 146 identified windships, traveling in groups and companies of from five to 974 persons. Passage times ranged from 23 to 177 days, the latter representing the ocean-to-ocean voyage of the ship *Brooklyn*. Of the 81 passages from Liverpool to New Orleans up to 1855, the average voyage took 54 days. The 45 passages from Liverpool to New York averaged 38 days. In the Pacific, voyages from Australia, New Zealand, and India were particularly long and wearisome, requiring from 80 to 112 days. The vessels transporting the Saints varied in rig—ships, barks, brigs, a barkentine, and a schooner. In size their tonnages ranged from 183 to 1,979.

For three decades Mormon missionaries and emigrants traveled the world in windships. These Saints traversed most of the great oceans and seas—the Atlantic Ocean, Pacific Ocean, Indian Ocean, Mediterranean Sea, Caribbean Sea, East China Sea, Japan Sea, North Sea, and Baltic Sea. Approximately 50,000 Mormon converts emigrated to America under sail. Of this total some 8,600 came in the 1840s, another 21,200 in the fifties, and about 20,700 in the sixties. During these years the American merchant marine dominated the seas, but the Civil War all but drove the Stars and Stripes out of the shipping business. Confederate raiders destroyed about 110,000 tons of American shipping, and Yankee shipowners sold in panic over 700,000 tons to foreign buyers.[9]

It was more than the Civil War, however, that caused the decline in United States shipping. For some time the Americans had been growing complacent. Yankee-built sailing craft were superior in almost every respect, and the efforts of American shipbuilders were directed toward expanding their sailing fleets. In the meantime, the British had turned their attention to the development of oceangoing steamships. There were many advantages in so doing. The British empire had enormous coal deposits, the finest machine works, a government eager to grant generous subsidies to shipbuilders, and a chain of coaling stations dotting the globe to fuel far-cruising steamers. As a result, in the sixties few, if any, American-flag steamships were trading in the Atlantic.

In one year—1868—the pattern of Mormon emigration changed abruptly. The Saints abandoned sailing vessels for steamships, and from that time, except for one Pacific voyage under sail, their ocean crossings were all under steam. No longer did Mormon passengers endure weeks of tedious and often miserable conditions on the smaller and more vulnerable sailing craft. In one giant step the Mormon emigrants were caught up in the machine age.

Over the next twenty-two years some 41,000 Saints came to America in 157 voyages aboard 21 different steamships. Although the emigrant companies ranged up to 976 persons, the average size declined from a high of 424 in the sixties to 273 in the 1870s and 242 in the following decade. Of the 157 passages 149 were made from Liverpool to New York. These voyages took from 8 to 17 days, but averaged 11 days compared with the average of 38 days in sailing vessels. Pacific crossings were naturally longer —one taking 33 days from Sydney to San Francisco, still a substantially faster time than required under sail.

Even though accommodations were better on steamships, the emigrant in steerage lived a Spartan existence. He was supplied with "little more than a bunk, a blanket, and a deep soup bowl."[10] His quarters were usually cramped and lacking in privacy, although some masters catered particularly to the Mormons and provided separate facilities for them. In a voyage during July 1880, for example, the steamer *Wyoming* had a partitioned section for the 120 traveling Saints.[11] Whatever the conditions, steerage passengers could always draw some comfort from the knowledge that a steamship crossing was considerably faster than that of a sailing ship. Deaths were much less frequent, and sickness was not nearly as widespread as on sailing craft.

In brief, the changes in water transportation over this period were dramatic. At first the steam engine was considered an imperfect supplement to sail, but soon sail was considered merely an alternative power source to steam. Virtually all steamships during the years of the Mormon migration were rigged with sails mounted on two to four masts. Ocean liners combined the silhouettes of square-riggers, barks, brigs, or barkentines with their funnels. The steamships also evolved from paddle wheels to single propellers to twin screws, from wood to iron to steel hulls, from single to compound engines, and from oil lamps to electric lighting. Finally, sails were discarded, and the steamship ruled the oceans.

For the Mormons as a people times went from bad to worse. Denounced from the pulpit and in the press—particularly for the practice of polygamy—they found enemies on every side. Soon their religion became a political issue, and acrimonious attacks were made by eager office-seekers and in Congress itself. The shrill voices raised against the Saints carried across the water to Europe, but not all of the prejudice and persecution originated in America. Missionaries in foreign lands were harassed and even occasionally jailed. Government officials in Denmark, Norway, and Sweden warned their people against the Mormons, and Prussia eventually went so far as to banish the elders.[12]

In America, critics of Mormonism worked to create a negative public image of the overseas converts. The immigrants were pictured as ignorant, base-born, and simple—as gleanings from the slums and fields of the Old World. Opposition to the foreigners also was prevalent among the non-Mormon element in Utah. However, while the local Gentiles greeted the Europeans with suspicion and hostility, the Utah Mormons welcomed them with brass bands, singing, and flags waving.[13]

The first open break with the United States government came in 1857 and 1858, when federal troops were sent to Utah. Fortunately, wiser heads realized the folly of this action, and bloodshed was avoided. Yet during this period missionaries were recalled, and proselyting in Europe lost momentum for a time.

Then came the Civil War. While the nation fought for its survival, the Mormon Church enjoyed a respite from attack. The Saints concentrated on securing and building Zion at home. Missionaries also returned to Europe and intensified their efforts to win new converts. As a result, the decade of the sixties was the high-water mark of Mormon emigration, with more than 24,000 Saints emigrating to America in those years.

After the Civil War the anti-Mormon campaign aimed to abolish polygamy through legislation, and one bill after another was introduced in Congress. The Cragin Bill of 1867, for example, would have denied polygamists a trial by jury. The Cullom Bill of 1869 would have placed Utah under almost the complete control of the federal government, and the Ashley Bill proposed that same year would have dismembered Utah and divided it among adjoining territories. In 1874 the Poland Act passed both houses and was signed into law, giving federal judges jurisdiction over civil and criminal cases and considerable latitude in selection of jurors. Two additional laws were passed—the Edmunds Act and Edmunds-Tucker Act —which were to have even greater impact on the church, polygamy, and immigration.[14]

In 1882 Congress legislated the Edmunds Act, which made "cohabitation" a punishable offense, disqualified polygamist voters, established a commission to regulate elections, and brought federal marshals into Utah for its enforcement. These marshals and their deputies pursued polygamists relentlessly, and the "underground" period of Mormon history began.

The Edmunds-Tucker Act was even harsher, however. Passed in 1887, this act dissolved the Perpetual Emigrating Fund, dissolved the church corporation as a legal entity, confiscated church-owned property, and abolished women's suffrage and other political rights. If this law was designed to destroy the Mormon Church, it nearly succeeded. The Saints were now on the defensive and engaged in their most crucial battle for survival.[15]

The anti-Mormon crusade also made it increasingly unpleasant for overseas converts arriving at New York. Entry through Castle Garden had been routine. Now port officials sought to exclude incoming Mormons as paupers. In July 1886 the 426 Saints from the steamer *Nevada* "were subjected to the most rigid questioning and examination by the officers at Castle Garden."[16] The superintendent detained 25 emigrants, including four families from Iceland, because they had no more than $25. The Mormon agent had to argue that he would provide them with railroad tickets to Utah, where there was no likelihood that they would become public charges.[17]

Six weeks later 45 of the 301 Saints from the steamship *Wyoming* were also detained. Commissioner Edward Stephenson finally allowed all to continue, except a woman and three children who were sent back to England.[18] However, it was necessary for Judge Andrews of the New York Supreme Court to issue a writ of habeas corpus for the release of the others.[19]

These obstructing tactics of the immigration officials persisted into 1890, despite repeated protests by the church. Finally a special commission appointed by the United States Treasury Department conducted an investigation of Mormon immigration. After visiting the Guion Line's offices and church headquarters in Liverpool and examining the records, this body declared that it had obtained "full information, and concluded the accusations against the Mormons respecting emigration from Europe were without foundation."[20]

It was soon evident that the Edmunds-Tucker Act was accomplishing its purpose. The full legal weight of the federal government was directed against plural marriage. United States marshals were hunting down and arresting polygamists, and the leadership of the Mormon Church was driven underground. Church property had been escheated, and carpetbaggers were moving into the resulting economic and political vacuum. Thus, with its temporal power seriously crippled, with the specter of bankruptcy clouding its future, and with its leadership increasingly powerless, the Mormon Church finally bowed to the inevitable. On the morning of October 6, 1890, the Church of Jesus Christ of Latter-day Saints approved in its general conference the "Manifesto"—an official declaration that the practice of polygamy was thereafter prohibited.

At this time Mormon emigration reached a turning point. There were many reasons for the decrease in the flow of converts from overseas. No doubt the dissolution of the Perpetual Emigrating Fund was a factor, although many Saints had paid their own way to Utah and received no aid from this financing mechanism. No doubt also the mounting secular pressures on the church diverted energy from proselyting to more critical activities. Furthermore, the heavy exodus of converts over the years had so weakened the foreign missions that it was difficult for missionaries to rebuild local organizations, particularly since the strongest and most dedicated were the members most likely to emigrate.[21]

There were also indications of a change in emphasis regarding the gathering. In 1890 George Q. Cannon of the First Presidency said, according to the *New York Times*, "Our converts are made abroad by missionaries just like those of any other Church, but instead of inducing them to come to this country, we really urge our missionaries to dissuade them in any way they can. It is not to our advantage to have any come who are not thoroughly grounded in the faith."[22] It would be some years before this new policy was fully applied, but eventually the concept of Zion was broadened to include those Saints in foreign lands.

Whatever other reasons contributed to the changing pattern of emigration, the important fact is that it did change. The era of large companies of Saints braving the seas and rivers passed into history. The curtain fell on a compelling drama staged in a setting of wind and wave, a drama of ships and Saints.

Appendixes

APPENDIX 1
Emigrant Companies

Vessel	Rig	Registry	Tons	Master	No. LDS Pass.	Port	Departure Date	Port	Arrival Date	Passage Days	Company Leader
Britannia	Ship	U.S.	630	E. Cook	41	Liv.	6- 6-40	N.Y.	7-20-40	44	J. Moon
North America	Ship	U.S.	611	A. Lowber	201	Liv.	9- 8-40	N.Y.	10-12-40	34	T. Turley
Isaac Newton	Ship	U.S.	600	L. Spaulding	50*	Liv.	10-15-40	N.O.	12- 2-40	48	S. Mulliner
Sheffield	Ship	U.S.	590	R. Porter	235	Liv.	2- 7-41	N.O.	3-30-41	51	H. Clark
Caroline	Bark	Br.	330	R. Turner	?	—	- -41	—	- -41		T. Clark
Echo	Ship	U.S.	668	A. Wood	109	Liv.	2-16-41	N.O.	4-16-41	59	D. Browett
Alesto	Ship	U.S.	420	H. Whiting	54	Liv.	3-17-41	N.O.	5-16-41	60	T. Smith
Rochester	Ship	U.S.	714	P. Woodhouse	130	Liv.	4-21-41	N.Y.	5-20-41	29	B. Young
Harmony	Ship	Br.	832	J. Jamison	50	Bristol	5-10-41	Quebec	7-12-41	63	T. Kingston
Caroline	Bark	Br.	330	R. Turner	100*	Bristol	8- 8-41	Quebec	10-22-41	75	T. Richardson
Tyrian	Ship	U.S.	511	D. Jackson	207	Liv.	9-21-41	N.O.	11- 9-41	49	J. Fielding
Chaos	Ship	U.S.	771	L. Pratt	170	Liv.	11- 8-41	N.O.	1-14-42	67	P. Melling
Tremont	Ship	U.S.	368	J. Gillespie	143	Liv.	1-12-42	N.O.	3-10-42	57	—
Hope	Ship	U.S.	881	F. Soule	270	Liv.	2- 5-42	N.O.	4- 1-42	55	J. Burnham
John Cumming	Ship	U.S.	721	G. Thayer	200*	Liv.	2-20-42	N.O.	4-26-42	65	—
Hanover	Ship	U.S.	577	J. Drummond	200*	Liv.	3-12-42	N.O.	5- 2-42	51	A. Fielding
Sidney	Ship	U.S.	450	R. Cowen	180	Liv.	9-17-42	N.O.	11-11-42	55	L. Richards
Medford	Ship	U.S.	545	U. Wilber	214	Liv.	9-25-42	N.O.	11-13-42	49	O. Hyde
Henry	Ship	U.S.	395	B. Pierce	157	Liv.	9-29-42	N.O.	11-10-42*	42	J. Snyder
Emerald	Ship	Br.	642	W. Leighton	250	Liv.	10-29-42	N.O.	1- 5-43*	68	P. Pratt
Swanton	Ship	U.S.	677	S. Davenport	212	Liv.	1-16-43	N.O.	3-16-43	59	L. Snow
Yorkshire	Bark	Br.	658	W. Bache	83	Liv.	3- 8-43	N.O.	5-10-43	63	T. Bullock
Claiborne	Ship	U.S.	663	J. Burgess	106	Liv.	3-21-43	N.O.	5-13-43	53	—
Metoka	Ship	U.S.	775	J. McLaren	280	Liv.	9- 5-43	N.O.	10-27-43	52	—
Champion	Bark	Br.	795	J. Cochrane	91	Liv.	10-21-43	N.O.	12- 6-43	46	—

Fanny	Bark	U.S.	529	T. Patterson	210	Liv.	1-23-44	N.O.	3- 7-44	44	W. Kay
Isaac Allerton	Ship	U.S.	595	T. Torrey	60	Liv.	2- 6-44	N.O.	3-22-44*	45	—
Swanton	Ship	U.S.	677	S. Davenport	81	Liv.	2-11-44	N.O.	4- 5-44	54	—
Glasgow	Ship	U.S.	594	J. Lambert	150	Liv.	3- 5-44	N.O.	4-13-44	39	H. Clark
Norfolk	Ship	U.S.	548	D. Elliot	143	Liv.	9-19-44	N.O.	11-11-44	53	—
Palmyra	Ship	U.S.	612	Barstow	200*	Liv.	1-17-45	N.O.	3-11-45	53	A. Fielding
Parthenon	Ship	U.S.	536	S. Woodbury	10*	Liv.	3-30-45	N.O.	5-12-45	43	—
Oregon	Ship	U.S.	649	J. Borland	125*	Liv.	9- 1-45	N.O.	10-28-45	57	—
Liverpool	Ship	U.S.	623	S. Davenport	45	Liv.	1-16-46	N.O.	3-25-46	68	H. Clark
Brooklyn	Ship	U.S.	445	A. Richardson	235	N.Y.	2- 4-46	S.F.	7-31-46	177	S. Brannan
Montezuma	Ship	U.S.	924	A. Lowber	10*	Liv.	8-15-46	N.Y.	9-17-46	33	—
America	Ship	U.S.	1137	Trussell	50*	Liv.	2- 1-47	N.O.	3-10-47	37	J. Taylor
Empire	Ship	U.S.	1049	J. Russell	24	Liv.	7- 6-47	N.Y.	8-10-47	35	L. Scovil
Carnatic	Bark	Br.	654	W. McKenzie	120	Liv.	2-20-48	N.O.	4-19-48	59	F. Richards
Sailor Prince	Ship	Br.	950	A. McKechnie	80	Liv.	3- 9-48	N.O.	4-28-48	50	M. Martin
Erin's Queen	Ship	Br.	821	H. Campbell	232	Liv.	9- 7-48	N.O.	10-28-48	51	S. Carter
Sailor Prince	Ship	Br.	950	A. McKechnie	311	Liv.	9-24-48	N.O.	11-20-48	57	L. Butler
Lord Sandon	Bark	Br.	678	G. Welsh	11	Liv.	12-30-48*	N.O.	2-17-49	49	—
Zetland	Ship	Br.	1283	H. Brown	358	Liv.	1-29-49	N.O.	4- 2-49	63	O. Spencer
Ashland	Ship	U.S.	422	W. Harding	187	Liv.	2- 6-49	N.O.	4-18-49	71	J. Johnson
Henry Ware	Ship	U.S.	540	E. Nason	225	Liv.	2- 7-49	N.O.	4- 8-49	60	R. Martin
Buena Vista	Ship	U.S.	547	E. Linnell	249	Liv.	2-25-49	N.O.	4-19-49	53	D. Jones
Hartley	Ship	U.S.	469	S. Cammett	220	Liv.	3- 5-49	N.O.	4-28-49	54	W. Hulme
Emblem	Ship	U.S.	610	W. Cammett	100*	Liv.	3-12-49	N.O.	5 -4-49	53	R. Deans
James Pennell	Ship	U.S.	571	J. Fullerton	236	Liv.	9- 2-49	N.O.	10-22-49	50	T. Clark
Berlin	Ship	U.S.	613	A. Smith	253	Liv.	9- 5-49	N.O.	10-22-49	47	J. Brown
Zetland	Ship	Br.	1283	H. Brown	250*	Liv.	11-10-49	N.O.	12-24-49	44	S. Hawkins
Argo	Ship	Br.	999	C. Mills	402	Liv.	1-10-50	N.O.	3 -8-50	57	J. Clinton
Josiah Bradlee	Ship	U.S.	648	C. Mansfield	263	Liv.	2-18-50	N.O.	4-18-50	59	T. Day
Hartley	Ship	U.S.	469	C. Morrill	109	Liv.	3- 2-50	N.O.	5- 2-50	61	D. Cook

*Asterisked items are estimates.

Vessel	Rig	Registry	Tons	Master	No. LDS Pass.	Departure Port	Departure Date	Port	Arrival Date	Passage Days	Company Leader
North Atlantic	Ship	U.S.	799	H. Cook	357	Liv.	9- 4-50	N.O.	11- 1-50	58	D. Sudworth
James Pennell	Ship	U.S.	571	J. Fullerton	254	Liv.	10- 2-50	N.O.	11-22-50	51	C. Layton
Joseph Badger	Ship	U.S.	891	T. Skolfield	227	Liv.	10-17-50	N.O.	11-22-50	36	J. Morris
Ellen	Ship	Br.	893	A. Phillips	466	Liv.	1- 8-51	N.O.	3-14-51	65	J. Cummings
George W. Bourne	Ship	U.S.	663	W. Williams	281	Liv.	1-22-51	N.O.	3-20-51	57	W. Gibson
Ellen Maria	Ship	U.S.	768	A. Whitmore	378	Liv.	2- 2-51	N.O.	4- 6-51	63	G. Watt
Olympus	Ship	U.S.	744	H. Wilson	245	Liv.	3- 4-51	N.O.	4-27-51	54	W. Howell
Kennebec	Ship	U.S.	926	J. Smith	333	Liv.	1-10-52	N.O.	3-14-52	64	J. Higbee
Ellen Maria	Ship	U.S.	768	A. Whitmore	369	Liv.	2-10-52	N.O.	4- 5-52	55	I. Haight
Niagara	Stmr.	Br.	1825	J. Stone	20*	Liv.	3- 6-52	Boston	3-19-52	13	J. Taylor
Rockaway	Ship	U.S.	815	G. Preble	30	Liv.	3- 6-52	N.O.	4-25-52	50	E. Morris
Italy	Ship	U.S.	749	J. Reed	28	Liv.	3-11-52	N.O.	5-10-52	60	O. Monster
Forest Monarch	Ship	Br.	977	E. Brewer	297	Liv.	1-16-53	N.O.	3-16-53	59	J. Forsgren
Ellen Maria	Ship	U.S.	768	A. Whitmore	332	Liv.	1-17-53	N.O.	3- 6-53	48	M. Clawson
Golconda	Ship	Br.	1124	G. Kerr	321	Liv.	1-23-53	N.O.	3-26-53	62	J. Gates
Jersey	Ship	U.S.	849	J. Day	314	Liv.	2- 5-53	N.O.	3-21-53	44	G. Halliday
Elvira Owen	Ship	U.S.	874	C. Owen	345	Liv.	2-15-53	N.O.	3-31-53	44	J. Young
International	Ship	U.S.	1003	D. Brown	425	Liv.	2-28-53	N.O.	4-23-53	54	C. Arthur
Falcon	Ship	U.S.	813	Wade	324	Liv.	3-26-53	N.O.	5-18-53	53	C. Bagnall
Camillus	Ship	U.S.	717	C. Day	228	Liv.	4- 6-53	N.O.	6- 7-53	62	C. Bolton
Envelope	Bark	Br.	402	Smith	30*	Sydney	4- 6-53	S.F.	7- 8-53	94	C. Wandell
R. K. Page	Ship	U.S.	995	W. Strickland	17	Liv.	9- 1-53	N.O.	10-28-53	57	Bender
Jessie Munn	Ship	Br.	875	J. Duckitt	335	Liv.	1- 3-54	N.O.	2-20-54	48	C. Larsen
Benjamin Adams	Ship	U.S.	1170	J. Drummond	384	Liv.	1-28-54	N.O.	3-22-54	53	H. Olsen
Golconda	Ship	Br.	1124	G. Kerr	464	Liv.	2- 4-54	N.O.	3-18-54	42	D. Curtis
Windermere	Ship	U.S.	1108	J. Fairfield	477	Liv.	2-22-54	N.O.	4-24-54	61	D. Garn
Old England	Ship	U.S.	917	J. Barstow	45	Liv.	3- 5-54	N.O.	4-26-54	52	J. Angus
John M. Wood	Ship	U.S.	1146	R. Hartley	397	Liv.	3-12-54	N.O.	5- 2-54	51	R. Campbell

Ship	Rig	Flag	Tons	Master	Pass.	From	Date	To	Date	No.	Agent
Julia Ann	Bark	U.S.	372	C. Davis	63	Newcastle	3-22-54	S. Pedro	6-12-54	83	W. Hyde
Germanicus	Ship	U.S.	1167	A. Fales	220	Liv.	4- 4-54	N.O.	6-12-54	69	R. Cook
Marshfield	Ship	U.S.	999	J. Torrey	366	Liv.	4- 8-54	N.O.	5-29-54	51	W. Taylor
Martha Whitmore	Ship	U.S.	649	P. Whitmore	10*	Liv.*	-54	N.O.*	-54	—	—
Clara Wheeler	Ship	U.S.	996	J. Nelson	29	Liv.	4-24-54	N.O.	7- 3-54	70	
Clara Wheeler	Ship	U.S.	996	J. Nelson	422	Liv.	11-24-54	N.O.	1-11-55	48	H. Phelps
Rockaway	Ship	U.S.	815	S. Goodwin	24	Liv.	1- 6-55	N.O.	2-26-55	51	S. Glasgow
James Nesmith	Ship	U.S.	991	H. Mills	440	Liv.	1- 7-55	N.O.	2-23-55	47	P. Hansen
Neva	Ship	U.S.	849	T. Brown	13	Liv.	1-9-55	N.O.	2-22-55	44	T. Jackson
Charles Buck	Ship	U.S.	1424	W. Smalley	403	Liv.	1-17-55	N.O.	3-14-55	56	R. Ballantyne
Isaac Jeanes	Ship	U.S.	843	W. Chipman	16	Liv.	2- 3-55	Phil.	3- 5-55	30	G. Riser
Siddons	Ship	U.S.	895	J. Taylor	430	Liv.	2-27-55	Phil.	4-20-55	52	J. Fullmer
Juventa	Ship	U.S.	1187	A. Watts	573	Liv.	3-31-55	Phil.	5- 5-55	35	W. Glover
Chimborazo	Ship	U.S.	916	P. Vesper	431	Liv.	4-17-55	Phil.	5-22-55	35	E. Stevenson
S. Curling	Ship	U.S.	1468	S. Curling	581	Liv.	4-22-55	N.Y.	5-22-55	30	I. Barlow
Tarquinia	Brig	U.S.	210	E. Meyers	72	Melb.	4-27-55	Hono.	7- 5-55a	69	B. Frost
William Stetson	Ship	U.S.	1147	J. Jordan	293	Liv.	4-26-55	N.Y.	5-27-55	31	A. Smethurst
Frank Johnson	Ship	U.S.	529	A. Lothrop	10*	Calcutta	5-29-55	S.F.	9-18-55	112	—
Cynosure	Ship	U.S.	1258	J. Pray	159	Liv.	7-29-55	N.Y.	9- 5-55	38	G. Seager
Julia Ann	Bark	U.S.	372	B. Pond	28	Sydney	9- 7-55	Wrecked, Scilly Is.	10-3-55		J. Penfield
Emerald Isle	Ship	U.S.	1736	G. Cornish	350	Liv.	11-30-55	N.Y.	12-29-55	29	P. Merrill
John J. Boyd	Ship	U.S.	1311	T. Austin	512	Liv.	12-12-55	N.Y.	2-16-56	66	K. Peterson
Caravan	Ship	U.S.	1363	W. Sands	457	Liv.	2-14-56	N.Y.	3-27-56	41	D. Tyler
Enoch Train	Ship	U.S.	1618	H. Rich	534	Liv.	3-23-56	Boston	5- 1-56	39	J. Ferguson
S. Curling	Ship	U.S.	1468	S. Curling	707	Liv.	4-19-56	Boston	5-23-56	34	D. Jones
Thornton	Ship	U.S.	1422	C. Collins	764	Liv.	5- 4-56	N.Y.	6-14-56	41	J. Willie
G. W. Kendall	Brig	U.S.	183	H. Wilson	9	Tahiti	5- 5-56	S.F.	6-27-56	52	Anderson
Horizon	Ship	U.S.	1775	W. Reed	856	Liv.	5-25-56	Boston	6-20-56	26	E. Martin
Jenny Ford	Bark	U.S.	397	S. Sargent	20*	Sydney	5-28-56	S. Pedro	8-15-56	80	A. Farnham
Wellfleet	Ship	U.S.	1353	I. Westcott	146	Liv.	5-31-56	Boston	7-13-56	43	J. Aubrey
Lucy Thompson	Ship	U.S.	1500	C. Pendleton	14	Liv.	7- 5-56	N.Y.	8- 8-56	34	J. Thompson

Vessel	Rig	Registry	Tons	Master	No. LDS Pass.	Departure Port	Departure Date	Arrival Port	Arrival Date	Passage Days	Company Leader
Columbia	Ship	U.S.	1051	C. Hutchinsen	223	Liv.	11-18-56	N.Y.	1- 1-57	44	J. Williams
Escort	Ship	U.S.	1454	E. A. Hussey	10*	Calcutta	12-10-56	N.Y.	3- 3-57	83	M. McCune
George Washington	Ship	U.S.	1534	J. Comings	817	Liv.	3-28-57	Boston	4-20-57	23	J. Park
Westmoreland	Ship	U.S.	999	R. Decan	544	Liv.	4-25-57	Phil.	5-31-57	36	M. Cowley
Tuscarora	Ship	U.S.	1232	R. Dunlevy	547	Liv.	5-30-57	Phil.	7- 3-57	34	R. Harper
Lucas	Ship	U.S.	350	J. Daggett	69	Sydney	6-27-57	S. Pedro	10- 8-57*	103	W. Wall
Wyoming	Ship	U.S.	891	E. Brooks	36	Liv.	7-18-57	Phil.	9- 3-57	47	C. Harmon
Underwriter	Ship	U.S.	1168	J. Roberts	25	Liv.	1-21-58	N.Y.	3-11-58	49	H. Harriman
Empire (II)	Ship	U.S.	1273	E. Coombs	64	Liv.	2-19-58	N.Y.	3-19-58	28	J. Hobson
John Bright	Ship	U.S.	1444	R. Cutting	89	Liv.	3-22-58	N.Y.	4-23-58	32	I. Iversen
Milwaukie	Ship	U.S.	738	C. Rhoades	10*	Melb.	12-28-58	S.F.	3-18-59	81	—
Gemsbok	Bark	U.S.	622	S. Mayo	5	P. Eliz.	1-22-59	Boston	3-18-59	55	—
Alacrity	Bark	Br.	317	J. Cooper	28	P. Eliz.	3- 9-59	Boston	5-19-59	71	J. Humphreys
William Tapscott	Ship	U.S.	1525	J. Bell	725	Liv.	4-11-59	N.Y.	5-14-59	33	R. Neslen
Antarctic	Ship	U.S.	1116	G. Stouffer	30	Liv.	7-10-59	N.Y.	8-21-59	42	J. Chaplow
Emerald Isle	Ship	U.S.	1736	G. Cornish	54	Liv.	8-20-59	N.Y.	10- 1-59	42	H. Hug
Underwriter	Ship	U.S.	1168	J. Roberts	594	Liv.	3-30-60	N.Y.	5- 1-60	32	J. Ross
William Tapscott	Ship	U.S.	1525	J. Bell	730	Liv.	5-11-60	N.Y.	6-15-60	35	A. Calkin
Manchester	Ship	U.S.	1067	G. Trask	379	Liv.	4-16-61	N.Y.	5-14-61	28	C. Spencer
Underwriter	Ship	U.S.	1168	J. Roberts	624	Liv.	4-23-61	N.Y.	5-22-61	29	M. Andrus
Monarch of the Sea	Ship	U.S.	1979	W. Gardner	955	Liv.	5-16-61	N.Y.	6-19-61	34	J. Woodward
Humboldt	Ship	Ger.	789	H. Boysen	323	Hamb.	4- 9-62	N.Y.	5-20-62	41	H. Hansen
Franklin	Ship	Ger.	708	R. Murray	413	Hamb.	4-15-62	N.Y.	5-29-62	44	C. Madsen
Electric	Ship	Ger.	1274	H. Johansen	336	Hamb.	4-18-62	N.Y.	6- 5-62	48	S. Christoffersen
Athena	Ship	Ger.	1058	D. Schilling	484	Hamb.	4-21-62	N.Y.	6- 7-62	47	O. Liljenquist
John J. Boyd	Ship	U.S.	1311	J. Thomas	702	Liv.	4-23-62	N.Y.	6- 1-62	39	J. Brown
Manchester	Ship	U.S.	1067	G. Trask	376	Liv.	5- 6-62	N.Y.	6-12-62	37	J. McAllister
William Tapscott	Ship	U.S.	1525	J. Bell	807	Liv.	5-14-62	N.Y.	6-25-62	42	W. Gibson

Ship	Rig	Nat.	Tons	Captain	Pass.	From	Date	To	Arrived	Days	Leader
Windermere	Ship	U.S.	1108	D. Harding	110	Le Havre	5-15-62	N.Y.	7- 8-62	54	S. Ballif
Antarctic	Ship	U.S.	1116	G. Stouffer	38	Liv.	5-18-62	N.Y.	6-27-62	40	W. Moody
Rowena	Bark	Br.	319	L. Stapleton	15	Pt. Eliz.	3-14-63	N.Y.	5-22-63	69	R. Grant
Henry Ellis	Ship	Br.	401	J. Phillips	32	Pt. Eliz.	3-31-63	N.Y.	5-28-63	58	Stock & Zyderlaam
John J. Boyd	Ship	U.S.	1311	J. Thomas	767	Liv.	4-30-63	N.Y.	5-29-63	29	W. Cluff
B. S. Kimball	Ship	U.S.	1192	H. Dearborn	657	Liv.	5- 8-63	N.Y.	6-15-63	38	H. Lund
Consignment	Ship	U.S.	1132	Tukey	38	Liv.	5- 8-63	N.Y.	6-20-63	43	A. Christensen
Antarctic	Ship	U.S.	1116	G. Stouffer	486	Liv.	5-23-63	N.Y.	7-10-63	48	J. Needham
Cynosure	Ship	U.S.ᵇ	1258	Drum or Wms.	775	Liv.	5-30-63	N.Y.	7-19-63	50	D. Stuart
Amazon	Ship	U.S.	1771	H. Hovey	895	London	6- 4-63	N.Y.	7-18-63	44	W. Bramall
Echo	Bark	Br.	256	E. Dent	9	Pt. Eliz.	4- 5-64	Boston	6-12-64	68	J. Talbot
Susan Pardew	Bark	Br.	378	J. Davis	18	Pt. Eliz.	4-10-64	Boston	6-11-64	62	W. Fotheringham
Monarch of the Sea	Ship	U.S.	1979	R. Kirkaldy	974	Liv.	4-28-64	N.Y.	6- 3-64	36	J. Smith
General McClellan	Ship	U.S.	1518	G. Trask	802	Liv.	5-21-64	N.Y.	6-23-64	33	T. Jeremy
Hudson	Ship	U.S.	1618	I. Pratt	863	London	6- 3-64	N.Y.	7-19-64	46	J. Kay
Mexicana	Brig	Br.	276	W. Sanderson	47	Pt. Eliz.	4-12-65	N.Y.	6-18-65	67	M. Atwood
Belle Wood	Ship	Br.	1399	T. W. Freeman	636	Liv.	4-29-65	N.Y.	5-31-65	32	W. Shearman
B. S. Kimball	Ship	U.S.	1192	H. Dearborn	558	Hamburg	5- 8-65	N.Y.	6-14-65	37	A. Winberg
David Hoadley	Ship	U.S.	981	I. Hayden	24	Liv.	5-10-65	N.Y.	6-19-65	40	W. Underwood
Bridgewater	Ship	U.S.	1479	C. Sisson	7	Liv.	6- 7-65	N.Y.	7-14-65	37	—
Albert	Bark	Br.	319	P. Holkins	15*	Melb.	10-17-65	S.F.	1-26-66	100	J. Spencer
John Bright	Ship	U.S.	1444	W. Dawson	747	Liv.	4-30-66	N.Y.	6- 6-66	37	C. Gillet
Caroline	Ship	Br.	1133	S. Adey	389	London	5- 5-66	N.Y.	6-11-66	37	S. Hill
American Congress	Ship	U.S.	863	Woodman	350	London	5-23-66	N.Y.	7- 4-66	42	J. Nicholson
Kenilworth	Ship	Br.	987	J. Brown	684	Hamburg	5-25-66	N.Y.	7-16-66	52	S. Sprague
Arkwright	Ship	U.S.	1266	D. Caulkins	450	Liv.	5-30-66	N.Y.	7- 6-66	37	J. Wixom
Cornelius Grinnell	Ship	U.S.	1118	A. Spencer	26	London	5-30-66	N.Y.	7-11-66	42	R. Harrison
Cavour	Bark	Nor.	369	A. Foyen	201	Hamburg	6- 1-66	N.Y.	7-31-66	60	N. Nielsen
Humboldt	Ship	Ger.	789	H. Boysen	328	Hamburg	6- 2-66	N.Y.	7-18-66	46	G. Brown
St. Mark	Ship	U.S.	1448	W. Howard	104	Liv.	6- 6-66	N.Y.	7-24-66	48	A. Stevens
Hudson	Ship	U.S.	1618	I. Pratt	20	London	6- 1-67	N.Y.	7-19-67	48	—

154

Vessel	Rig	Registry	Tons	Master	No. LDS Pass.	Departure Port	Departure Date	Arrival Port	Arrival Date	Passage Days	Company Leader
Manhattan	Stmr.	Br.	2869	J. Williams	482	Liv.	6-21-67	N.Y.	7- 4-67	13	A. Hill
John Bright	Ship	U.S.	1444	J. Howart	720	Liv.	6- 4-68	N.Y.	7-13-68	39	J. McGaw
Emerald Isle	Ship	U.S.	1736	Gillespie	876	Liv.	6-20-68	N.Y.	8-14-68	55	H. Hals
Constitution	Ship	Br.	1327	W. Hatten	457	Liv.	6-24-68	N.Y.	8 -5-68	42	H. Cluff
Minnesota	Stmr.	Br.	2869	J. Price	534	Liv.	6-30-68	N.Y.	7-12-68	12	J. Parry
Colorado	Stmr.	Br.	2927	R. Cutting	600	Liv.	7-14-68	N.Y.	7-28-68	14	W. Preston
Minnesota	Stmr.	Br.	2869	J. Price	338	Liv.	6- 2-69	N.Y.	6-14-69	12	E. Morris
Minnesota	Stmr.	Br.	2869	J. Price	598	Liv.	7-15-69	N.Y.	7-28-69	13	O. Olsen
Colorado	Stmr.	Br.	2927	J. Williams	365	Liv.	7-28-69	N.Y.	8-10-69	13	J. Pace
Minnesota	Stmr.	Br.	2869	J. Price	443	Liv.	8-25-69	N.Y.	9- 6-69	12	M. Ensign
Manhattan	Stmr.	Br.	2869	W. Forsyth	242	Liv.	9-22-69	N.Y.	10- 7-69	15	J. Lawson
Minnesota	Stmr.	Br.	2869	J. Price	294	Liv.	10- 6-69	N.Y.	10-17-69	11	J. Needham
Colorado	Stmr.	Br.	2927	J. Williams	16	Liv.	10-20-69	N.Y.	11- 1-69	12	C. Wilden
Colorado	Stmr.	Br.	2927	T. F. Freeman	20	Liv.	6-28-70	N.Y.	7-12-70	14	—
Manhattan	Stmr.	Br.	2869	W. Forsyth	269	Liv.	7-13-70	N.Y.	7-26-70	13	K. Maeser
Minnesota	Stmr.	Br.	2869	E. Whineray	357	Liv.	7-20-70	N.Y.	8- 1-70	12	J. Smith
Idaho	Stmr.	Br.	3132	J. Price	186	Liv.	9- 7-70	N.Y.	9-21-70	14	F. Hyde
Nevada	Stmr.	Br.	3125	W. Green	26	Liv.	9-14-70	N.Y.	9-26-70	12	B. Walter (?)
Manhattan	Stmr.	Br.	2869	W. Forsyth	59	Liv.	11-16-70	N.Y.	12- 2-70	16	R. Thompson
Wyoming	Stmr.	Br.	3238	E. Whineray	10	Liv.	5-10-71	N.Y.	5-22-71	12	J. Parry
Wonga Wonga	Stmr.	Br.	1002	Stewart	20*	Sydney	6- 4-71	S.F.	7- 8-71	33	E. Kearsley
Wyoming	Stmr.	Br.	3238	E. Whineray	248	Liv.	6-21-71	N.Y.	7- 3-71	12	G. Lake
Minnesota	Stmr.	Br.	2869	T. W. Freeman	397	Liv.	6-28-71	N.Y.	7-13-71	15	W. Cluff
Colorado	Stmr.	Br.	2927	T. F. Freeman	146	Liv.	7-12-71	N.Y.	7-25-71	13	H. Park
Nevada	Stmr.	Br.	3125	W. Forsyth	93	Liv.	7-26-71	N.Y.	8- 7-71	12	L. Smith
Minnesota	Stmr.	Br.	2869	T. W. Freeman	60	Liv.	8- 9-71	N.Y.	8-21-71	12	W. Douglass
Nevada	Stmr.	Br.	3125	W. Forsyth	263	Liv.	9- 6-71	N.Y.	9-18-71	12	J. Hart
Nevada	Stmr.	Br.	3125	W. Forsyth	300	Liv.	10-18-71	N.Y.	11- 1-71	14	G. Peterson

Nevada^c	Stmr.	U.S.	2143	J. Blethen	11	Auck.	12-30-71	S.F.*	1-30-72*	30*	—
Manhattan	Stmr.	Br.	2869	J. Price	221	Liv.	6-12-72	N.Y.	6-26-72	14	D. Brinton
Nevada	Stmr.	Br.	3125	W. Forsyth	426	Liv.	6-26-72	N.Y.	7- 8-72	12	E. Peterson
Wisconsin	Stmr.	Br.	3238	T. W. Freeman	179	Liv.	7-31-72	N.Y.	8-12-72	12	G. Ward
Minnesota	Stmr.	Br.	2869	J. Morgan	602	Liv.	9- 4-72	N.Y.	9-17-72	13	G. Wilkins
Minnesota	Stmr.	Br.	2869	J. Morgan	203	Liv.	10-16-72	N.Y.	10-29-72	13	T. Dobson
Manhattan	Stmr.	Br.	2869	J. Price	35	Liv.	12- 4-72	N.Y.	12-21-72	17	D. Kennedy
Nevada	Stmr.	Br.	3125	W. Forsyth	246	Liv.	6- 4-73	N.Y.	6-16-73	12	C. Wilcken
Wisconsin	Stmr.	Br.	3238	T. W. Freeman	976	Liv.	7- 2-73	N.Y.	7-15-73	13	D. Calder
Nevada	Stmr.	Br.	3125	W. Forsyth	283	Liv.	7-10-73	N.Y.	7-23-73	13	E. Box
Wyoming	Stmr.	Br.	3238	J. Morgan	510	Liv.	9- 3-73	N.Y.	9-20-73	17	J. Fairbanks
Idaho	Stmr.	Br.	3132	J. Moore	522	Liv.	10-22-73	N.Y.	11- 4-73	13	J. Hart
Nevada	Stmr.	Br.	3125	J. Price	155	Liv.	5- 6-74	N.Y.	5-21-74	15	L. Herrick
Nevada	Stmr.	Br.	3125	J. Price	243	Liv.	6-11-74	N.Y.	6-23-74	12	J. Birch
Idaho	Stmr.	Br.	3132	W. Forsyth	806	Liv.	6-24-74	N.Y.	7- 6-74	12	P. Carstensen
Minnesota	Stmr.	Br.	2869	T. Jones	81	Liv.	7- 8-74	N.Y.	7-21-74	13	J. Keller
Wyoming	Stmr.	Br.	3238	C. Beddoe	558	Liv.	9- 2-74	N.Y.	9-14-74	12	J. Graham
Wyoming	Stmr.	Br.	3238	C. Beddoe	155	Liv.	10-14-74	N.Y.	10-26-74	12	W. Fife
Wyoming	Stmr.	Br.	3238	J. Guard	176	Liv.	5-12-75	N.Y.	5-24-75	12	H. Gowans
Wisconsin	Stmr.	Br.	3238	W. Forsyth	167	Liv.	6-16-75	N.Y.	6-27-75	11	R. Burton
Idaho	Stmr.	Br.	3132	C. Beddoe	765	Liv.	6-30-75	N.Y.	7-14-75	14	C. Larsen
Wyoming	Stmr.	Br.	3238	J. Price	300	Liv.	9-15-75	N.Y.	9-27-75	12	R. Morris
Dakota	Stmr.	Br.	4332	W. Forsyth	120	Liv.	10-14-75	N.Y.	10-24-75	10	B. Eardley
Montana	Stmr.	Br.	4321	C. Beddoe	20	Liv.	1-19-76	N.Y.	1-31-76	12	I. Coombs
Nevada	Stmr.	Br.	3125	T. W. Freeman	131	Liv.	5-24-76	N.Y.	6- 5-76	12	J. Woodhouse
Idaho	Stmr.	Br.	3132	C. Beddoe	628	Liv.	6-28-76	N.Y.	7-10-76	12	N. Flygare
Nevada	Stmr.	Br.	3125	J. Guard	5	Liv.	8-23-76	N.Y.	9- 5-76	13	W. Binder
Wyoming	Stmr.	Br.	3238	T. Jones	322	Liv.	9-13-76	N.Y.	9-23-76	10	P. Barton
Wyoming	Stmr.	Br.	3238	T. Jones	118	Liv.	10-25-76	N.Y.	11- 4-76	10	D. Udall
Wyoming	Stmr.	Br.	3238	T. Jones	186	Liv.	6-13-77	N.Y.	6-23-77	10	J. Rowberry
Wisconsin	Stmr.	Br.	3238	W. Forsyth	714	Liv.	6-27-77	N.Y.	7- 7-77	10	

Vessel	Rig	Registry	Tons	Master	No. LDS Pass.	Departure Port	Departure Date	Arrival Port	Arrival Date	Passage Days	Company Leader
Wisconsin	Stmr.	Br.	3238	W. Forsyth	482	Liv.	9-19-77	N.Y.	9-30-77	11	H. Park
Idaho	Stmr.	Br.	3132	W. Holmes	150	Liv.	10-17-77	N.Y.	10-29-77	12	W. Paxman
Nevada	Stmr.	Br.	3125	W. Gadd	354	Liv.	5-25-78	N.Y.	6- 5-78	11	T. Judd
Montana	Stmr.	Br.	4321	C. Beddoe	221	Liv.	6-15-78	N.Y.	6-25-78	10	T. Brandley
Nevada	Stmr.	Br.	3125	T. Owen	569	Liv.	6-29-78	N.Y.	7-10-78	11	J. Cook
Wyoming	Stmr.	Br.	3238	H. Gadd	609	Liv.	9-14-78	N.Y.	9-25-78	11	H. Naisbitt
Nevada	Stmr.	Br.	3125	C. Rigby	20*	Liv.	9-21-78	N.Y.	10- 3-78	12	J. Christensen
Wyoming	Stmr.	Br.	3238	H. Gadd	145	Liv.	10-19-78	N.Y.	10-29-78	10	A. Miner
Malay	Bkt.	U.S.	812	Love	10*	Sydney	2-21-79	S.F.	5-10-79*	77	—
Wyoming	Stmr.	Br.	3238	H. Gadd	170	Liv.	4-19-79	N.Y.	4-30-79	11	C. Nibley
Wyoming	Stmr.	Br.	3238	T. Jones	162	Liv.	5-24-79	N.Y.	6- 3-79	10	A. McDonald
Wyoming	Stmr.	Br.	3238	G. Murray	622	Liv.	6-28-79	N.Y.	7- 8-79	10	W. Williams
Wyoming	Stmr.	Br.	3238	G. Murray	336	Liv.	9- 6-79	N.Y.	9-16-79	10	N. Flygare
Arizona	Stmr.	Br.	5147	T. Jones	224	Liv.	10-18-79	N.Y.	10-27-79	9	W. Bramall
Wyoming	Stmr.	Br.	3238	C. Rigby	120	Liv.	4-10-80	N.Y.	4-21-80	11	J. Bunting
Wisconsin	Stmr.	Br.	3238	E. Bentley	332	Liv.	6- 5-80	N.Y.	6-15-80	10	J. Jones
Australia	Stmr.	Br.	1938	Cargill	25*	Sydney	6-17-80	S.F.	7-15-80	27	F. May
Wisconsin	Stmr.	Br.	3238	E. Bentley	727	Liv.	7-10-80	N.Y.	7-21-80	11	N. Rasmussen
Nevada	Stmr.	Br.	3125	T. Jones	338	Liv.	9- 4-80	N.Y.	9-14-80	10	J. Rider
Wisconsin	Stmr.	Br.	3238	E. Bentley	258	Liv.	10-23-80	N.Y.	11- 2-80	10	J. Nicholson
Wyoming	Stmr.	Br.	3238	C. Rigby	186	Liv.	4-16-81	N.Y.	4-26-81	10	D. Dunbar
City of Sydney	Stmr.	U.S.	3016	Dearborn	27	Auck.	4-26-81	S.F.	5-17-81	20	G. Batt
Wyoming	Stmr.	Br.	3238	C. Rigby	297	Liv.	5-21-81	N.Y.	6- 1-81	11	J. Matthews
Nevada	Stmr.	Br.	3125	T. Jones	11	Liv.	6-11-81	N.Y.	6-23-81	12	R. Runolfsen
Wyoming	Stmr.	Br.	3238	C. Rigby	775	Liv.	6-25-81	N.Y.	7- 7-81	12	S. Roskelly
Nevada	Stmr.	Br.	3125	T. Jones	22	Liv.	7-16-81	N.Y.	7-27-81	11	J. Eyvindson
Wyoming	Stmr.	Br.	3238	C. Rigby	644	Liv.	9- 3-81	N.Y.	9-13-81	10	J. Finlayson
Wisconsin	Stmr.	Br.	3238	E. Bentley	396	Liv.	10-22-81	N.Y.	11- 2-81	11	L. Martineau

Nevada	Stmr.	Br.	3617ᵈ	T. Jones	342	Liv.	4-12-82	N.Y.	4-24-82	12	J. Donaldson
Nevada	Stmr.	Br.	3617	T. Jones	392	Liv.	5-17-82	N.Y.	5-27-82	10	W. Webb
Nevada	Stmr.	Br.	3617	A. Bremmer	933	Liv.	6-21-82	N.Y.	7- 2-82	11	R. Irvine
Arizona	Stmr.	Br.	5147	S. Brooks	18	Liv.	7-22-82	N.Y.	8- 1-82	10	—
Wyoming	Stmr.	Br.	3238	J. Douglas	662	Liv.	9- 2-82	N.Y.	9-12-82	10	W. Cooper
Abyssinia	Stmr.	Br.	3253	E. Bentley	416	Liv.	10-21-82	N.Y.	11- 3-82	13	G. Stringfellow
Nevada	Stmr.	Br.	3617	A. Bremmer	352	Liv.	4-11-83	N.Y.	4-22-83	11	D. McKay
Nevada	Stmr.	Br.	3617	A. Bremmer	427	Liv.	5-16-83	N.Y.	5-27-83	11	B. Rich
Nevada	Stmr.	Br.	3617	A. Bremmer	697	Liv.	6-20-83	N.Y.	7- 1-83	11	H. Magleby
Wisconsin	Stmr.	Br.	3238	C. Rigby	18	Liv.	7-14-83	N.Y.	7-25-83	11	J. Sutton
Nevada	Stmr.	Br.	3617	A. Bremmer	682	Liv.	8-29-83	N.Y.	9-10-83	12	P. Goss
Wisconsin	Stmr.	Br.	3238	C. Rigby	369	Liv.	10-27-83	N.Y.	11- 7-83	11	J. Pickett
Nevada	Stmr.	Br.	3617	A. Bremmer	319	Liv.	4- 9-84	N.Y.	4-19-84	10	C. Fjeldsted
Arizona	Stmr.	Br.	5147	S. Brooks	287	Liv.	5-17-84	N.Y.	5-26-84	9	E. Williams
Arizona	Stmr.	Br.	5147	S. Brooks	531	Liv.	6-14-84	N.Y.	6-23-84	9	E. Nye
Nevada	Stmr.	Br.	3617	A. Bremmer	14	Liv.	8- 2-84	N.Y.	8-13-84	11	H. Attley
Wyoming	Stmr.	Br.	3238	J. Douglas	496	Liv.	8-30-84	N.Y.	9- 9-84	10	B. Bennett
City of Berlin	Stmr.	Br.	5491	S. Kennedy	93	Liv.	10-23-84	N.Y.	11- 2-84	10	C. Ek
Arizona	Stmr.	Br.	5147	S. Brooks	163	Liv.	11- 1-84	N.Y.	11-11-84	10	J. Smith
Wisconsin	Stmr.	Br.	3238	E. Bentley	187	Liv.	4-11-85	N.Y.	4-22-85	11	L. Lund
Wisconsin	Stmr.	Br.	3238	E. Bentley	274	Liv.	5-16-85	N.Y.	5-27-85	11	N. Hodges
Wisconsin	Stmr.	Br.	3238	E. Bentley	541	Liv.	6-20-85	N.Y.	7- 1-85	11	J. Hansen
Wisconsin	Stmr.	Br.	3238	E. Bentley	329	Liv.	8-29-85	N.Y.	9- 8-85	10	J. Thornley
Nevada	Stmr.	Br.	3617	J. Douglas	313	Liv.	10-24-85	N.Y.	11- 4-85	11	A. Lund
Nevada	Stmr.	Br.	3617	J. Douglas	179	Liv.	4-17-86	N.Y.	4-27-86	10	E. Woolley
Arizona	Stmr.	Br.	5147	S. Brooks	15	Liv.	5-15-86	N.Y.	5-24-86	9	I. Gadd
Nevada	Stmr.	Br.	3617	J. Douglas	279	Liv.	5-22-86	N.Y.	6- 1-86	10	M. Pratt
Nevada	Stmr.	Br.	3617	J. Douglas	426	Liv.	6-26-86	N.Y.	7- 7-86	11	C. Olsen
Alaska	Stmr.	Br.	6392	G. Murray	23	Liv.	7-10-86	N.Y.	7-18-86	8	—
Wyoming	Stmr.	Br.	3238	C. Rigby	301	Liv.	8-21-86	N.Y.	8-31-86	10	D. Kunz
British King	Stmr.	Br.	3412	J. Kelly	307	Liv.	10-13-86	Phil.	10-27-86	14	J. Greenwood

Vessel	Rig	Registry	Tons	Master	No. LDS Pass.	Departure Port	Departure Date	Arrival Port	Arrival Date	Passage Days	Company Leader
Nevada	Stmr.	Br.	3617	J. Cushing	194	Liv.	4-16-87	N.Y.	4-28-87	12	D. Callister
Nevada	Stmr.	Br.	3617	J. Cushing	187	Liv.	5-21-87	N.Y.	6- 1-87	11	E. Davis
Wyoming	Stmr.	Br.	3238	C. Rigby	159	Liv.	6- 4-87	N.Y.	6-15-87	11	J. Nielsen
Wisconsin	Stmr.	Br.	3238	E. Bentley	646	Liv.	6-18-87	N.Y.	6-28-87	10	Q. Nichols
Wisconsin	Stmr.	Br.	3238	E. Bentley	406	Liv.	8-27-87	N.Y.	9- 8-87	12	J. Hart
Nevada	Stmr.	Br.	3617	J. Douglas	278	Liv.	10- 8-87	N.Y.	10-18-87	10	J. Wells
Alameda	Stmr.	U.S.	3158	Morse	25*	Sydney	4-18-88*	S.F.	5-13-88	24	J. Blythe
Wisconsin	Stmr.	Br.	3238	E. Bentley	74	Liv.	4-28-88	N.Y.	5-10-88	12	F. Bramwell
Wyoming	Stmr.	Br.	3238	C. Rigby	137	Liv.	5-19-88	N.Y.	5-29-88	10	W. Wood
Arizona	Stmr.	Br.	5147	S. Brooks	11	Liv.	5-26-88	N.Y.	6- 4-88	9	—
Wisconsin	Stmr.	Br.	3238	E. Bentley	210	Liv.	6- 2-88	N.Y.	6-13-88	11	C. Dorius
Nevada	Stmr.	Br.	3617	J. Cushing	70	Liv.	6- 9-88	N.Y.	6-20-88	11	J. Stucki
Wyoming	Stmr.	Br.	3238	C. Rigby	118	Liv.	6-23-88	N.Y.	7- 2-88	9	H. Bowring
Wisconsin	Stmr.	Br.	3238	E. Bentley	7	Liv.	7- 7-88	N.Y.	7-18-88	11	R. Lindsay
Wyoming	Stmr.	Br.	3238	C. Rigby	136	Liv.	7-28-88	N.Y.	8- 8-88	11	H. Christiansen
Wisconsin	Stmr.	Br.	3238	E. Bentley	155	Liv.	8-11-88	N.Y.	8-24-88	13	L. Naylor
Wyoming	Stmr.	Br.	3238	C. Rigby	83	Liv.	9- 1-88	N.Y.	9-11-88	10	A. Johnson
Wisconsin	Stmr.	Br.	3238	T. Dunn	145	Liv.	9-15-88	N.Y.	9-25-88	10	W. Phillips
Wyoming	Stmr.	Br.	3238	C. Rigby	123	Liv.	10- 6-88	N.Y.	10-15-88	9	N. Lindelof
Wisconsin	Stmr.	Br.	3238	J. Morrall	125	Liv.	10-20-88	N.Y.	10-30-88	10	J. Quigley
Arizona	Stmr.	Br.	5147	S. Brooks	7	Liv.	11-17-88	N.Y.	11-27-88	10	L. Moench
?e					26	Amst.	4-27-89	N.Y.	—		M. Krumperman
Arizona	Stmr.	Br.	5147	S. Brooks	—	Liv.	5-11-89	N.Y.	5-20-89	9	H. Barrell
Wisconsin	Stmr.	Br.	3238	J. Morrall	142	Liv.	5-18-89	N.Y.	5-29-89	11	M. Dailey
Wyoming	Stmr.	Br.	3238	C. Rigby	359	Liv.	6- 8-89	N.Y.	6-19-89	11	L. Anderson
Wisconsin	Stmr.	Br.	3238	J. Morrall	172	Liv.	6-22-89	N.Y.	7- 3-89	11	J. Volker
Wyoming	Stmr.	Br.	3238	C. Rigby	191	Liv.	8-17-89	N.Y.	8-27-89	10	J. Weibye
Wisconsin	Stmr.	Br.	3238	J. Morrall	172	Liv.	8-31-89	N.Y.	9-11-89	11	W. Payne

Ship	Type	Flag	Tons	Master	No.	Port	Date	Port	Date		Agent
Wyoming	Stmr.	Br.	3238	C. Rigby	113	Liv.	9-21-89	N.Y.	10- 1-89	10	R. Larsen
Wisconsin	Stmr.	Br.	3238	J. Morrall	142	Liv.	10- 5-89	N.Y.	10-17-89	12	E. Bennett
Wyoming	Stmr.	Br.	3238	C. Rigby	161	Liv.	10-26-89	N.Y.	11- 6-89	11	A. Skanchy
Nevada	Stmr.	Br.	3617	J. Cushing	11	Liv.	11-16-89	N.Y.	11-27-89	11	R. Morse
Wisconsin	Stmr.	Br.	3238	J. Morrall	52	Liv.	4-19-90	N.Y.	4-29-90	10	O. Worthington
Wyoming	Stmr.	Br.	3238	C. Rigby	156	Liv.	5- 3-90	N.Y.	5-13-90	10	A. Anderson
Wisconsin	Stmr.	Br.	3238	J. Morrall	122	Liv.	5-24-90	N.Y.	6- 4-90	11	J. Hayes
Wyoming	Stmr.	Br.	3238	C. Rigby	304	Liv.	6- 7-90	N.Y.	6-19-90	12	E. Willardson
Wisconsin	Stmr.	Br.	3238	J. Morrall	113	Liv.	6-28-90	N.Y.	7-10-90	12	A. Maw
Wisconsin	Stmr.	Br.	3238	J. Morrall	86	Liv.	8- 2-90	N.Y.	8-13-90	11	L. Jordan
Wyoming	Stmr.	Br.	3238	C. Rigby	128	Liv.	8-16-90	N.Y.	8-26-90	10	J. Ostlund
Wisconsin	Stmr.	Br.	3238	J. Morrall	116	Liv.	9- 6-90	N.Y.	9-17-90	11	J. Stucki
Wyoming	Stmr.	Br.	3238	C. Rigby	197	Liv.	9-20-90	N.Y.	10- 1-90	11	J. Jensen
Wisconsin	Stmr.	Br.	3238	J. Morrall	—	Liv.	10-11-90	N.Y.	10-23-90	12	J. Golightly

*Asterisked items are estimates.

ªVoyage incomplete.

ᵇAbout this time the *Cynosure* was sold to British owners.

ᶜThe *Nevada* was a side-wheel steamship that traded in the Pacific.

ᵈRegistered tonnage revised.

ᵉPossibly the Dutch ship *Edam*, which arrived in New York from Amsterdam on May 13, 1889; passenger list is almost illegible.

APPENDIX 2
Emigrant Vessel Types and Tonnages, By Decade

	1840–1849	1850–1859	1860–1869	1870–1879	1880–1890	TOTAL
Sailing Vessel Passages	52	77	46	1		176
Ships	45	69	40			154
Barks	7	6	5			18
Brigs		2	1			3
Barkentine				1		1
(Repeat Voyages)						(32)
Vessels Utilized						144
Steamship Passages		1	10	59	87	157
(Repeat Voyages)						(136)
Steamships Utilized						21
Registered Tonnages						
Sailing Vessels						
Smallest	330	183	256			183
Largest	1,283	1,775	1,979	812[a]		1,979
Median	618	977	1,151			875
Average	663	977	1,137			924
Steamships						
Smallest			2,869	1,002	1,938	1,002
Largest		1,825[b]	2,927	5,147	6,392	6,392
Median			2,869	3,132	3,238	3,238
Average			2,886	3,157	3,537	3,341
Total Vessels Utilized						165

[a]Bkt. *Malay*   [b]SS *Niagara*

APPENDIX 3

Building Locations for Emigrant Vessels, Alphabetically, With Years and Builders

Sailing Vessels

UNITED STATES

Connecticut   3
> East Haven (1)
>> Schooner *Emma Packer*[a] (1849)
> Mystic (2)
>> Sp. *Belle Wood* (1854, G. Greenman)
>> Sp. *Electric* (1853, Irons & Grinnell)

Maine   62
> Bath (18)
>> Sp. *Benjamin Adams* (1852, W. and J. Drummond)
>> Sp. *Caravan* (1855, Willard Hall)
>> Sp. *Cynosure* (1853, Johnson Rideout)
>> Sp. *Elvira Owen* (1852, R. Morse & Sons)
>> Sp. *Emerald Isle* (1853, Trufant & Drummond)
>> Sp. *Falcon* (1849, G. F. & J. Patten)
>> Sp. *Glasgow* (1837, B. Patten)
>> Sp. *Hanover* (1838, Levi Houghton)
>> Sp. *Italy* (1846, John Larrabee)
>> Sp. *Kennebec* (1850, Johnson Rideout)
>> Sp. *Liverpool* (1837, Johnson Rideout)
>> Sp. *Marshfield* (1852, John Larrabee)
>> Sp. *Old England* (1849, Amos L. Allen)
>> Sp. *Rockaway* (1848, Thomas Harward)
>> Sp. *Sheffield* (1836, G. F. & J. Patten)
>> Sp. *Swanton* (1838, Benjamin Pattee)
>> Sp. *Tremont* (1830, Johnson Rideout)
>> Sp. *William Tapscott* (1852, W. Drummond)
> Biddeford (1)
>> Sp. *John M. Wood* (1853, Edmund Perkins)
> Boothbay (1)
>> Bg. *G. W. Kendall* (1846)
> Brunswick (3)
>> Sp. *Consignment* (1856, Samuel Dunning)
>> Sp. *James Pennell* (1848, Charles S. Pennell)
>> Sp. *Joseph Badger* (1848, Samuel Dunning)
> Cape Elizabeth (1)
>> Sp. *Frank Johnson* (1850, B. W. Pickett)

[a]In 1855 this schooner rescued survivors of the wrecked bark *Julia Ann* and transported them to the Society Islands.

Damariscotta (1)
    Sp. *Lucy Thompson* (1852)
East Machias (1)
    Bk. *Jenny Ford* (1854)
Ellsworth (1)
    Sp. *Horizon* (1854)
Frankfort (1)
    Sp. *Caroline*, ex *Arey* (1856, Williams & Arey)
Georgetown (1)
    Sp. *Escort* (1854, Joseph Berry)
Kennebunk (9)
    Sp. *Ashland* (1843)
    Sp. *Camillus* (1848)
    Sp. *George W. Bourne* (1849, G. W. Bourne)
    Sp. *Hartley* (1845, Jacob Perkins)
    Sp. *Henry Ware* (1847)
    Sp. *International* (1851, Clement Littlefield)
    Sp. *Neva* (1852, Stephen Ward)
    Sp. *Olympus* (1849, Jacob Perkins)
    Sp. *Windermere* (1851)
Newcastle (3)
    Sp. *American Congress* (1849)
    Sp. *Brooklyn* (1834, Joseph Russell)
    Sp. *Oregon* (1839)
Portland (2)
    Sp. *Emblem* (1839, Samuel Dyer)
    Sp. *Tyrian* (1841, Samuel Dyer)
Richmond (3)
    Sp. *Ellen Maria* (1849, Harrison Springer)
    Sp. *Martha Whitmore* (1854, Dexter Jack)
    Sp. *R. K. Page* (1852, T. J. Southard)
Robbinston (2)
    Bk. *Julia Ann* (1850)
    Sp. *Metoka* (1841)
Rockland (3)
    Sp. *B. S. Kimball* (1857)
    Sp. *Charles Buck* (1853)
    Sp. *Franklin*, ex *Yankee Ranger* (1854)
Thomaston (8)
    Sp. *Empire* (1,273 tons,[b] built 1851)
    Sp. *General McClellan* (1862, Samuel Watts)
    Sp. *Germanicus* (1853)
    Sp. *James Nesmith* (1850)

---

[b]Tonnage given to distinguish vessels of the same name.

Sp. *Juventa* (1853)
Sp. *S. Curling* (1854)
Sp. *St. Mark* (1860)
Sp. *William Stetson* (1851)
Warren (2)
  Sp. *Chimborazo* (1851)
  Sp. *Claiborne* (1840)
Yarmouth (1)
  Sp. *Milwaukie* (1853, Joseph Seabury)

MASSACHUSETTS   25
Boston (8)
  Sp. *Antarctic* (1850, Donald McKay)
  Bk. *Gemsbok* (1857, R. E. Jackson)
  Sp. *Chaos* (1840, Gad Leavitt)
  Sp. *Cornelius Grinnell* (1850, Donald McKay)
  Sp. *Enoch Train* (1854, Paul Curtis)
  Bk. *Fanny* (1836, Herman Holmes)
  Sp. *Norfolk* (1841, Nathaniel Cushing)
  Sp. *Wellfleet* (1853, Paul Curtis)
Chelsea (2)
  Sp. *George Washington* (1851, John A. Taylor)
  Bkt. *Malay* (1852)
Duxbury (1)
  Sp. *Hope* (1841, Samuel N. Cushing)
Haverhill (1)
  Sp. *Henry* (1831)
Kingston (1)
  Sp. *Alesto* (1840, Lysander Bartlett)
Marblehead (1)
  Bk. *Albert* (1862, Joshua Brown)
Medford (8)
  Sp. *Berlin* (1842, S. Lapham)
  Sp. *Clara Wheeler* (1850, John Taylor)
  Sp. *Josiah Bradlee* (1849, John Taylor)
  Sp. *Lucas* (1839, Paul Curtis)
  Sp. *Medford* (1837, F. Waterman & H. Elwell)
  Sp. *Palmyra* (1838, Sprague G. James)
  Sp. *Parthenon* (1836, B. & J. D. Curtis)
  Sp. *Sidney* (1836, Waterman & Jewell)
Newburyport (2)
  Sp. *Kenilworth*, ex *American Volant* (1853, John Currier)
  Sp. *Buena Vista* (1848)
Quincy (1)
  Sp. *Athena* (1857, G. Thomas)

NEW HAMPSHIRE   9

    Portsmouth (9)
       Sp. *America* (1846, Raynes & Tobey)
       Sp. *Arkwright* (1855)
       Sp. *Empire* (1,049 tons,[b] built 1844, Raynes & Fernald)
       Sp. *Isaac Allerton* (1838, George Raynes)
       Sp. *Isaac Newton* (1836, George Raynes)
       Sp. *Jersey* (1848, George Raynes)
       Sp. *John Cumming* (1836, George Raynes)
       Sp. *Manchester* (1860, Tobey & Littlefield)
       Sp. *North Atlantic* (1849, George Raynes)

NEW JERSEY   1

    Perth Amboy (1)
       Bg. *Tarquinia* (1840, David Crowell)

NEW YORK   16

    New York City (16)
       Sp. *Amazon* (1854, J. Westervelt)
       Sp. *Britannia* (1826, Brown & Bell)
       Sp. *Columbia* (1846, W. H. Webb)
       Sp. *Constitution* (1846, Brown & Bell)
       Sp. *David Hoadley* (1853)
       Sp. *Echo* (1834, C. Bergh & Co.)
       Sp. *Hudson* (1863, J. A. & D. D. Westervelt)
       Sp. *John Bright* (1854, W. H. Webb)
       Sp. *John J. Boyd* (1855, S. G. Bogart)
       Sp. *Monarch of the Sea* (1854, Roosevelt Coyce & Co.)
       Sp. *Montezuma* (1843, Webb & Allen)
       Sp. *North America* (1831, Brown & Bell)
       Sp. *Rochester* (1839, Brown & Bell)
       Sp. *Siddons* (1837, Brown & Bell)
       Sp. *Thornton* (1854, W. H. Webb)
       Sp. *Underwriter* (1850, Westervelt & Mackey)

PENNSYLVANIA   5

    Philadelphia (5)
       Sp. *Bridgewater* (1855, W. Cramp & Sons)
       Sp. *Isaac Jeanes* ('1854, William Cramp)
       Sp. *Tuscarora* (1848)
       Sp. *Westmoreland* (1851)
       Sp. *Wyoming* (1845)

UNITED STATES TOTAL   121

ALL OTHER COUNTRIES

CANADA   15

 New Brunswick (10)
  Sp. *Ellen* (1850)
  Sp. *Emerald* (1839)
  Sp. *Jessie Munn* (1852 at Bathurst)
  Sp. *Harmony* (1840, W. & I. Olive at Carleton)
  Bk. *Envelope* (1850 at Miramichi)
  Sp. *Sailor Prince* (1847 at Miramichi)
  Bk. *Yorkshire* (1842, McIntosh at Richibucto)
  Sp. *Argo* (1847, John Clark at Saint John)
  Sp. *Golconda* (1852, at Saint John)
  Bk. *Carnatic* (1846, H. Mahoney at Saint Martins)
 Nova Scotia (1)
  Sp. *Zetland* (1848, James Malcolm at St. Mary's Bay)
 Quebec (4)
  Sp. *Erin's Queen* (1846)
  Sp. *Forest Monarch* (1851, Pierre Valin)
  Bk. *Lord Sandon* (1841)
  Bk. *Champion* (1838 at New Richmond)

UNITED KINGDOM   7

 England (6)
  Bk. *Susan Pardew* (1863)
  Bg. *Unity* (1848 at Whitehaven)[c]
  Bk. *Alacrity* (1856 at Sunderland)
  Bk. *Echo* (1859, Peverall & Co. at Sunderland)
  Sp. *Henry Ellis* (1852, Bennet at Sunderland)
  Bk. *Rowena* (1861 at Sunderland)
 Scotland (1)
  Bg. *Mexicana* (1856 at Dundee)

GERMANY   1

 Lubeck (1)
  Sp. *Humboldt* (1853, Meyer)

INDIA   1

 Cochin (1)
  Bk. *Caroline* (1825)

NORWAY   1

 Langesund (1)
  Bk. *Cavour* (1865)

ALL OTHER COUNTRIES TOTAL   25

Total Sailing Vessels   **146**

---

[c]In 1855 this brig, owned by three Mormons, brought a small company of Saints from Port Elizabeth, South Africa, to London, from where they emigrated to America.

Steamships

UNITED STATES

New York   1
    Brooklyn (1)
        SS *Nevada* (2,143 tons,[b] built 1867, J. Simonson)

Pennsylvania   2
    Chester (2)
        SS *City of Sydney* (1875, J. Roach & Son)
        SS *Alameda* (1883, Cramp & Sons)

United States Total   3

UNITED KINGDOM

England   9
    Jarrow-on-Tyne (3)
        SS *Colorado* (1867, Palmer's Shipbuilding & Iron Co.)
        SS *Dakota* (1872, Palmer's Shipbuilding & Iron Co.)
        SS *Wisconsin* (1870, Palmer's Shipbuilding & Iron Co.)
    Newcastle (6)
        SS *Idaho* (1869, Palmer's Shipbuilding & Iron Co.)
        SS *Manhattan* (1866, Palmer's Shipbuilding & Iron Co.)
        SS *Minnesota* (1866, Palmer's Shipbuilding & Iron Co.)
        SS *Montana* (1872, Palmer's Shipbuilding & Iron Co.)
        SS *Nevada* (3,125 tons,[b] 1868, Palmer's Shipbuilding
          & Iron Co.)
        SS *Wyoming* (1870, Palmer's Shipbuilding & Iron Co.)

Ireland   1
    Belfast (1)
        SS *British King* (1881, Harland & Wolff, Ltd.)

Scotland   7
    Glasgow (5)
        SS *Abyssinia* (1870, J. & G. Thomson, Ltd.)
        SS *Alaska* (1881, John Elder)
        SS *Arizona* (1879, John Elder)
        SS *Australia* (1875)
        SS *Wonga Wonga* (1854)
    Greenock (2)
        SS *City of Berlin* (1875, Caird & Co.)
        SS *Niagara* (1848, Robert Steele & Co.)

United Kingdom Total   17
Unidentified   1

Total Steamships   21

TOTAL SAILING AND STEAM VESSELS[d]   167

---

[d]This figure excludes North Sea ships and American river craft.

APPENDIX 4

Twenty-four Voyages with Highest Death Toll at Sea, In Descending Order

Vessel	Year	No. of Deaths	Vessel	Year	No. of Deaths
Ship *John J. Boyd*	1856	"Many"	Ship *Brooklyn*	1846	10
Ship *Franklin*	1862	48	Ship *Electric*	1862	10[a]
Ship *Athena*	1862	38	Ship *Ellen*	1851	10
Ship *Emerald Isle*	1868	37	Ship *Hudson*	1864	10[b]
Ship *Berlin*	1849	28	Ship *William Tapscott*	1860	10
Ship *B. S. Kimball*	1865	28	Ship *Windermere*	1854	10
Ship *Clara Wheeler*	1855	23	Ship *Forest Monarch*	1853	9
Ship *Humboldt*	1862	14	Ship *Monarch of the Sea*	1861	9
Ship *James Nesmith*	1855	13	Ship *Benjamin Adams*	1854	8
Ship *Jessie Munn*	1854	12	Ship *International*	1853	7
Ship *Kenilworth*	1866	12	Ship *North America*	1840	6
Ship *Antarctic*	1863	11	Ship *John M. Wood*	1854	6

SOURCE: Church Emigration record and mission records.
[a]Partial list; no doubt toll higher.
[b]One additional child died at Castle Garden.

APPENDIX 5
EMIGRANT VOYAGES, BY PORT, SIZE, AND DECADE

	1840–1849	1850–1859	1860–1869	1870–1879	1880–1890	TOTAL
Port of Embarkation						
Liverpool	48	66	35	57	83	289
Bristol	2					2
New York	1					1
Sydney (including Newcastle)		5		2	2	9
Melbourne		2	1			3
Auckland				1	1	2
Calcutta		2				2
Hamburg			8			8
Le Havre			1			1
Pt. Elizabeth (Algoa Bay)		2	5			7
London			6			6
Amsterdam					1	1
Other	1	1				2
	52	78	56	60	87	333
Port of Debarkation						
New Orleans	43	38				81
New York	5	16	53	57	83	214
Quebec	2					2
San Francisco	1	4	1	3	3	12
Boston		8	2			10
San Pedro		3				3
Philadelphia		7			1	8
Honolulu		1				1
Other	1	1				2
	52	78	56	60	87	333
NUMBER OF PASSENGERS*	8,600	21,200	24,600	16,500	20,700	91,600
Emigrant Companies—Size						
Smallest	10	5	7	5	7	5
Largest	358	856	974	976	933	976
Median	157	272	428	212	176	200
Average	157	266	424	273	242	271

*Includes estimated non-organized emigrants and returning missionaries.

APPENDIX 6
Passage Times, By Vessel Type, Route, and Decade

	1840–1849		1850–1859		1860–1869		1870–1879		1880–1890		TOTAL	
	Pass.	Days	Pass.	Days	Pass.	Days	Pass.	Days	Pass.	Days	Pass.	Days
SAILING VESSELS												
Liverpool–New Orleans	43		38								81	
Shortest		37		36								36
Longest		71		70								71
Median		53		54								53
Average		54		54								54
Liverpool–New York	5		15		25						45	
Shortest		29		28		28						28
Longest		44		66		55						66
Median		34		38		37						37
Average		35		39		38						38
Bristol–Quebec	2										2	
Shortest		63										63
Longest		75										75
Average		69										69
New York–San Francisco*	1	177									1	177
Liverpool–Boston			5								5	
Shortest				23								23
Longest				43								43
Median				34								34
Average				33								33
Liverpool–Philadelphia			7								7	
Shortest				30								30
Longest				52								52
Median				35								35
Average				38								38
Sydney–San Francisco			1	94			1	77			2	85
Unknown (*Caroline* 1841)	1										1	
Melbourne–San Francisco			1	81	1	100					2	91
Sydney–Scilly Islands (*Julia Ann* wreck)			1	26							1	26
Tahiti–San Francisco			1	52							1	52
Melbourne–Honolulu (Incomplete)			1	69							1	69
Calcutta–San Francisco			1	112							1	112
Calcutta–New York			1	83							1	83

	1840–1849 Pass.	1840–1849 Days	1850–1859 Pass.	1850–1859 Days	1860–1869 Pass.	1860–1869 Days	1870–1879 Pass.	1870–1879 Days	1880–1890 Pass.	1880–1890 Days	TOTAL Pass.	TOTAL Days
Sydney and Newcastle (Aust.)–San Pedro			3								3	
Shortest				80								80
Longest				103								103
Average				89								89
Port Elizabeth–Boston			2		2						4	
Shortest				55		62						55
Longest				71		68						71
Average				63		65						64
Hamburg–New York					8						8	
Shortest						37						37
Longest						60						60
Median						47						47
Average						47						47
Le Havre–New York					1	54					1	54
London–New York					6						6	
Shortest						37						37
Longest						48						48
Median						43						43
Average						43						43
Port Elizabeth–New York					3						3	
Shortest						58						58
Longest						69						69
Median						67						67
Average						65						65
STEAMSHIPS												
Liverpool–New York					10		57		82		149	
Shortest						11		9		8		8
Longest						15		17		13		17
Median						13		12		11		12
Average						13		12		11		11
Liverpool–Boston			1	13							1	13
Sydney–San Francisco							1		2		3	
Shortest								33		24		24
Longest										27		33
Auckland–San Francisco							1	30	1	20	2	25
Liverpool–Philadelphia									1	14	1	14
Amsterdam–New York									1	?	1	?
Total Passages	52		78		56		60		87		333	

*Voyage of ship *Brooklyn*.

APPENDIX 7

Steamboats Used by Mormon Emigrants

Steamboat	Year Built	Tons	Dimensions in Feet
Isaac Newton[a]	1846	1332	320.6 x 40 x 10.7
John Simonds	1852	1024	295 x 40.5 x 8
Uncle Sam	1848	903	271 x 37.7 x 9.2
Illinois[b]	1838	755	205 x 29 x 13
Grand Turk	1848	688	241 x 39.7 x 7.7
Illinois	1852	682	278.5 x 37 x 6.8
Atlantic	1848	667	241.7 x 36 x 8
Oceana	1854	607	240.5 x 37.8 x 7
L. M. Kennett	1852	598	272 x 34 x 6.7
Josiah Lawrence	1848	593	252.8 x 33.4 x 7.3
James Robb	1852	593	276.5 x 34 x 6.5
Mameluke	1848	570	236 x 36 x 7
Concordia	1847	499	224 x 31 x 7.5
Alex. Scott	1842	487	230 x 28 x 7.8
Michigan	1853	482	225 x 35 x 6.4
Iowa	1848	455	222.5 x 31 x 6.8
Colorado	1864	439	225 x 35 x 6.8
Amazon	1855	410	227 x 35.5 x 5.3
Clara	1851	351	200.5 x 32 x 5.8
West Wind	1860	350	208 x 33 x 5.3
Pride of the West	1845	321	199 x 28 x 6
Julia Chouteau	1842	319	176 x 27 x 7
Polar Star	1852	310	203 x 28.8 x 5.8
Omaha	1856	307	200 x 29 x 5.5
Golden State	1852	298	172 x 29 x 6.3
Equinox	1852	297	168 x 31 x 6
St. Mary	1855	295	204 x 34.3 x 4.4
Washington City[c]	1852	282	168 x 28.7 x 6.2
Robert Campbell	1849	269	190 x 26.7 x 5.5
El Paso	1850	260	174 x 26 x 6
Goddess of Liberty	1841	248	167 x 26 x 6
Statesman	1851	248	172 x 28 x 5.4
F. X. Aubrey[d]	1853	247	169 x 28 x 5.5
Ben Bolt	1853	228	167 x 29 x 5
Dacotah (Dahcota)	1849	223	— — —

[a]This vessel was used on the Hudson River.

[b]This vessel was used on Lake Erie.

[c]This vessel was used on the Ohio and upper Mississippi rivers. All other steamboats traveled the Mississippi and Missouri rivers primarily, although they might have occasionally made trips on the Ohio and other tributaries of the Mississippi-Missouri river system.

[d]The only stern-wheel paddle steamboat. All others listed were side-wheelers.

Steamboat	Year Built	Tons	Dimensions in Feet		
Saluda	1846	223	179	x 26	—
Sacramento	1848	221	175	x 25	x 5.2
Amaranth	1841	220	167	x 25	x 5.5
Mandan	1847	204	163	x 26.3	x 5
Saranak	1846	199	156	x 26	x 5.1
Dove	1842	168	147	x 24	x 5
Congress[a]	1825	168	127	x 22.8	x 6.8
Chautauque[a]	1839	162	123.7	x 18.2	x 7.5
St. Croix	1844	159	157	x 23	x 4.6
Highland Mary	1848	159	162.5	x 22.5	x 4.5
Louisa	1839	152	—	—	—
Galena	1841	135	136	x 22	x 4.8
Mustang	1848	129	123	x 23.7	x 4.8
Chieftain[c]	1830	116	115.6	x 18.3	x 5.3
William Penn[c]	1839	105	80	x 21	x 6
Ariel	1837	95	125	x 17.5	x 4.5
Nauvoo (Ex *Des Moines*)	1838	93	123	x 20.3	x 4.2
Maid of Iowa	1842	60	115	x 18.3	x 3

NOTE: Several steamboats have defied identification either because their names were incorrectly recorded or their registrations were lost or never filed. In April 1841, for example, emigrants from the ship *Sheffield* went from New Orleans to St. Louis aboard the *Aster*, for which no registration can be found. Saints from the ship *North America* traveled up the Erie Canal from Albany to Buffalo in October 1840 aboard the steamboat *Silver Arrow* and met some other Mormons from the steamboat *J. D. Hawks*. No registrations of these steamboats were on file in the National Archives, Washington, D.C.

APPENDIX 8
Number of Mormon Passengers Carried by Individual Steamship Lines, In Descending Order

Steamship Line	Number Voyages	Number Passengers
Guion Line (Britain)		
SS *Wyoming*	38	10,473
SS *Nevada*	35	9,600*
SS *Wisconsin*	33	8,900*
SS *Minnesota*	11	3,907
SS *Idaho*	6	3,057
SS *Manhattan*	6	1,308
SS *Arizona*	9	1,270*
SS *Colorado*	5	1,147
SS *Abyssinia*	1	416
SS *Montana*	2	241
SS *Dakota*	1	120
SS *Alaska*	1	23
		40,462
American Steamship Company (U.S.)		
SS *British King***	1	307
Inman Line (Britain)		
SS *City of Berlin*	1	93
Oceanic Steamship Company (U.S.)		
SS *Alameda*	1	25*
SS *Australia*	1	25*
Pacific Mail Steamship Company (U.S.)		
SS *City of Sydney*	1	27
Cunard Line (Britain)		
SS *Niagara*	1	20*
California, New Zealand & Australian Mail Steamship Co. (Britain)		
SS *Wonga Wonga*	1	20*
United States, New Zealand and Australia Mail Steamship Co. (U.S.)		
SS *Nevada* (U.S.)	1	11
Other (Unidentified)	1	26
Total	157	41,016

*Estimated
**Sailed under both British and American flags at different times.

APPENDIX 9
Total Mormon Passengers Carried by Individual Emigrant Vessels

Vessel	Voyages	Total Passengers	Vessel	Voyages	Total Passengers
SS *Wyoming*	38	10,473	SS *Arizona*	9	1,270*
SS *Nevada*	35	9,600*	Sp. *Underwriter*	3	1,243
SS *Wisconsin*	33	8,900*	Sp. *B. S. Kimball*	2	1,215
SS *Minnesota*	11	3,907	SS *Colorado*	5	1,147
SS *Idaho*	6	3,057	Sp. *Ellen Maria*	3	1,079
Sp. *William Tapscott*	3	2,262	Sp. *Cynosure*	2	934
Sp. *John J. Boyd*	3	1,981	Sp. *Amazon*	1	895
Sp. *Monarch of the Sea*	2	1,929	Sp. *Hudson*	2	883
Sp. *John Bright*	3	1,556	Sp. *Horizon*	1	856
SS *Manhattan*	6	1,308	Sp. *George Washington*	1	817
Sp. *S. Curling*	2	1,288	Sp. *General McClellan*	1	802
Sp. *Emerald Isle*	3	1,280			

*Estimated

APPENDIX 10
The Twenty-five Largest Mormon Emigrant Companies, In Descending Order

Vessel	Year	No.	Vessel	Year	No.
SS *Wisconsin*	1873	976	Sp. *Cynosure*	1863	775
Sp. *Monarch of the Sea*	1864	974	Sp. *John J. Boyd*	1863	767
Sp. *Monarch of the Sea*	1861	955	SS *Idaho*	1875	765
SS *Nevada*	1882	933	Sp. *Thornton*	1856	764
Sp. *Amazon*	1863	895	Sp. *John Bright*	1866	747
Sp. *Emerald Isle*	1868	876	Sp. *William Tapscott*	1860	730
Sp. *Hudson*	1864	863	SS *Wisconsin*	1880	727
Sp. *Horizon*	1856	856	Sp. *William Tapscott*	1859	725
Sp. *George Washington*	1857	817	Sp. *John Bright*	1868	720
Sp. *William Tapscott*	1862	807	SS *Wisconsin*	1877	714
SS *Idaho*	1874	806	Sp. *S. Curling*	1856	707
Sp. *General McClellan*	1864	802	Sp. *John J. Boyd*	1862	702
SS *Wyoming*	1881	775			

APPENDIX 11

SHIPMASTERS OF MORE THAN TWO MORMON EMIGRANT VOYAGES

Shipmaster/Vessel	Voyages per Vessel	Total Voyages
Charles Edward Rigby		23
SS *Wyoming*	20	
SS *Wisconsin*	2	
SS *Nevada*	1	
Edward Bentley		15
SS *Abyssinia*	1	
SS *Wisconsin*	14	
William Forsyth		14
SS *Idaho*	1	
SS *Manhattan*	3	
SS *Nevada*	6	
SS *Wisconsin*	3	
SS *Dakota*	1	
James Price		11
SS *Idaho*	1	
SS *Manhattan*	2	
SS *Minnesota*	5	
SS *Nevada*	2	
SS *Wyoming*	1	
John Preston Morrall		11
SS *Wisconsin*	11	
Thomas Jones		11
SS *Arizona*	1	
SS *Minnesota*	1	
SS *Nevada*	5	
SS *Wyoming*	4	
Samuel Brooks		8
SS *Arizona*	8	
Arthur Wellesley Bremmer		7
SS *Nevada*	7	
John Douglas		7
SS *Nevada*	5	
SS *Wyoming*	2	
Charles James Beddoe		6
SS *Idaho*	2	

Shipmaster/Vessel	Voyages per Vessel	Total Voyages
SS *Montana*	2	
SS *Wyoming*	2	
Thomas William Freeman		6
Sp. *Belle Wood*	1	
SS *Minnesota*	2	
SS *Nevada*	1	
SS *Wisconsin*	2	
John A. R. Cushing		4
SS *Nevada*	4	
Henry Gadd		4
SS *Nevada*	1	
SS *Wyoming*	3	
Stephen Davenport		3
Sp. *Swanton*	2	
Sp. *Liverpool*	1	
James Morgan		3
SS *Minnesota*	2	
SS *Wyoming*	1	
George Siddons Murray		3
SS *Alaska*	1	
SS *Wyoming*	2	
George C. Stouffer		3
Sp. *Antarctic*	3	
G. D. S. Trask		3
Sp. *Manchester*	2	
Sp. *General McClellan*	1	
Amherst Whitmore		3
Sp. *Ellen Maria*	3	
Edward Whineray		3
SS *Minnesota*	1	
SS *Wyoming*	2	
James A. Williams		3
SS *Colorado*	2	
SS *Manhattan*	1	

ABBREVIATIONS

CE Church Emigration

JH Journal History

MH Manuscript History
These documents are available in the Church of
Jesus Christ of Latter-day Saints, Historical Department,
Library-Archives Division, Salt Lake City, Utah.

NA National Archives, Washington, D.C.

♪Notes

Chapter One
A CALL ACROSS THE DEEP

NOTE: The reader may refer to the Bibliography for complete titles and bibliographical information. In this section short forms are used wherever possible.

1. Orson F. Whitney, *Life of Heber C. Kimball*, pp. 124–31, 213–14; Heber C. Kimball, *Journal*, pp. 13–15; John R. Spears, *Captain Nathaniel Brown Palmer*, pp. 154–63. See also Port of New York Documents, NA, crew list showing Captain Palmer as master of the *Garrick* on the July 1837 voyage. Accounts differ as to the exact hour of departure, but Kimball records ten o'clock. Kimball and Hyde had been ordained apostles in 1835, Richards would be ordained an apostle in 1840.

2. Matthias F. Cowley, *Wilford Woodruff*, p. 113.

3. Whitney, *Heber C. Kimball*, p. 285; *Manuscript History of Brigham Young*, reprinted from the *Millennial Star* by Elden J. Watson, pp. 68–69.

4. Joseph Smith, *History of the Church of Jesus Christ of Latter-day Saints*, IV, 384–88.

5. Orson Hyde, *A Sketch of the Travels and Ministry of Elder Orson Hyde*, p. 24.

6. Ibid., pp. 16–18.

7. Howard H. Barron, *Orson Hyde: Missionary, Apostle, Colonizer*, p. 135.

8. MH, French Polynesian Mission, CA. Noah Rogers' Journal, 1843 through November 6, 1845, CA. According to a letter from the Old Dartmouth Historical Society Whaling Museum, dated December 8, 1975, this voyage was almost a total failure. Captain Plaskett's drunkenness was no doubt a contributing cause. In April 1844 the master fell from aloft, injuring his head. The whaler put into Tahiti and was abandoned there by officers and crew. She was taken in charge by the American consul and sent home under J. Hogan Brown, the sailing master of the U.S. brig *Perry*. The *Timoleon* arrived in New Bedford July 12, 1845, with only 100 barrels of sperm oil. In his journal Noah Rogers mentions that Captain Plaskett was jailed in Papeete for threatening a Dr. Winslow, and French authorities ordered him to stay aboard his ship.

9. MH, French Polynesian Mission; Rogers, Journal. The *Artarevedre*'s name was also spelled *Artrovedre*, *Artrevida*, and *Artarvedre*. The Chief of Archives Service,

French Polynesia, in a letter to the author dated January 13, 1977, stated that the vessel was apparently the 40-ton two-masted schooner listed in an official bulletin; all registrations of ships were destroyed by a bombardment of Tahiti in 1914. The vessel, which another unofficial source listed at 25 tons, was used frequently by the missionaries and was skippered by Captain Sajat (also spelled Lajat and Sajot).

10. MH, French Polynesian Mission. Rogers, Journal.

11. Ibid. Andrew Jenson, *Latter-day Saint Biographical Encyclopedia*, IV, 377.

12. *Deseret News*, March 26, 1950.

13. Jenson, *Encyclopedia*, III, 699. See also Louis J. Rasmussen, *San Francisco Ship Passenger Lists*, IV, 15.

14. Cowley, *Wilford Woodruff*, p. 235. Daughters of Utah Pioneers, *Lessons for April 1969*, pp. 440–41, includes a letter of Wilford Woodruff to an unknown addressee dated March 2, 1846.

15. Eliza R. Snow, *Biography and Family Record of Lorenzo Snow*, p. 114; JH, CA, May 4, 27, 1850. Registration Document, December 12, 1849, NA, records that Hoodless was master and part owner. He was master in 1850 when the vessel was affiliated with the Black Star Line.

16. MH, Hawaiian Mission, 1850; JH, September 25, 1850, which quotes excerpts from a letter from George Q. Cannon. The ten missionaries were Hiram Clark, Thomas Whittle, Henry W. Bigler, Thomas Morris, John Dixon, William Farrer, James Hawkins, Hiram H. Blackwell, James Keeler, and George Q. Cannon.

17. Parley P. Pratt, *Autobiography*, pp. 433–36, 442–51.

18. Andrew Jenson, *Church Chronology*, p. 46. At this same conference the revelation on celestial marriage was first made public.

19. Journals of Richard Ballantyne, holograph, 9 vols. (first 5 vols. cover mission to India 1852–55), CA. Logbook of the Ship *Monsoon*, holograph by Captain Zenas Winsor, January 30 to April 24, 1853, Old Dartmouth Historical Society Whaling Museum, New Bedford, Mass. The thirteen missionaries traveling on this ship were Richard Ballantyne, William F. Carter, Benjamin Franklin Dewey, William Fotheringham, Nathaniel Vary Jones, Truman Leonard, Elam Ludington (also Elam Luddington and Elim Luddington), Amos Milton Musser, Robert Owens (also Owen), Levi Savage, Robert Skelton, Samuel Amos Woolley, and Chauncey Walker West. Dewey, Ludington, Savage, and West were called to the Siam Mission but traveled to Calcutta with those assigned to the East Indian Mission. The 774-ton *Monsoon* was built in 1851 by Trufant & Drummond at Bath, Maine.

20. Ballantyne, Journals. Ballantyne copied this portion of Captain Thomas D. Scott's logbook.

21. Ballantyne, Journals; Rogers, Journal. Ballantyne made the following passages: San Pedro to San Francisco, 10 days; San Francisco to Calcutta, 85 days; Calcutta to Madras, 34 days; Madras to London, 134 days; Liverpool to New Orleans, 56 days. Rogers spent 203 days at sea from New Bedford to Tubuai, another four days from Tubuai to Papeete, and 126 days from Papeete to New Bedford.

22. MH, Australasian Mission, 1854–55, CA.

23. MH, East Indian Mission. See also *Millennial Star*, XVII, pp. 189–91.

24. MH, East Indian Mission. West's account is included under the date of January 9, 1854 (News 5: 230, 264, 286). No registration for the *Hiageer* has been located. According to the Public Record Office in London, the ship *John Gray* was 578 tons and

was built at Greenock in 1842, with three masts, three decks, a square stern, and a figurehead of a man. Her master was Duncan McDonald; she was wrecked in 1867.

25. MH, East Indian Mission, includes under date of July 29, 1856, Musser's letter describing his experience. The 1,350-ton clipper ship *Viking* was built at Bath, Maine, in 1853 and was wrecked on Princess Island off Simoda while carrying Chinese coolies from Hong Kong to San Francisco in 1863.

26. Few details of Leonard's mission are known, except for his letters published in the *Millennial Star*, XVI, 223; XVII, 588–90; XVIII, 45–46; and in the *Deseret News*, V, 158–59. CE, CA, 1856.

27. Ballantyne's letter to F. D. Richards, December 13, 1854, in *Millennial Star*, XVII, 28.

28. MH, East Indian Mission, May 2, 1856, The *Earl of Eglinton* was 1,274 tons, built in 1854 at Scotland.

29. Juanita Brooks, ed., *On the Mormon Frontier: The Diary of Hosea Stout*, II, 472–88. Also letter from the Rijksmuseum "Nederlands Scheepvaart Museum" dated March 30, 1977, providing details of the *Jan van Hoorn*. According to the Maritiem Museum "Prins Hendrik" of Rotterdam, letter of March 22, 1976, Captain Jacob Bouten was born in Groningen in 1815 and was a well-known and capable master.

30. Brooks, *Hosea Stout*, 11, 472–88; Public Record Office, London and Richmond.

31. MH, *Hawaiian Mission*.

32. Ibid., September 27, 1854; June 21, 1857.

33. MH, Australasian Mission, May 10, 1857.

34. MH, Hawaiian Mission, December 24, 1854. NA, ship registrations.

35. MH, Hawaiian Mission, January 29, 1855; April 1, 1856; August 1, 1856; Jenson, *Encyclopedia*, III, 713.

36. Jenson, *Encyclopedia*, I, 70.

37. MH, Australasian Mission, March 31, 1852; Archives Office of Tasmania, letter of February 22, 1978; Rasmussen, *Ship Passenger Lists*, IV, 134; Public Record Office, registration documents.

38. William Hyde's Journal, CA; letter of Josiah W. Fleming to his family, quoted in MH, Australasian Mission, March 30, 1853. The bark *Pacific*'s tonnage is confused; Sydney harbor records list her at 195 tons, but Sydney newspapers, April 1, 1853, report her at 355 tons. One number could be net, the other gross, tonnage.

39. Absalom P. Dowdle letter to George Q. Cannon, December 11, 1856; MH, Australasian Mission, December 12, 1856. There appears to be a mistake in passage time of the *General Wool*. Mission records state 104 days, but if the vessel cleared port August 23, as reported by the *Daily Alta California*, and left the next day, reaching Sydney November 27, the time would be about 94 days.

40. Jenson, *Encyclopedia*, IV, 130. The identity of the *Louis Napoleon* is not certain. The only vessel that seems likely is a British three-masted bark of 302 tons, built in 1856 at Nova Scotia. Documents in the Public Record Office show her wrecked in 1863 with no details—an earlier date from the February or March 1864 date in the biographical account; such confusion of dates is not uncommon. The fact that the vessel is listed as a bark may not be significant since rigs can be changed or the biography may have used "ship" as a generic term.

41. Letter of Jesse Haven to the First Presidency of the church dated January 18, 1856. This long letter provides a valuable history of the South African Mission. MH, South African Mission, December 15, 1855.

42. Ibid.; also *Millennial Star*, XVIII, 111. Letter from William H. Walker dated November 28, 1855; letter from Leonard I. Smith dated February 9, 1856. Both elders give accounts of the purchase of the *Unity* and the voyage to London. MH, South African Mission, November 27 and 28, 1855.

43. Whitney, *Heber C. Kimball*, pp. 97, 107. Registration documents indicate that the 367-ton *United States* was built in 1834 at Huron, Ohio, with the usual two stacks and two decks, and was lost in 1849. Her 386-ton namesake was built in 1832 at Oswegatchian, New York, and broken up in 1842.

44. Watson, *Brigham Young*, pp. 58–59; William M. Lytle Files, NA, hereafter Lytle List or Lytle Files.

45. Watson, *Brigham Young*, pp. 104–5.

46. Lytle List indicates that the *Rapids* was a side-wheeler of 109 tons, built in 1839 and abandoned in 1843. The side-wheeler *Adelaide* was registered at 87 tons, built in 1841, and abandoned in 1848. The side-wheeler *Raritan* was registered at 138 tons and operated from 1840 to 1846. The *Nautilus* was built in 1840 and abandoned four years later.

47. Whitney, *Heber C. Kimball*, p. 347. Lytle List indicates that the *Osprey* was built in 1842 and abandoned in 1848.

48. Watson, *Brigham Young*, p. 167; Lytle List.

49. Whitney, *Heber C. Kimball*, pp. 350–52. Lytle lists the side-wheeler *Balloon* at 204 tons, built in 1839 at New York and lost in 1872.

50. Cowley, *Wilford Woodruff*, p. 233. Registration documents list the *Oswego* as a two-masted 151-ton screw-driven steam schooner, built in 1842, abandoned in 1853, master D. W. Davis.

51. Jenson, *Encyclopedia*, III, 713-14; Jenson, *Church Chronology*, April 13, 1870.

52. MH, Hawaiian Mission, October 26, 1850. The side-wheeler *Senator* was registered at 754 tons, built in 1848 by William R. Brown at New York City, and dismantled in 1882. The 240-ton side-wheeler *West Point* was built in New York in 1849 and operated on the Sacramento River between 1850 and 1868.

53. Jenson, *Encyclopedia*, I, 334; Eugene W. Smith, *Passenger Ships of the World*, pp. 2, 3, 107. The *Glasgow* was built in 1851 at Glasgow and registered at 1,950 tons, single-screw, four masts and a funnel; she burned off Nantucket in 1865.

54. Ibid.; C. R. Vernon Gibbs, *Passenger Liners of the Western Ocean*, pp. 61–62; NA, Passenger Lists of Port of New York; Smith, *Passenger Ships*, pp. 7, 46, 91, 184, 702. The *Niagara* was built in 1848 at Greenock, Scotland, with paddle-wheels, three masts, a funnel, a wooden hull, a tonnage of 1,825, and a clipper bow; she was wrecked in 1875 with no loss of life. MH, British Mission, March 5 and May 12, 1852; Jenson, *Encyclopedia*, IV, 374. The *Transit* was a paddle steamer of 263 tons built in 1831.

55. Jenson, *Encyclopedia*, I, 485; Smith, *Passenger Ships*, pp. 16, 64. A pioneer vessel of the Collins Line, the *Atlantic*, of 2,856 tons, had three masts and one funnel; she was built in 1849 and broken up in 1871. See also MH, British Mission, February 10, 1859. The *City of Washington* was built in 1855 for the Inman Line. She was

2,381 tons, had three masts and one funnel, and was wrecked in 1873; her sister ship was the *City of Baltimore*.

56. Jenson, *Encyclopedia*, III, 738. Wood sailed for England on the *City of Washington* in July 1863, but his health failed and he was sent home several months later. He died crossing the plains in 1864. *Record of American and Foreign Shipping* (hereafter American Lloyds), 1864, p. 621, lists the *Etna* at 1,967 tons, bark rig, built in 1855 at Greenock, Scotland. Smith, *Passenger Ships*, pp. 90–91, reports her tonnage at 2,215.

57. Jenson, *Encyclopedia*, II, 372. Ship registrations in the NA show that the *Ada Hancock* was formerly named *Milton Willis* and was built in 1859 at San Francisco. She was a wooden screw steamer with one deck, a square stern, and a billethead.

58. Jenson, *Encyclopedia*, I, 125. Smith, *Passenger Ships*, p. 243, lists the 3,871-ton *Scotia* as built in 1862 at Glasgow, Scotland, with two masts and two funnels; the vessel was wrecked in 1904. See also Jenson, *Encyclopedia*, I, 146; Teasdale was ordained an apostle in 1882, Carrington in 1870. The single-screw steamer *City of Antwerp* was built in 1867 and registered at 2,391 tons.

59. Warren Armstrong, *The Atlantic Highway*, p. 60; Gibbs, *Passenger Liners*, pp. 204–5.

60. Jenson, *Encyclopedia*, III, 742. The *Knickerbocker* was a 1,642-ton screw steamer built in 1873 at Wilmington, Delaware.

61. MH, Australasian Mission, 1883. Smith, *Passenger Ships*, p. 300. The *City of New York* was built in 1875 in Chester, Pa. The 3,019-ton single-screw steamer operated in the Pacific Mail Steamship Line; she was wrecked in 1893. *Daily Alta California*, November 30, 1883, reports her arrival at San Francisco. Barber sailed from Auckland on November 7. See also Jenson, *Church Chronology*, p. 121; *Lloyd's Register*, 1884–85. *Milo*, 795 tons and screw-driven, was built in 1882 at Hartlepool, England.

62. MH, Australasian Mission, May 26, 1886; Jenson, *Church Chronology*, p. 149; *Daily Alta California*, June 14, 1886; Smith, *Passenger Ships*, pp. 312, 330. The single-screw 2,598-ton *Mararoa*, with two masts and one funnel, was built in 1885 at Dumbarton, Scotland, and was owned by the Union Steamship Co. of New Zealand. She made a few runs across the Pacific but was considered too small; she was scrapped in 1938. The single-screw 2,489-ton *Zealandia* was built with four masts and one funnel at Glasgow, Scotland, in 1875 and operated by the Oceanic Steamship Co. She was wrecked in the Atlantic in 1917; her sister ship was the *Australia*. The single-screw 3,158-ton *Mariposa*, with two masts and one funnel, was built in 1883 at Philadelphia. She operated in the Oceanic Steamship Co. fleet and was lost in 1917.

Chapter Two

THE GATHERING

1. Smith, *History of the Church*, II, 492; *Doctrine and Covenants*, 29:7–8.

2. Whitney, *Heber C. Kimball*, p. 288; Smith, *History of the Church*, IV, 119, 185–87.

3. Smith, *History of the Church*, IV, 541.

4. *Millennial Star*, XXI, 41.

5. Jane C. Robinson Hindley, *Reminiscences and Diaries*, 1855, CA.

6. P. A. M. Taylor, *Expectations Westward*, pp. 113–42. Also see Milton R. Hunter, *Brigham Young, The Colonizer*, pp. 86–100, and William Mulder, *Homeward to Zion*, pp. 7–17.

7. James Linforth, *Route from Liverpool to the Great Salt Lake Valley*, pp. 16–17.

8. Andrew Jenson, *Encyclopedic History of the Church of Jesus Christ of Latter-day Saints*, pp. 650–51; Leonard J. Arrington, *Great Basin Kingdom*, pp. 98–99. See also CE, 1850, 1855, and 1863; Hunter, *Brigham Young*, pp. 86-89; Taylor, *Expectations Westward*, pp. 122–25 and Mulder, *Homeward to Zion*, pp. 142–47.

9. CE, 1849; *Millennial Star*, XII, 133.

10. Jenson, *History*, pp. 650–51. The Assembly of the State of Deseret passed an act incorporating the Perpetual Emigrating Fund Company on September 14, 1850. When the Territory of Utah was established, the company was rechartered on October 4, 1851.

11. Arrington, *Great Basin Kingdom*, pp. 98–99.

12. Linforth, *Route from Liverpool*, pp. 12–16.

13. CE, 1855; Linforth, *Route from Liverpool*, p. 15.

14. See Mulder, *Homeward to Zion*, pp. 110, 130; Taylor, *Expectations Westward*, p. 125, and Jenson, *Encyclopedia*, I, 364.

15. Refer to Appendix 1 for extensive data concerning the voyages of the gathering.

16. Watson, *Brigham Young*, p. 69.

17. Dixon Scott, *Liverpool*, p. 51, and Edward Howell, *Liverpool As It Is*, passim.

18. Kate B. Carter, comp., "Sailing Vessels and Steamboats," Daughters of Utah Pioneers, *Lessons for April, 1969* (hereafter DUP Lesson Book, 1969), p. 448, quoted from *Millennial Star*, XI, 71.

19. CE, 1852; *Millennial Star*, XIV, 73.

20. CE, 1852.

21. *Millennial Star*, XV, 89, 282; *Morgenstjernen*, I, 180.

22. *Millennial Star*, XVI, 41, 447; *Morgenstjernen*, II, 52.

23. *Morgenstjernen*, II, 52; also CE, 1854.

24. CE, 1854.

25. Ibid., 1855.

26. Ibid.; ship's name spelled *Geiser* in this record.

27. MH, Scandinavian Mission.

28. CE, 1857, 1859.

29. Ibid., 1860.

30. Ibid., 1863.

31. DUP Lesson Book, 1969, p. 491, and *Lloyd's Register*, 1867–1868.

32. Mulder, *Homeward to Zion*, p. 170.

Chapter Three
WINDSHIPS AND MARINERS

1. Watson, *Brigham Young*, p. 77; Whitney, *Heber C. Kimball*, p. 293. See also Passenger List, Port of New York, July 20, 1840, and Ship Registrations, NA.

2. James B. Allen and Thomas G. Alexander, eds., *Manchester Mormons, The Journal of William Clayton*, p. 169.

3. Capt. Alan Villiers, *Men, Ships, and the Sea*, pp. 214–17.

4. Peter Kemp, ed., *The Oxford Companion to Ships and the Sea* (London, 1976), pp. 737–41; W. A. McEwen and A. H. Lewis, *Encyclopedia of Nautical Knowledge*, pp. 472–74; John Durant and Alice Durant, *Pictorial History of American Ships*, pp. 40–45.

5. William Avery Baker, *A Maritime History of Bath, Maine, and the Kennebec River Region*, I, 164, credits Kennebunk with 9, Thomaston 8, Brunswick 3, Newcastle 3, Richmond 3, and Rockland 3.

6. See William Armstrong Fairburn, *Merchant Sail*, 6 vols., passim.

7. See Baker, *Maritime History*, I, 252, 292–93, and 300–4, for information cited in this and the next three paragraphs.

8. Ship Registrations, NA; CE, 1851, 1852, 1853.

9. See Baker, *Maritime History*, I, 369–402.

10. Ibid., 438–507; Jack Coggins, *Ships and Seamen of the American Revolution*, pp. 43–48; Howard I. Chapelle, *The History of American Sailing Ships*, pp. 273–95; Carl C. Cutler, *Queens of the Western Ocean*, p. 261.

11. Cutler, *Queens*, pp. 314–15.

12. Villiers, *Men, Ships, and the Sea*, pp. 214–17.

13. Basil Lubbock, *The Western Ocean Packets*, pp. 7–8.

14. Villiers, *Men, Ships, and the Sea*, pp. 214–17.

15. Cutler, *Queens*, pp. 371–456.

16. Ibid.

17. Allen and Alexander, *Manchester Mormons*, pp. 173–74.

18. Basil W. Bathe, *Seven Centuries of Sea Travel*, pp. 89–91.

19. MH, Scandinavian Mission, 1962.

20. *Millennial Star*, XXIII, 328, 475, 478, 522, and Mulder, *Homeward to Zion*, p. 170.

21. *Millennial Star*, XXX, 426, 494, 588. Mulder, *Homeward to Zion*, p. 171.

22. CE, 1852.

23. DUP Lesson Book, 1969, p. 489, account of Olof Jenson.

24. Ibid., pp. 479–81. See also *Millennial Star*, XVI, 94, 256, 272, 297, 447. *Morgenstjernen*, II, 52.

25. *Millennial Star*, X, 203; CE, 1848.

26. *Millennial Star*, XIX, 313, 411, 445.

27. Walter Blair and W. K. Chandler, eds., *Readings in Poetry* (New York and London, 1935), p. 55.

28. Cutler, *Queens*, p. 247.

29. Smith, *History of the Church*, V, 380. The *Yorkshire* is listed as a bark in *Lloyd's Register* for 1843, although she could have been ship-rigged on this voyage.

30. DUP Lesson Book, 1969, pp. 437–40, letter of Ann Pichforth.

31. Ibid., pp. 440–41, letter of Wilford Woodruff dated March 2, 1846.

32. CE, 1850.

33. *Millennial Star*, XIII, 9.

34. Ibid., XV, 89, 282, 368.

35. Patience Loader Rosa Archer, "Autobiography, 1827–1872," typescript, Brigham Young University Library, pp. 151–58.

36. MH, South African Mission.

37. Ballantyne, Journals.

38. Pratt, *Autobiography*, pp. 434–36, 449–50.

39. CE, 1844.

40. Ibid., 1849, 1850.

41. Ibid., 1853; *Millennial Star*, XV, 169, 358, 361, 443.

42. *Millennial Star*, XVI, 270, 297, 440, 462.

43. CE, 1855; *Millennial Star*, XVIII, 206.

44. *Millennial Star*, XVIII, 353.

45. MH, Australasian Mission, 1856; Alonzo Colton, Journal, CA.

46. DUP Lesson Book, 1969, pp. 466–70.

47. CE, 1857.

48. Ibid., 1862.

49. DUP Lesson Book, 1969, pp. 480–81.

50. CE, 1863, 1864, 1865.

51. Carl C. Cutler, *Greyhounds of the Sea* (New York, 1930), p. 313.

52. CE, 1868. The passenger manifest, NA, lists a Captain Gillespie as master of the *Emerald Isle* during the 1868 voyage. The Mormons commemorate July 24 as Pioneer Day; on that day in 1847 the first Mormon company entered Salt Lake Valley.

Chapter Four

A SAGA OF SAIL

1. Allen and Alexander, *Manchester Mormons*, pp. 172–84.

2. Pratt, *Autobiography*, p. 361.

3. Snow, *Lorenzo Snow*, pp. 65–66.

4. John Henry Evans, *Charles Coulson Rich*, pp. 177–78.

5. Hubert Howe Bancroft, *History of California*, V, 544–50; Jenson, *Historical Record*, pp. 875–76; Kate B. Carter, comp., "The Ship Brooklyn," DUP, *Lessons for May, 1960*, pp. 525–87. Crew list, February 4, 1846, NA; passenger manifest, Port of Honolulu, June 22, 1846, State Archives.

6. *Millennial Star*, XI, 315, XII, 43, 75.

7. CE, 1851, includes the accounts of Howell and Nowers.

8. Linforth, *Route from Liverpool*, pp. 23–30.

9. Letter of Christopher Arthur to Samuel W. Richards, quoted in CE, 1853; *Millennial Star*, XV, 169, 358, 361.

10. Jenson, *Historical Record*, V, 162–63.

11. Jenson, *History*, pp. 383–84.

12. Ballantyne, Journals; Ballantyne family records; CE, 1855.

13. MH, South African Mission, 1855. Stock, Parker, and Roper purchased the *Unity* for £2,500 when other vessels either refused the company passage or demanded exorbitant fares for poor steerage accommodations.

14. MH, East Indian Mission, 1855; MH, Australasian Mission, 1857.

15. *Millennial Star*, XXI, 286, 419; XXII, 331, 459, 538; XXIV, 348, 588. CE, 1859, 1860, 1862.

16. CE, 1861, 1864. *Millennial Star*, XXVI, 426; XXVII, 16. Registration Documents, NA, convert the old tonnage of 1,979 to the new basis of 2,164 tons after 1864. Captain William R. Gardner of Providence, Rhode Island, was master in 1861 and Robert Kirkaldy in 1864.

17. DUP Lesson Book, 1969, pp. 484–85; *Millennial Star*, XVII, 16.

18. Miner G. Atwood's Journal, holograph, 3 vols., April 12 to June 30, 1865, excerpted in MH, South African Mission, 1865. *Millennial Star*, XXVII, 442–45.

19. MH, Australasian Mission, 1879.

Chapter Five

QUEENS OF THE RIVERS

1. Jenson, *History*, p. 152; Mulder, *Homeward to Zion*, p. 24.

2. Leonard V. Huber, *Louisiana, A Pictorial History*, p. 106. Most blacks lived on plantations and outlying farms. Before the Civil War there were about 13,000 blacks in New Orleans out of a population of 168,000; see Huber's *New Orleans, A Pictorial History*, pp. 54, 124.

3. Huber, *Louisiana*, p. 114. Hodding Carter, *Lower Mississippi*, and Huber, *New Orleans*, provide useful background.

4. Henry Sinclair Drago, *The Steamboaters*, pp. v-viii.

5. E. W. Gould, *Fifty Years on the Mississippi*, pp. 431–33; Drago, *The Steamboaters*, p. 17; Hodding Carter, *Lower Mississippi*, passim.

6. Frank Donovan, *River Boats of America*, p. 9; Gould, *Fifty Years*, p. 432; Drago, *The Steamboaters*, p. vii; Paul O'Neil, *The Rivermen*, pp. 24, 28, 44.

7. Quoted in Donovan, *River Boats*, pp. 106-7.

8. Ibid., p. 104.

9. All tonnages, dimensions, and other descriptive details of individual steamboats were obtained from the Lytle Files and original Ship Registrations and Enrollments, NA.

10. Smith, *History of the Church*, IV, 569; DUP Lesson Book, 1969, pp. 432–33.

11. CE, 1842, 1843.

12. Ibid., 1841, 1842. Two years earlier the *Goddess of Liberty* had carried Saints from St. Louis to Nauvoo for a fare of one dollar each. This company had crossed the Atlantic aboard the ship *Sheffield*.

13. Dallin H. Oaks and Joseph I. Bentley, "Joseph Smith and Legal Process: In the Wake of the Steamboat *Nauvoo*," pp. 736–81; Registrations, NA.

14. JH, various dates in 1843, 1844, 1854, and 1864; DUP Lesson Book, 1969, pp. 436–37; Jenson, *History*, p. 462; Registrations, NA.

15. CE, 1845.

16. Jenson, *Encyclopedia*, IV, 740.

17. CE, 1848.

18. CE, 1849.

19. JH, April 11, 1849. Lytle Files show that *Mandan* burned with no loss of life.

20. CE, 1849, 1851. Lytles Files indicate that the *Grand Turk* was lost in 1856. However, *Way's Directory*, p. 124, states that she was burned at New Orleans on February 6, 1854.

21. JH, April 25, 1849.

22. CE, 1849.

23. Registrations, NA.

24. Ibid.; CE, 1850.

25. DUP Lesson Book, 1969, p. 454.

26. CE, 1851; Registrations, NA.

27. CE, 1851.

28. CE, 1852; O'Neil, *Rivermen*, pp. 89–92. James T. Lloyd, *Lloyd's Steamboat Directory*, pp. 290–91. *Millennial Star*, XIV, 41, 154, 220, 283. No one knows for certain how many Mormons were killed in the *Saluda* disaster. Estimates have been as high as 200, but church records indicate that only about 90—and no more than 110—Mormons were aboard, and probably no more than a third were killed.

29. *Way's Directory*, p. 172; Lytle Files.

30. *Way's Directory*, p. 146; Lytle Files. Further details of this river trip are lacking.

31. See CE, 1854; also Lytle Files and Registrations, NA, for the information cited here and in the next two paragraphs.

32. Ibid.; also Fred Erving Dayton, *Steamboat Days*, p. 339.

33. See CE, 1855; also Lytle Files and Registrations, NA, for the information cited here and in the next two paragraphs.

34. DUP Lesson Book, 1969, p. 427.

35. Allen and Alexander, *Manchester Mormons*, pp. 185–96; Lytle Files and Registrations, NA.

36. See CE, 1855; also Lytle Files and Registrations, NA, for information cited here and in the next two paragraphs.

37. O'Neil, *Rivermen*, p. 25.

38. CE, 1859; Registration, NA.

39. CE, 1860; Lytle Files; Donovan, *River Boats*, p. 76.

40. CE, 1862; Lytle Files and Registrations, NA.

41. CE, 1865; *Way's Directory*, p. 74; Lytle Files.

Chapter Six
ENGINES OF THE SEA

1. J. R. T. Hughes and Stanley Reiter, "The First 1,945 British Steamships," *The Journal of the American Statistical Association*, pp. 360–81.

2. Jenson, *Church Chronology*, p. 45; MH, British Mission, 1852; Passenger Lists, NA.

3. Byron S. Miller, *Sail, Steam, and Splendor*, pp. 32–37; John Malcolm Brinnin, *The Sway of the Grand Saloon*, pp. 90–93.

4. N. R. P. Bonsor, "The Guion Line," *The Belgian Shiplover*, XXVI–XXVII (Brussels, April 1974–January 1975), pp. 393–99; Gibbs, *Passenger Liners*, pp. 202–5.

5. Brigham Young wrote to Richards, May 23, 1868: "To enable our immigration to avail themselves of the healthiest portion or portions of the year, for better withstanding the changes of the habits, diet and climate, and for other good and sufficient reasons, we wish you to employ none but steamships . . ." (Young Letterbooks, CA). F.D. Richards Diary, June 21, 1867, and March 7, 1868, CA.

6. *Millennnial Star*, XXXVI, 376. Joseph F. Smith Diary, April–May 1874; William Budge to Samuel Goddard, July 15, 1879; Daniel H. Wells to Anthon H. Lund, March 3, 1885, and to James Jack, March 7, 1885; all, CA.

7. Budge to George H. Taylor, September 7, 1879; Budge to John Taylor, October 18, 1879, and October 16, 1880; all, CA. Lund's obituary for George Ramsden, "A Good Friend Gone," *Millennial Star*, LVIII, 360. Lund to Heber J. Grant, March 22, 1905, CA.

8. Smith, *Passenger Ships*, p. 711. Gibbs, *Passenger Liners*, pp. 202–3.

9. At the time of their emigrant voyages, both the *British King* and the *Australia* were registered to British owners. According to Smith, *Passenger Ships*, pp. 689, 728, the *British King* was listed in the American Steamship Line in 1881 and the *Australia* in the Oceanic Steamship Line in 1875. It is possible that both were chartered.

10. Miller, *Sail, Steam, and Splendor*, pp. 67–70. Melvin Maddocks, *The Great Liners*, p. 58.

11. Brinnin, *Sway of the Grand Saloon*, pp. 155–58.

12. Ibid., pp. 261–62.

13. Miller, *Sail, Steam, and Splendor*, p. 45.

14. Ibid., pp. 99–100.

15. Maddocks, *The Great Liners*, p. 55.

16. These were: *Colorado*, sunk in 1872 by a collision in the River Mersey; *Dakota*, wrecked off Wales in 1877; *Idaho*, wrecked in 1878; *Manhattan*, wrecked off South Africa in 1902; *Montana*, stranded on the Welsh Coast in 1880; and *Niagara*, wrecked in 1875 after being converted to a sailing ship. In addition, these steamships used by the missionaries were also lost: *City of Antwerp* in 1890, *City of New York*, wrecked in 1893, *City of Washington* in 1873, *Glasgow* in 1865, and *Scotia* in 1904. References to these ships in Gibbs and Eugene Smith books.

17. For information cited here and to the end of the chapter, see Miller, *Sail, Steam, and Splendor*, pp. 82–83; *Millennial Star* XXIV, 605.

Chapter Seven
GREYHOUNDS OF STEAM

1. *Millennial Star*, XXX, 442, 445, 461; Gibbs, *Passenger Liners*, p. 203.

2. MH, British Mission, June 28, 1871; July 22, 1871; September 4, 1872.

3. Passenger Lists, Port of New York, NA; CE, 1868, 1869, 1870, 1871; American Lloyd's, 1868.

4. CE, 1874; Smith, *Passenger Ships*, p. 66.

5. Ibid., p. 182.

6. MH, British Mission, MH, Scandinavian Mission, and CE include many references to the 35 voyages. Masters were identified from Passenger Lists and shipping news in various issues of the *New York Commercial Advertiser*.

7. Gibbs, *Passenger Liners*, p. 203; Smith, *Passenger Ships*, p. 281; CE, 1871–90; Passenger Lists, NA.

8. Passenger Lists, NA; American Lloyd's, 1884; CE, 1872–90.

9. CE, 1873, 1877, 1880; MH, British Mission, July 10, 1880; JH, July 29, 1880.

10. John A. Widtsoe, *In the Gospel Net*, pp. 76–77.

11. Smith, *Passenger Ships*, pp. 74, 173; Gibbs, *Passenger Liners*, p. 204; *Lloyd's*, 1876–77; MH, British Mission, October 14, 1875; June 15, 1878; Jenson, *Church Chronology*, January 19, 1876.

12. CE, 1879–1889; Gibbs, *Passenger Liners*, pp. 204–5; Armstrong, *Atlantic Highway*, pp. 59, 65.

13. Brinnin, *Sway of the Grand Saloon*, pp. 267–68.

14. Ibid.

15. Smith, *Passenger Ships*, pp. 17, 55, 59, 711; Gibbs, *Passenger Liners*, pp. 204–5.

16. Jenson, *Church Chronology*, January 21, 1882; Smith, *Passenger Ships*, p. 1; Gibbs, *Passenger Liners*, p. 68.

17. Jenson, *Church Chronology*, October 24, 1884; Smith, *Passenger Ships*, pp. 31, 58; Gibbs, *Passenger Liners*, pp. 119–20; American Lloyd's, 1879.

18. Jenson, *Church Chronology*, July 10, 1886; Smith, *Passenger Ships*, p. 3.

19. CE, 1886; Smith, *Passenger Ships*, pp. 38, 40, 277, 689; *Lloyd's*, 1885-1886, 1886-1887.

20. MH, Netherlands Mission, April 27, 1889; *Millennial Star*, LI, 300. The company presumably sailed by steamer to New York, arriving about May 15. The only record of a Dutch vessel arriving about that time was the SS *Edam* on May 13, 1889. Unfortunately the passenger list is quite illegible. I suspect, however, that the *Edam* is the correct ship. According to Eugene W. Smith, she was built in 1878 and was rated at 3,329 tons with four masts and one funnel.

21. MH, Australasian Mission, June 4, 1871; Smith, *Passenger Ships*, p. 329.

22. Jenson, *History*, p. 580; Smith, *Passenger Ships*, p. 315.

23. MH, Australasian Mission, June 17, 1880; Port of San Francisco Certificate of Registry, NA, San Bruno.

24. MH, New Zealand Mission, April 26, 1881; *Daily Alta California*, May 19, 1881; American Lloyd's, 1879.

25. MH, Australasian Mission, April 23, 1888.

Chapter Eight
EBB TIDE

1. Taylor, *Expectations Westward*, pp. 144–46. Leonard J. Arrington and Davis Bitton, *The Mormon Experience*, pp. 136–37. Mormon passenger totals include some returning missionaries and occasional non-Mormons traveling with emigrant companies. There are no statistics for emigrants who traveled independently. After allowing for these factors, an estimate of at least 85,000 appears to be reasonable. Statistics, Scandinavian Mission, show some 19,500 emigrants from 1850 through 1890.

2. Charles Dickens, *The Uncommercial Traveller* (New York and London, 1902), pp. 214, 224.

3. *Parliamentary Papers*, 1854, XIII, esp. Qq. 4985, 5016, 5049–54, 5073, 5076–79, 5085, 5167–83. Cited by Taylor, *Expectations Westward*, p. 173, and Arrington and Bitton, *The Mormon Experience*, p. 132.

4. Philip McCutchan, *Tall Ships, The Golden Age of Sail*, pp. 64–65.

5. *Millennial Star*, XVI, 797.

6. Brinnin, *Sway of the Grand Saloon*, p. 512, 515.

7. Cutler, *Greyhounds of the Sea*, pp. 412–33.

8. Basil Lubbock, *The Down Easters*, pp. 10, 52, 58, 72–73, 107–8, 253, 255, 262.

9. Durant and Durant, *Pictorial History*, p. 166.

10. Villiers, *Men, Ships, and the Sea*, p. 285.

11. CE, July 1880.

12. Mulder, *Homeward to Zion*, p. 292.

13. Arrington and Bitton, *The Mormon Experience*, p. 137.

14. Mulder, *Homeward to Zion*, p. 289. James B. Allen and Glen M. Leonard, *The Story of the Latter-day Saints*, pp. 343–44; Arrington, *Great Basin Kingdom*, pp. 359–61.

15. Allen and Leonard, *Latter-day Saints*, pp. 394–95, 404–412; Arrington, *Great Basin Kingdom*, pp. 359–61.

16. Jenson, *Church Chronology*, p. 134.

17. Mulder, *Homeward to Zion*, p. 299.

18. Jenson, *Church Chronology*, p. 135.

19. Mulder, *Homeward to Zion*, p. 299. Although Mulder speaks of another company arriving in September, it was the same company that left Liverpool on August 21, arrived the thirty-first and was processed through Castle Garden September 1. See Jenson, *Church Chronology*, pp. 134–35.

20. Mulder, *Homeward to Zion*, p. 300.

21. Arrington and Bitton, *The Mormon Experience*, pp. 139–40.

22. Quoted in ibid.

Bibliography

No adequate history of Mormon migration can be written without reliance on LDS Church and government archives. Particularly important are the Journal History, the Church Emigration record and Company Rosters, and the Manuscript Histories of the missions. These sources include transcripts from private journals, personal letters, newspaper articles, and other primary data. Their value lies in the nature of the compilation as a synthesis of voluminous material bearing on specific events with corrections, notes, and commentary. These sources facilitate reference to the original documents used as their factual basis. Since there are well over a hundred available private journals, diaries, and autobiographical sketches, such compilations are obviously indispensable. In some notes, I have cited these historical sources for convenience when to cite the original manuscripts directly would result in a multitude of footnotes and reconciliation of details.

Government archives, both in the United States and other nations, are often the only sources of passenger lists, ship registrations, crew lists, and port records. Some of these documents are faded, torn, or missing; others have been destroyed by fire, earthquake, or war. In such cases, I have developed data about ships, masters, passage times, dates, and ports from contemporary newspapers or periodicals.

MANUSCRIPTS AND DOCUMENTS

The Archives Office of New South Wales, Sydney, Australia.
>   Passenger lists at Fort Jackson.
Archives Office of Tasmania, Hobart, Tasmania.
>   Ship Registration documents.
Church of Jesus Christ of Latter-day Saints, Genealogical Department, Salt Lake City, Utah.
>   W.P.A. Passenger Lists, National Archives, microfilm copies, 1840–1876, for the ports of Boston, New Orleans, New York, and Philadelphia.
Church of Jesus Christ of Latter-day Saints, Historical Department, Library-Archives Division, Salt Lake City, Utah.

[191]

Church Emigration, 1840-1890.

Journal History, a daily history of the church, including portions of the History of Brigham Young.

Journals, diaries, and autobiographies: Richard Ballantyne, 1852–1855; Alonzo Colton, 1855–1856; Addison Pratt; Matthew McCune, 1855–1856; Noah Rogers, 1843–1845; and others used less extensively.

History of the Australasian Mission, 1851–1897.

History of the British Mission, 1840–1890.

History of the East Indian Mission, 1849–1856.

History of the French Polynesian Mission, 1844–1852.

History of the German Mission, 1852–1861.

History of the Hawaiian Mission, 1850–1858.

History of the Netherlands Mission, 1889.

History of the Scandinavian Mission, 1850–1890.

History of the South African Mission, 1853–1865.

Government Archives, South Africa, Pretoria and Cape Town, South Africa.

Customs Bills of Entry.

Port records of ship clearances.

HM Customs and Excise House, Registrar of British Ships, Liverpool, England.

Customs Bills of Entry and Bills of Lading.

Registers of British Ships.

La Trobe Library, The State Library of Victoria, and Victorian Public Records Office, Melbourne, Australia.

Register of Australian and New Zealand Shipping.

Inwards Shipping Index, 1839–1900.

Museum Für Hamburgische Geschichte, Hamburg, West Germany.

Shipping Registers and Records, Port of Hamburg.

National Archives, and Records Service, Industrial and Social Branch, Civil Archives Division, Washington, D.C., and Federal Archives and Record Center, San Bruno, California.

Customs and port records of arrivals and departures of vessels and American Consulate Documents at foreign ports.

First and Last Documents, Ship Registrations for numerous seaports and inland waterway ports.

W.P.A. Passenger Lists for the ports of Boston, New York, New Orleans, and Philadelphia.

The New Brunswick Museum, Saint John, New Brunswick, Canada.

Shipping registers of the ports of Saint John and Miramichi.

Old Dartmouth Historical Society Whaling Museum, New Bedford, Massachusetts.

Logbook, Ship *Monsoon*, January 30–April 23, 1853.

Papers of Captain Zenas Winsor.

Public Archives of Canada, Ottawa, Canada.

Registrations of ships built in Canada.

Public Record Office, Kew, Richmond, and London, England.

Registrations of British vessels.

Shipping and customs records.

Rijksmuseum "Nederlands Scheepvaart Museum," Amsterdam, Netherlands.

Ship registrations.

Shipping records.

Staatsarchiv, City Archives, Hamburg, West Germany.
  Hamburg port and customs records.
  Ship registrations.
Stadtarchiv Wismar, East Germany.
  Ship registrations at Wismar.
Town Clerk's Office, Kennebunkport, Maine.
  Shipbuilding records.

Major Published Sources

Baker, William Avery. *A Maritime History of Bath, Maine, and the Kennebec River Region.* 2 vols. Bath: Marine Research Society of Bath, 1973.

Cutler, Carl C. *Greyhounds of the Sea; The Story of the American Clipper Ship.* New York: Halcyon House, 1930.

———, *Queens of the Western Ocean; The Story of America's Mail and Passenger Sailing Lines.* Annapolis: United States Naval Institute, 1961.

Fairburn, William Armstrong. *Merchant Sail.* 6 vols. Lovell, Maine: Fairburn Marine Educational Foundation, 1945–55.

Gibbs, Commander C. R. Vernon, Royal Navy. *Passenger Liners of the Western Ocean.* New York: John De Graff, 1957.

Heyl, Erik. *Early American Steamers.* 6 vols. Buffalo: privately published, 1969.

Lloyd, James T. *Lloyd's Steamboat Directory.* Cincinnati: James T. Lloyd & Co., 1856.

Lloyd's Register of Shipping. London, 1835–1890.

Lytle, William M. *Merchant Steam Vessels of the United States 1807–1868* ("The Lytle List"). Mystic, Connecticut: The Steamship Historical Society of America, 1952.

Lytle, William M., and Forrest R. Holdcamper. *Merchant Steam Vessels of the United States, 1790–1868* ("The Lytle-Holdcamper List"). Staten Island, N.Y.: The Steamship Historical Society of America, 1975.

Rasmussen, Louis J. *San Francisco Ship Passenger Lists.* 4 vols. Colma, California: San Francisco Historic Record & Genealogy Bulletin.

Record of American and Foreign Shipping ("American Lloyd's"). New York: American Shipmasters' Association, 1867–1910.

Smith, Eugene W. *Passenger Ships of the World, Past and Present.* Boston: George H. Dean Company, 1963.

The Mercantile Navy List and Annual Appendage to the Commercial Code of Signals for all Nations. London: Bradbury and Evans, 1857.

Way, Frederick, Jr., ed. *Way's Directory of Western River Packets.* Sewicky, Pa.: published by the author, 1950.

Other Published Works

Allen, James B., and Thomas G. Alexander, eds. *Manchester Mormons, The Journal of William Clayton.* Santa Barbara and Salt Lake City: Peregrine Smith, 1974.

Allen, James B., and Glen M. Leonard. *The Story of the Latter-day Saints.* Salt Lake City: Deseret Book Company, 1976.

Armstrong, Warren. *The Atlantic Highway.* New York: John Day, 1962.

Arrington, Leonard J. *The Great Basin Kingdom: An Economic History of the Latter-day Saints, 1830–1900*. Cambridge: Harvard University Press, 1958.

Arrington, Leonard J., and Davis Bitton. *The Mormon Experience; A History of the Latter-day Saints*. New York: Alfred A. Knopf, 1979.

Bancroft, Hubert Howe. *History of California*. Vol. V, San Francisco: The History Company, 1886.

Barron, Howard H. *Orson Hyde: Missionary, Apostle, Colonizer*. Salt Lake City: Horizon Publishers, 1977.

Bates, Alan. *The Western Rivers Steamboat Cyclopoedium or American Riverboat*. Leonia, New Jersey: n.p., 1968.

Bathe, Basil W. *Seven Centuries of Sea Travel—From the Crusades to the Cruises*. New York: Tudor Publishing Company, 1973.

Benson, Richard M. *Steamships and Motorships of the West Coast*. New York: Bonanza Books, 1968.

Berrett, William E., and Alma B. Burton. *Readings in L.D.S. Church History*. 2 vols. Salt Lake City; Deseret Book Company, 1953–1955.

Bonsor, N. R. P. "The Guion Line." *The Belgian Shiplover* (Brussels), XXVI–XXVII (4/74–1/75), pp. 393–99.

Braynard, Frank O. *Famous American Ships*. New York: Hastings House, 1956.

Brett, Henry. *White Wings*. 2 vols. Christchurch, New Zealand: Capper Press, 1976.

Brewington, M. V. *Shipcarvers of North America*. New York: Dover Publications, 1972.

Brinnin, John Malcolm. *The Sway of the Grand Saloon*. New York: Delacorte Press, 1971.

Brooks, Juanita, ed. *On the Mormon Frontier: The Diary of Hosea Stout, 1844–1861*. 2 vols. Salt Lake City, University of Utah Press and Utah State Historical Society, 1964 and 1982.

Carson, Rachel. *The Sea Around Us*. New York: Golden Press, 1958.

Carter, Hodding. *Lower Mississippi*. New York: Rinehart, 1942.

Carter, Kate B., comp. "The Ship Brooklyn." Daughters of Utah Pioneers. *Lessons for May, 1960*, pp. 525–88.

———, comp. "Sailing Vessels and Steamboats." Daughters of Utah Pioneers. *Lessons for April, 1969*, pp. 421–92.

Chapelle, Howard I. *The History of American Sailing Ships*. New York: Bonanza Books, 1935.

Chappell, Phil E. *A History of the Missouri River*. Reprinted from the Ninth Volume, Kansas State Historical Collections, 1906.

Chittenden, Hiram Martin. *History of Early Steamboat Navigation on the Missouri River; Life and Adventures of Joseph La Barge*. Vol. I. New York: Francis P. Harper, 1903.

Church Almanac (1977–1982). Salt Lake City: Deseret News.

Clark, Arthur H. *The Clipper Ship Era*. New York and London: G. P. Putnam's Sons, 1910.

Coggins, Jack. *Ships and Seamen of the American Revolution*. Harrisburg, Pa.: Promontory Press, 1969.

Condon, George E. *Stars in the Water; The Story of the Erie Canal.* Garden City, New York: Doubleday, 1974.

Cotter, Edward P. *The Port of Liverpool.* Washington, D.C.: United States Government Printing Office, 1929.

Cowley, Matthias F. *Wilford Woodruff, History of His Life and Labors.* Salt Lake City: The Deseret News, 1916.

Cucari, Attilio. *Sailing Ships.* Chicago, New York, and San Francisco: Rand McNally, 1978.

Davis, Charles G. *Rigs of the Nine Principal Types of American Sailing Ships.* Salem, Mass.: Peabody Museum, 1974.

Dayton, Fred Erving. *Steamboat Days.* New York, Frederick A. Stokes Company, 1925.

Dickens, Charles. *The Uncommercial Traveller.* New York and London: Harper & Brothers, 1902.

Donovan, Frank. *River Boats of America.* New York: Thomas Y. Crowell, 1966.

Drago, Harry Sinclair. *The Steamboaters; from the Early Side-wheelers to the Big Packets.* New York: Bramhall House, 1967.

Durant, John, and Alice Durant. *Pictorial History of American Ships.* New York: Castle Books, 1953.

Evans, John Henry. *Charles Coulson Rich.* New York, 1936.

Everett, Amelia D. "The Ship Brooklyn." *California Historical Quarterly,* September 1958, pp. 229–40.

Flanders, Robert Bruce. *Nauvoo: Kingdom on the Mississippi.* Urbana: University of Illinois Press, 1965.

Freuchen, Peter. *Peter Freuchen's Book of the Seven Seas.* New York: Julian Messner, 1958.

Fry, Henry. *The History of North Atlantic Steam Navigation.* London: Sampson Low, Marston and Company, 1896.

Gibbs, Jim. *West Coast Windjammers in Story and Pictures.* New York: Bonanza Books, 1948.

Gould, E. W. *Fifty Years on the Mississippi, Or Gould's History of River Navigation.* St. Louis: Nixon-Jones Printing Company, 1889.

Green, Doyle L. "Mission to Polynesia." *The Improvement Era* (Salt Lake City), March, April, July, August, and October 1949, pp. 142–812.

Hafen, LeRoy R., and Ann W. Hafen. *Handcarts to Zion.* Glendale, Calif.: The Arthur H. Clark Company, 1960.

Hart, Edward L. *Mormon in Motion; The Life and Journals of James H. Hart.* Salt Lake City: Winsor Books, 1978.

Hill, Ralph Nading. *Sidewheeler Saga; A Chronicle of Steamboating.* New York and Toronto: Rinehart & Company, 1953.

Hilton, George F. *The Night Boat.* Berkeley, Calif.: Howell North Books, 1968.

Howe, Octavius T., and Frederick Matthews. *American Clipper Ships.* 2 vols. Salem, Mass.: Marine Research Society, 1926–1927.

Howell, Edward. *Liverpool As It Is.* Liverpool: Privately printed, 1860(?).

Huber, Leonard V. *Louisiana, A Political History.* New York: Charles Scribner's Sons, 1975.

————. *New Orleans, A Pictorial History*. New York: Crown Publishers, 1971.

Hughes, J. Quentin. *Liverpool*. Design Yearbook Limited, n.p., n.d.

Hughes, J. R. T., and Stanley Reiter. "The First 1,945 British Steamships." *The Journal of the American Statistical Association*, LIII, June 1958, pp. 360–81.

Hunter, Louis C. *Steamboats on the Western Rivers; An Economic and Technological History*. Cambridge: Harvard University Press, 1949.

Hunter, Milton R. *Brigham Young, The Colonizer*. Salt Lake City: Deseret News Press, 1940.

Hyde, Orson. *A Sketch of the Travels and Ministry of Elder Orson Hyde*. Salt Lake City: Deseret News Press, 1869.

Jenson, Andrew, *Church Chronology*. Salt Lake City: The Deseret News, 1899.

————. *Encyclopedic History of the Church of Jesus Christ of Latter-day Saints*. Salt Lake City, Deseret News Publishing Company, 1941.

————. *Latter-day Saint Biographical Encyclopedia*. 4 vols. Salt Lake City: Deseret News, 1901–1936.

Jenson, Richard L., and Gordon Irving. "The Voyage of the Amazon." *The Ensign*, March 1980, pp. 16–19.

Kemple, John Haskell. *San Francisco Bay, A Pictorial Maritime History*. New York: Bonanza Books, 1947.

Kemp, Peter, ed. *The Oxford Companion to Ships and the Sea*. London: Granada Publishing Ltd., 1979.

Kimball, Heber C. *Heber C. Kimball's Journal*. Salt Lake City, 1882.

Laing, Alexander. *American Sail; A Pictorial History*. New York: Bonanza Books, 1961.

————. *Clipper Ship Men*. Garden City, N.Y.: Garden City Publishing Co., 1950.

Lane, Carl D. *American Paddle Steamboats*. New York: Coward-McCann, 1943.

Lass, William E. *A History of Steamboating on the Upper Missouri River*. Lincoln, Neb.: University of Nebraska Press, 1962.

Lawson, Will. *Pacific Steamers*. Glasgow: Brown, Son & Ferguson, Ltd., 1927.

Leonard, Glen M. "Truman Leonard: Pioneer Mormon Farmer." *Utah Historical Quarterly*, Summer 1976, pp. 240–60.

Lewis & Dryden. *Marine History of the Pacific Northwest*. Edited by George Newell. 2 vols. Seattle: The Superior Publishing Company, 1966–1967.

Lewis, Edward V., Robert O'Brien, and the editors of *Life*. *Ships*. New York: Time Inc. 1965.

Linforth, James. *Route from Liverpool to the Great Salt Lake Valley*. Liverpool and London: Franklin D. Richards, 1855.

Lubbock, Basil. *The Down Easters, American Deep-water Sailing Ships, 1869–1929*. Glasgow: Brown, Son & Ferguson, Ltd., 1971.

————. *The Western Ocean Packets*. Glasgow: Brown, Son, & Ferguson, Ltd., 1956.

Lund, A. William. "The Ship Brooklyn." *The Improvement Era*, October 1951, pp. 708–33.

MacMullen, Jerry. *Paddle-Wheel Days in California*. Stanford: Stanford University Press, 1944.

McEwen, W. A., and A. H. Lewis. *Encyclopedia of Nautical Knowledge.* Cambridge, Md.: Cornell Maritime Press, 1953.

McCutchan, Philip. *Tall Ships, The Golden Age of Sail.* New York: Crown Publishers, 1976.

McKay, Richard C. *Some Famous Sailing Ships and Their Builder Donald McKay.* New York and London: G. P. Putnam's Sons, The Knickerbocker Press, 1931.

Maddocks, Melvin, and the editors of Time-Life Books. *The Great Liners.* Alexandria, Va.: Time-Life Books, 1978.

Matthews, Frederick C. *American Merchant Ships, 1850–1900.* 2 vols. Salem, Mass.: Marine Research Society, 1930-1931.

Miller, Byron S. *Sail, Steam, and Splendor; A Pictorial History of Life Aboard the Transatlantic Liners.* New York: Times Books, 1977.

Morris, Richard B., ed. *Encyclopedia of American History.* New York: Harper & Brothers, 1953.

Mulder, William. *Homeward to Zion; The Mormon Migration from Scandinavia.* Minneapolis: University of Minnesota Press, 1957.

Mulder, William, and Russell A. Mortensen. *Among the Mormons.* New York: Alfred A. Knopf, 1958.

Murphy, Thomas W. *The Landing; A Remembrance of Her People and Shipyards.* Kennebunk, Maine: Privately printed, 1977.

Neff, Andrew Love. *History of Utah, 1847 to 1869.* Salt Lake City: The Deseret News Press, 1940.

Oaks, Dallin H., and Joseph I. Bentley. "Joseph Smith and Legal Process: In the Wake of the Steamboat *Nauvoo.*" *Brigham Young University Law Review,* Vol. 1976, No. 3, pp. 735–81.

O'Niel, Paul, and the editors of Time-Life Books. *The Rivermen.* New York: Time-Life Books, 1975.

Parry, J. H. *Romance of the Sea.* Washington, D.C.: The National Geographic Society, 1981.

Petersen, William J. *Steamboating on the Upper Mississippi.* Iowa City: The State Historical Society of Iowa, 1937.

Pratt, David H. "Life on Board a Mormon Emigrant Ship." Paper presented at World Conference on Records, sponsored by LDS Church, Salt Lake City, 1980.

Pratt, Louisa Barnes. "Obituary of a Mormon Elder." *The Phrenological Journal,* LVI, March 1873, pp. 203–4.

Pratt, Parley Parker. *The Autobiography of Parley Parker Pratt.* Chicago: Published for Pratt Bros. by Law, King & Law, 1888.

Roberts, B. H. *A Comprehensive History of The Church of Jesus Christ of Latter-day Saints.* 6 vols. Salt Lake City: Deseret News Press, 1930.

Robinson, John, and George Francis Dow. *The Sailing Ships of New England.* 2 vols. Salem, Mass.: Marine Research Society, 1922-1924.

Scharffs, Gilbert W. *Mormonism in Germany, A History of the Church of Jesus Christ of Latter-day Saints in Germany between 1840 and 1880.* Salt Lake City: Deseret Book Company, 1970.

Scott, Dixon. *Liverpool.* London: Adams and Charles Black, 1907.

Smith, Joseph. *History of the Church of Jesus Christ of Latter-day Saints.* 7 vols. Salt Lake City: The Deseret Book Company, 1951.

Snow, Eliza R. *Biography and Family Record of Lorenzo Snow.* Salt Lake City: Deseret News Company, 1884.

Spears, John R. *Captain Nathaniel Brown Palmer, An Old-Time Sailor of the Sea.* New York: The Macmillan Company, 1922.

Staff, Frank. *The Transatlantic Mail.* Adlard Coles Ltd., 1856.

Taylor, P. A. M. *Expectations Westward, The Mormons and the Emigration of Their British Converts in the Nineteenth Century.* Ithaca, N. Y.: Cornell University Press, 1966.

Villiers, Capt. Alan. *Men, Ships, and the Sea.* Washington, D.C.: National Geographic Society, 1973.

————. *Vanished Fleets; Sea Stories from Old Van Dieman's Land.* New York: Charles Scribner's Sons, 1974.

Watson, Elden Jay. *Manuscript History of Brigham Young 1801–1844.* Salt Lake City, 1968.

Whipple, A. B. C., and the editors of Time-Life Books. *The Clipper Ships.* Alexandria, Va.: Time-Life Books, 1980.

Whitney, Orson F. *History of Utah.* 2 vols. Salt Lake City: George Q. Cannon & Sons, 1892–1893.

————. *Life of Heber C. Kimball, An Apostle: The Father and Founder of the British Mission.* Salt Lake City: Kimball Family, 1888.

Widtsoe, John A. *In the Gospel Net; The Story of Anna Karina Gaarden Widtsoe.* Salt Lake City: Bookcraft, 1966.

Wright, Benj. C. *San Francisco Ocean Trade Past and Future.* San Francisco: A. Carlisle & Co., 1911.

Zobell, Albert L. *Under the Midnight Sun; Centennial History of Scandinavian Missions.* Salt Lake City: Deseret Book Company, 1950.

NEWSPAPERS AND JOURNALS

Daily Alta California (San Francisco), 1852–1880.

Daily Crescent (New Orleans), 1854.

Daily Picayune (New Orleans), 1842, 1843, 1849.

Deseret News (Salt Lake City), 1850–1890.

The Historical Record (Salt Lake City), ed. and pub. by Andrew Jenson, V (1886), VI (1887).

The Latter-day Saints' Millennial Star (Liverpool), 1840–1890.

Louisiana Courier (New Orleans), 1841, 1842.

Missouri Historical Review, XXI (1926–27).

Morgenstjernen (Salt Lake City), 1882, 1883, 1884, 1885.

The Mormon (New York City), ed. by John Taylor, 1855–1856.

New Orleans Commercial Bulletin, 1844.

New Orleans Price Current, 1847.

New Orleans Tropic, 1844.

New York Commercial Advertiser, 1871, 1881, 1882, 1884, 1889.

New York Times, 1879.
Pacific Commercial Advertiser (Honolulu), 1857.
The Polynesian (Honolulu), 1857, 1858.
Quebec Gazette, 1841.
Sacramento Daily Record Union, 1884.
San Francisco Mercantile Gazette and Shipping Register, 1858–1859.
Sydney Morning Herald (Australia), 1853, 1857.

Acknowledgments

Except for general historical information, the basic facts in this work were researched personally or by correspondence from many public and private institutions. These primary sources included Mormon emigration and shipping records, customs passenger lists, ship registrations, customs bills of entry and bills of lading, early town records, American and foreign newspapers, letters of emigrants and missionaries, and private diaries and journals. In addition, numerous maps, pictures, prints, and photographs were provided by public and private custodians over many years.

Such a research undertaking was possible only through the generous cooperation and assistance of a large number of individuals and institutions. Of the individuals to whom I am particularly indebted, special mention should be made of the following:

Dr. Leonard J. Arrington, the Lemuel Redd Professor of Western History at Brigham Young University; Dr. Davis C. Bitton, Professor of History at the University of Utah; and staff members of the Library-Archives Division, Historical Department of the Church of Jesus Christ of Latter-day Saints. Of these staff members Linda Haslam was especially helpful in steering me to source materials and responding to numerous inquiries. Richard L. Jensen was also most generous in volunteering data from his own research and suggesting valuable sources. To my journalist friend Harold Lundstrom I express appreciation for his help in verifying certain facts.

Brigham D. Madsen, Professor of History at the University of Utah, and S. George Ellsworth, Professor of History at Utah State University, read the manuscript for the University of Utah Press and made many useful recommendations for revision. Thomas Patterson, Manager of Geographic Research Laboratories at the University of Utah, produced the maps for this volume.

Mr. Kenneth R. Hall, Archivist, Industrial and Social Branch of the National Archives at Washington, D.C., was unstinting in his assistance, granting me access to ship registration books, permitting me to use the Lytle Files on steamboats, and patiently answering a thousand and one questions. Without his help the research would have suffered immeasurably.

[201]

Mrs. S. M. Smith, Registrar of British Ships at the Liverpool Custom House, graciously made available ship registrations and customs records and guided me through the historic documents of this great port. To her I feel greatly indebted.

When limitations on my time made it impossible to research the hundreds of documents in the Public Record Office in London and Richmond, England, Mr. G. H. Somner provided the professional services required and developed much information that might have been unobtainable otherwise.

Since some data required translation from foreign languages, I am particularly appreciative of the skills of Dr. Theodore E. Verhaaren and Mr. Donald B. Norton. They made the unintelligible intelligible for me.

Others were also most helpful and should be recognized: Ms. Astrid Johnson, Librarian of Norsk Sjøfartsmuseum; Dr. Henning Henningsen, Director of Handels-Og Søfartsmuseet På Kronborg; N. E. Upham, Assistant Keeper of the Department of Ships, and Miss D. A. Pipe, Research Assistant, at the National Maritime Museum; Ms. S. Bell, Archivist at the Public Archives of Canada; Mrs. M. Robertson, Archivist at The New Brunswick Museum; S. M. Riley, Assistant, Department of Maritime History, Merseyside County Museums; Ms. Patricia Reynolds, La Trobe Librarian at The State Library of Victoria; Bernhard Havighorst, Bremen, West Germany; Dr. Walter Kresse of the Museum Für Hamburgische Geschichte; Mr. B. C. W. Lap, Curator of the Maritiem Museum "Prins Hendrik" of Rotterdam; Dr. Jürgen Meyer, Ship and Fishery Department of the Altonaer Museum; Adrian Osler, Keeper of Shipping, Tyne and Wear County Council Science Museum; David Hull, Matilda Dring, Isabel Bullen, and Barbara Bernhart of The San Francisco Maritime Museum; Mrs. Carolyn Ritger and Paul B. Hensley of The Mariners Museum; Harold E. Brown of the Maine Maritime Museum; Wesley Catlin of the California State Library; Marguerite K. Ashford, Bernice P. Bishop Museum; Rose Lambert, Louisiana State Museum; Collin B. Hamer, Jr., New Orleans Public Library; Kathy Flynn, Photographic Assistant, Peabody Museum; Georgia Weyer Hamilton, Head Cataloguer, Mystic Seaport, Inc.; and Richard C. Kugler, Director, Old Dartmouth Historical Society Whaling Museum.

Grateful appreciation is also expressed for the use of the facilities and services of the following institutions:

Church of Jesus Christ of Latter-day Saints, Genealogical Department and Historical Department, Salt Lake City, Utah.
National Archives and Records Service, Industrial and Social Branch, Civil Archives Division, Washington, D.C., and Federal Archives and Record Center, San Bruno, California.
HM Customs and Excise House, Liverpool, England.
Public Record Office, Kew, Richmond, and London, England.
San Francisco Maritime Museum, San Francisco, California.
Brigham Young University Library, Special Collections, Provo, Utah.
San Francisco Public Library, Special Collections, San Francisco, California.
Merseyside County Museums, Liverpool, England.
National Maritime Museum, Greenwich, England.
Tyne and Wear County Council Science Museum, Newcastle-upon-Tyne, England.
Stewart Bale Ltd., Commercial, Architectural and Shipping Photographers, Liverpool, England.

Algemeen Rijksarchief Te 'sGravenhage, The Hague, Netherlands.
Rijksmuseum "Nederlands Scheepvaart Museum," Amsterdam, Netherlands.
Maritiem Museum "Prins Hendrik," Rotterdam, Netherlands.
Bureau Veritas, Paris, France.
Lloyd's Register of Shipping, London, England.
Handels-Og Søfartsmuseet På Kronborg, Danish Maritime Museum, Helsingør, Denmark.
Norsk Sjøfartsmuseum, Oslo, Norway.
Archives Nationales, Paris, France.
Musée de la Marine, Paris, France.
Staatsarchiv, City Archives, Hamburg, West Germany.
Altonaer Museum, Ship and Fishery Department, Hamburg, West Germany.
Museum Für Hamburgische Geschichte, Hamburg, West Germany.
Stadtarchiv Wismar, Wismar, East Germany.
Archives Office of Tasmania, Hobart, Tasmania.
Government Archives, South Africa, Cape Town and Pretoria, South Africa.
Service des Archives Polynesie Français, Papeete, Tahiti.
Public Archives of Canada, Ottawa, Canada.
The New Brunswick Museum, Saint John, New Brunswick, Canada.
La Trobe Library, The State Library of Victoria, Melbourne, Australia.
The Archives Authority of New South Wales, The Archives Office of New South Wales, Sydney, Australia.
Bernice P. Bishop Museum, Honolulu, Hawaii.
Hawaii State Library, Honolulu, Hawaii.
California State Library, Sacramento, California.
California Historical Society, San Francisco, California.
Bancroft Library, University of California, Berkeley, California.
Palo Alto Public Library, Palo Alto, California.
The Huntington Library, San Marino, California.
Boston Public Library, Boston, Massachusetts.
New York Public Library, New York City, New York.
Old Dartmouth Historical Society Whaling Museum, New Bedford, Massachusetts.
The National Maritime Historical Society, Brooklyn, New York.
Mystic Seaport, Inc., Mystic, Connecticut.
South Street Seaport Museum, New York City, New York.
Smithsonian Institution, Washington, D.C.
Missouri Historical Society, St. Louis, Missouri.
Maine Maritime Museum, Bath, Maine.
Maine Historical Society, Portland, Maine.
Philadelphia Maritime Museum, Philadelphia, Pennsylvania.
New Orleans Public Library, New Orleans, Louisiana.
Louisiana State Museum, New Orleans, Louisiana.
The Library of Congress, Washington, D.C.
The Mariners Museum, Newport News, Virginia.
U.S. Naval Photographic Center, Washington, D.C.
Kennebunk Public Library, Kennebunk, Maine.
Brick Store Museum, Kennebunk, Maine.
Kennebunkport Historical Society, Kennebunkport, Maine.
Kennebunkport Public Library, Kennebunkport, Maine.
Town Clerk's Office, Kennebunkport, Maine.

The Steamship Historical Society of America, Inc., Staten Island, New York.
Utah State Historical Society, Salt Lake City, Utah.
Free Public Library, Council Bluffs, Iowa.
The New-York Historical Society, New York City, New York.
Peabody Museum of Salem, Massachusetts.
South African Public Library, Cape Town, South Africa.
M. H. de Young Memorial Museum, San Francisco, California.
State of Hawaii Public Archives, Honolulu, Hawaii.

Index

NOTE: Many of the vessels, their builders and their captains, as well as emigrant company leaders, involved in the Mormon maritime migration are not discussed in the text. The reader is referred to the Appendixes for extensive data on all aspects of this phase of the Mormon gathering.